D1715041

THE MAY 1968 EVENTS IN FRANCE

Also by Keith A. Reader

THE CINEMA: A HISTORY
CULTURES ON CELLULOID
* INTELLECTUALS AND THE LEFT IN FRANCE SINCE 1968
LA VIE EST A NOUS (*with G. Vincendeau*)

* *From the same publishers*

The May 1968 Events in France

Reproductions and Interpretations

Keith A. Reader
Reader in French Cultural Studies
University of Kingston, Surrey

with

Khursheed Wadia
Senior Lecturer in French
Wolverhampton University

First published in Great Britain 1993 by
MACMILLAN PRESS LTD
Houndmills, Basingstoke, Hampshire RG21 6XS
and London
Companies and representatives
throughout the world

A catalogue record for this book is available
from the British Library.

ISBN 0-333-49757-0

First published in the United States of America 1993 by
ST. MARTIN'S PRESS, INC.,
Scholarly and Reference Division,
175 Fifth Avenue,
New York, N.Y. 10010

ISBN 0-312-09014-5

Library of Congress Cataloging-in-Publication Data
Reader, Keith
The May 1968 events in France: reproductions and interpretations
/ Keith A. Reader, with Khursheed Wadia.
p.   cm.
Includes bibliographical references.
ISBN 0-312-09014-5
1. Riots—France—Paris. 2. France—History—1958– 3. Student
movements—France—Paris—History—20th century. 4. Radicalism–
–France—Paris—History—20th century. I. Wadia, Khursheed.
II. Title.
DC420.R43 1993
944'.360836—dc20   92-27879
                                                                        CIP

This book is printed on paper suitable for recycling and made
from fully managed and sustained rain forests

Transferred to digital printing 1998
02/780

To G.D. (who first drew my attention to how important the events were), and to my mother (my first
'event').

Contents

Acknowledgements

My thanks go in the first instance to the Nuffield Foundation, for the grant that enabled me to spend the summer of 1989 in Paris researching this book, and to my colleagues in the School of Languages at Kingston University, for enabling me to take study leave in the summer term of 1991 to write the book. Library staff at the Bibliothèque de Documentation Internationale Contemporaine at Nanterre, the Institut des Sciences Politiques, the Maison des Sciences de l'Homme, and the Vidéothèque de Paris (all in Paris) were extremely helpful, as were the long-suffering inter-library loans team at Kingston. Help, ideas and inspiration came from Richard Alwyn, Philippe Binet, David Caute, Claire Duchen, Jill Forbes, Eleonore Kofman, Colin MacCabe, Jean-Paul Morel (whose generosity with his own library saved me much time in Paris), Richard Nice, Pascal Ory, Jean-François Sirinelli, Michael Worton and others. Diana Holmes put me in contact with Khursheed Wadia without whose contribution the book would have been much impoverished. My May 1968 special-subject groups at Kingston acted as guinea-pigs (and sometimes punchbags) for many of the ideas and suggestions herein. The Kingston languages office staff – especially Sarah Bacon – were towers of strength.

I would like to thank the editors of the *Revue française des Sciences politiques* for permission to include an article from that journal by Philippe Bénéton and Jean Touchard, which I have translated and include here as Chapter 2.

More personally, I should like to thank my mother, my cat, Bessie, and Eleonore for (very different kinds of) loving support, Tim Farmiloe at Macmillans for his forbearance as deadlines expired and idiotic questions were asked, Hugues Joscaud for the generous and convivial hospitality he offered on a number of visits to Paris, Madame Auffray of the Institut Francophone de Paris for providing me with accommodation during a last-minute bibliographical visit, and all the friends who stayed with me in Paris during the summer of 1989 and secured my sanity at the cost of their own.

List of Abbreviations

AFP   Agence France Presse – France's leading news agency

CFDT   Confédération française démocratique du travail – second largest French trade union grouping, more *gauchiste* than the CGT

CGT   Confédération générale du travail – largest French trade union grouping, closely allied with the PCF

FER   Fédération des étudiants révolutionnaires – Trotskyist group

JCR/LCR   Jeunesse (later Ligue) communiste révolutionnaire – Trotskyist group

MLF   Mouvement de libération des femmes

OAS   Organisation de l'armée secrète – colonialist paramilitaries in Algeria

ORTF   Office de radiodiffusion télévision française

PCF   Parti communiste française

PCMLF   Parti communiste (marxiste-léniniste) française – Maoist

PS   Parti socialiste

PSU   Parti socialiste unifié – loosely *gauchiste* grouping

SNE-S(up)   Syndicat national de l'enseignement secondaire/supérieur – teaching unions affiliated to the CGT

UEC   Union des étudiants communistes

UJCml   Union des jeunesses communistes (marxiste-leniniste)

UNEF   Union nationale des étudiants de France

1 What Happened in May 1968?

To describe the event implies that the event was written. How can an event be written? What can the 'writing of the event' mean?[1]

The diversity of expressions used to describe what happened in France in May 1968 clearly indicates how difficult it is to say precisely what the 'events', to use the commonest term, were. 'Crisis', 'strike', 'revolt', 're-volution', '(student) commune', 'civil war', '*chienlit*/dog's breakfast' (to use the somewhat euphemistic English translation of the time), or the simple chronological 'May' (followed or not by '{19}68') are the other terms most often found.[2] This heterogeneity in speaking of a historical moment is remarkable; however strong and contradictory the feelings they arouse, the Paris Commune, the Russian Revolution, the Munich putsch are each generally known by one name. Why should 'May' be so different?

The main reason is the disparity between the all-consuming intensity of the events while they lasted and the overwhelming reimposition of the political status quo immediately afterwards. It is noteworthy that Bénéton and Touchard speak of 'the crisis of May and June 1968', for occupations, barricades, demonstrations continued through the first half of June, but in an increasingly isolated and despairing manner. Once de Gaulle had made his major radio speech on 30 May, followed that evening by a vast demonstration of support for him on the Champs-Élysées, the energy that had sustained the movement drained away with unexampled rapidity. The landslide Gaullist electoral victory a month to the day after the General's speech came as a surprise to very few.

Yet it followed a month in which France had virtually come to a halt, precipitated by large-scale student protests and occupations that led to the greatest general strike in European history, involving nine million workers and losing 15 000 000 working days. It is this junction of student and worker protest that marks France's 1968 as distinctive, much further-reaching than the other student movements that swept most of the world in that year.[3] De Gaulle said of May, with a characteristically ambiguous combination of chauvinism and irony: 'As always, France led the way'.[4] The paradox that so vast a social and cultural movement led to so massive a reassertion of the political status quo underlies Edgar Morin's view that:

What we have to understand is at once the immensity and the insignifi-
cance of May 68. But to do that we have to resurrect the sphinx-like
quality of the events.[5]

The term 'sphinx' has overtones of on the one hand Freud's celebrated
allusion to the riddle of 'femininity' ('those of you who are women . . . you
are yourselves the problem'),[6] on the other the enigmatic quality of François
Mitterrand, often referred to as 'the sphinx'. I mention these because
whether Morin intended them or not they serve to show one of the most
remarkable aspects of May – its cultural polyvalence and semantic richness,
residing less in the size of its vocabulary than in the range of its echoes. The
impact of psychoanalysis and feminism, and Mitterrand's election as President in 1981 and subsequent domination of the French political stage, are
both widely recognised as in some sense important – and ambiguous –
consequences of 'May', so that the use of the term 'sphinx' is unlikely to
appear innocent to the educated French reader. This connotative saturation
suggests how 'May' appears as a prism in which the major cultural changes
of twentieth-century France are multiply refracted.

HOW TO SPEAK OF MAY?

The variety of names by which the events are known already goes to
suggest this. To speak of them as a 'crisis' lays particular stress on their
institutional dimension; France at the height of the events was without
effective government, and the Fifth Republic, less than ten years old at the
time, seemed on the verge of decomposition with no tangible alternative in
sight. 'Revolt' and 'revolution', by contrast, emphasise their euphoric,
transformational quality, the distinction made by Camus in *L'Homme Révolté/
The Rebel* between existential revolt (good) and political revolution (bad)
here losing its ethical charge and reflecting rather how far the observer felt
that fundamental change in French society was possible. Thus, Jean
Joussellin's *Les Révoltes des jeunes/The Revolt of the Young* sees May
(situated in the world-wide context of '1968') as the twentieth-century's
major youth revolt, while for Gérard Mendel in *La Révolte contre le père/
The Revolt against the Father* its Oedipal component was crucial. The
aftermath of the events unsurprisingly produced a host of works referring to
them as a 'revolution', whether following Trotsky betrayed (André Barjonet's
La Révolution trahie de 1968/Revolution Betrayed in 1968), for Maoists in
preparation (André Glucksmann's *Stratégie et révolution en France/Strat-
egy and Revolution in France*), or for the hostile Right a creation of fantasy

(Raymond Aron's *La Révolution introuvable/The Undiscoverable Revolution*). Morin's comment in 1986 that 'the word revolution is now for me a polluted one'[7] illustrates how far the term, at any rate in the maximalist sense in which it was bandied about in 1968, has fallen into disfavour. We may speak of 'the Thatcherite revolution' or the 'quiet revolutions' in Eastern Europe, but if only because of the absence of overt violence the word obviously means something other than it did. It would certainly be difficult now to speak of May as a 'revolution' with an entirely straight face – a point underlined by the title of Dany Cohn-Bendit's twentieth-anniversary retrospective, *Nous l'avons tant aimée, la révolution/How we loved the Revolution*, whose English title, *Revolution Revisited*, sadly loses its elegiac irony.

'Civil war', as in Serge July, Alain Geismar and Erlyne Morane's *Vers la guerre civile/Towards civil war*, and Edgar Morin's 'La Commune étudiante'/'The student commune' (in *Mai 68: la brèche*), can be seen as opposed variants on 'revolution', stressing respectively the bloodshed avoided in May but seen by Maoists in particular as inevitable thereafter and the festive, celebratory quality attested to by virtually all those who took part. Morin likens May to a *'jeu-kermesse'*[8] – at once game and popular fair – but his use of 'commune' also implicitly likens the events to the Paris Commune of 1871, which of course ended in the very bloodshed evoked by the term 'civil war'. . . .

The terms *'chienlit'* and '(general) strike' have the clearest political connotations of all. *'Chienlit'* etymologically means 'one who shits in his bed', so that the rendering as 'dog's breakfast' (from *chien*/dog) favoured by the English press in May is more than a little feeble. (It was also used in the eighteenth-century to denote a masked carnival personage, so that its scatological overtones are of a markedly playful kind.) The term was used first by the neo-Fascist weekly *Minute* (2 May), then, notoriously, by de Gaulle at the height of the events (*'Les réformes, oui! La chienlit, non!!* Reforms, yes! A shitty mess, no!'), and my Larousse dictionary gives 1968 as the term's first use to refer to 'a disordered or chaotic situation', so that it has truly passed into the contemporary French language as a result of May. Predictably, the one title to use the term, *La Chienlit*, a special issue (edited by Dominique Venner) of the extreme Right-wing journal *Le Crapouillot*, is a hostile 'dictionary' satirising individuals and concepts, central among which is that of *contestation* – the challenging and question-ing of almost every aspect of social organisation so widespread in May and for three or four years thereafter, a term left in French in the present text because so closely linked with its context as to be effectively untranslatable. A splendid countervailing instance of the linguistic verve so characteristic of May is provided by the Beaux-Arts poster caricaturing de Gaulle with the legend: '*La chienlit, c'est lui!*/He's the shitty mess!'

'(General) strike' is even more clearly Communist than '*chienlit*' is Gaullist. The PCF strongly condemned the early manifestations of student discontent, especially when these were the work of what is called 'ultra-Left' (in other words, anarchist, Maoist, or Trotskyist) groups. Georges Marchais (later to become its General Secretary) wrote a venomous editorial in *L'Humanité* on 3 May in which he declared that 'these false revolutionaries must be energetically unmasked, for objectively they serve the interests of the Gaullist power and the large capitalist monopolies', reserving his choicest bile for the 'German anarchist' Cohn-Bendit. It was only when the working class became involved after the police brutality of the night of 10 May that the PCF changed its tune, supporting the workers who went on strike and sometimes even occupied their factories. Thenceforth the line was clear: the police repression was inexcusable, the workers' demands for improved conditions and salary increases justified and to be fought for until (so they hoped) the election of a Left-wing government. The term 'strike', in the work of Communists as different as the then General Secretary Waldeck Rochet and the Party's leading philosopher Louis Althusser, thus suggests that the significance of May was to be found in factories and workplaces rather than in occupied temples of culture such as the Sorbonne or the Théâtre de l'Odéon. Much as Morin's 'commune' evoked Paris in 1871, so the '(general) strike' of the PCF would have touched off memories of 1936 and the Popular Front, when workers all over France occupied their factories to secure improved salaries and conditions from the newly-elected Left-wing government. To refer to the events as a 'strike', that is to say, effectively meant that they could not also be thought of as a 'revolution'.

Given the connotative density of the terms we have so far discussed, it is not surprising that there was a need for a 'neutral' expression, nor that the two chosen ('the events' and 'May') are so blandly uninformative. Even without its ideological overtones, 'revolution' would be a straightforward misnomer, for the régime was not overthrown; 'crisis' is too negative, 'revolt' and 'strike' omit important elements, and the other terms cited appear too emotive. A simple chronological label (which in other contexts can coexist with one more specific – '1066', 'October') was an obvious alternative, and the use of 'events' (according to my *Collins English Dictionary* 'anything that takes place or happens, especially something important') about as uncontroversial a solution as could be imagined.

I shall argue later that – as my Barthesian epigraph suggests – even the term 'event' has conceptual overtones and implications important in contemporary French intellectual life. For the moment, however, it is time to turn to the chronology of the months of May and June. So lengthy an introduction was necessary in order to emphasise the peculiar difficulty of defining the object of our study, a difficulty to be neither miraculously abolished nor accepted with weary resignation, but rather engaged with as a fundamental part of 'writing the event(s)'. The question in the chapter-title can perhaps now be rephrased: not so much 'What happened in France in May 1968?' as 'What separate yet linked events go to form the "events" in May?' In order to answer that, we shall need to look at developments in the years before 1968.

THE YEARS BEFORE 1968

Varying forms of discontent among both students and workers had been manifest for some years before May. The period since the Second World War (to be described later by Jean Fourastié as 'the thirty glorious years')[9] had been one of rapid growth and spreading material prosperity, in which France had transformed itself from a largely agricultural to a modern industrial consumer society. In 1958, only 10 per cent of French households had a refrigerator; by the time de Gaulle resigned in 1969, the figure was 75 per cent.[10] The paradox that the paternalistic, even authoritarian de Gaulle presided over a period of unexampled economic growth and prosperity (albeit unevenly distributed) already suggests one of the founding contradictions of May, between material abundance and outmoded political and social structures. Another is figured in the title of an earlier work by Fourastié (1958), *Le grand espoir du XXe siècle/The great hope of the twentieth-century*, sub-titled 'Technical progress, economic progress, social progress', and preceded by Jean Monnet's exhortation to 'live better by producing better'.[11] The limitations of such materialistic optimism became plain in the intervening decade, where to quote Alain Delale and Gilles Ragache 'the whole of France was concentrated around a few dozen "growth poles". Everywhere else became deserted or went into decline.'[12] It is scarcely to be wondered at that such starry-eyed faith in material progress came to look extremely jaded ten years later.

Developments in the student world, too, appear significant in retrospect. The number of students grew by 224 per cent between 1958 and 1968, but resources were anything but adequate to the increase. The University of Nanterre, catering for students from the western – thus most affluent – parts of Paris, opened in 1964 before its library had even been completed, in an urban and cultural desert with minimal public-transport links to Paris; small wonder that it was there that the 'events' began. . . . Ideologically too the student milieu was changing. The UEC which, as the Communist Party's student wing, had long been the dominant force on the student Left, had been riddled with dissent since the early 1960s. The main dissident currents were the so-called 'Italians', drawing on the way in which the Italian Communist Party had democratised itself and criticising the Stalinist centralism of the PCF; the 'Chinese', looking towards (their version of) Mao's China rather than the USSR; and the Trotskyists, who considered socialism in one country an impossibility and criticised all self-styled Socialist or Communist societies as bureaucratic distortions. 1966 saw the breakway of the 'Chinese' to form the UJCml and of many Trotskyists to form the JCR – groups that seemed insignificant at the time, but were to have much greater influence in May.[13]

A more bizarre occurrence was the electoral takeover of the student union at the University of Strasbourg in 1966 by a group describing themselves as 'situationists'. Their pamphlet *De la misère en milieu étudiant considérée sous ses aspects économique, politique, psychologique, sexuel et notamment intellectuel, et de quelques moyens pour y remédier/ On the wretchedness of student life in its economic, political, psychological, sexual and above all intellectual aspects, and a few suggestions for improving it* described students as 'products of modern society, just like Godard and Coca-Cola',[14] and advocated forms of direct democracy and festive revolution that strikingly foreshadowed May. The student union takeover was annulled by a court of law (so much for the concept of democracy in the student milieu!), but the situationists and their ideas, to which we shall return, had made an impact, notably at Nanterre and Nantes.

This is not, of course, to say that the average French student before (or even in) 1968 lived in a constant state of ideological frenzy, solicited by different Left-wing groups like so many barkers at a fairground. S/he probably felt distant from a Gaullist régime, and its appointed university authorities, whose attitude seemed high-handed and out of touch with the reality of overcrowded classrooms and irrelevant or uninspiring courses. S/he might well have had vaguely Leftist sympathies, influenced by the manifest inequalities of income in prosperous France and by the Algerian war that had finished only in 1962. S/he, if Parisian and not exceptionally fortunate, was likely to be faced with the unwelcome choice between living a protracted adolescent existence at home and conditions often no less constricting, and quite possibly less comfortable, in a university residence or bed-sitting room. Either way, an independent life – especially a sexual one – could seem an almost unattainable dream.

Young workers might well have had more financial independence, and felt closer to the 'youth culture' of the early 1960s (which spawned French rock stars such as Johnny Hallyday and Richard Anthony), but the hierarchical authoritarianism of Gaullist France was replicated in factory structures even more clearly than in the universities. Housing problems for workers, too, were similar to those for students, except that instead of a university residence the young worker was likely to find her/himself in an (often religious) hostel. That there should have been smouldering discontent among young people in search of their autonomy was no more surprising in itself than that workers should have been dissatisfied with their salaries and conditions at a time of major industrial reconstruction. The two coincided to make May remarkable, but did not fuse, which as much as anything else limited its political effects.

January 1968 saw a strike at the SAVIEM lorry factory in Caen, where resentment not only at inadequate salaries, but at rigorous hierarchisation and excessive rates of production, went beyond the mild token action advocated by the unions to issue in an all-out strike and a mass demonstration in the centre of the city. This led to a pitched battle that went on until 5 a.m., culminating in the attempted seizure of the prefecture (the regional seat of government). Two hundred were injured (including thirty-six policemen), and five young workers were later given prison sentences. The brushing aside of union calls for moderation, like the spontaneous violence directed against police and government, were to be repeated, massively amplified, in May.

The same month saw a clash on the campus of Nanterre (where the previous November there had been a ten-day student strike), between the minister for youth and sport, François Missoffe, and a sociology student called Daniel Cohn-Bendit. Missoffe, invited to inspect a new swimming-pool, was taken to task by Cohn-Bendit for making no mention of sexual problems in his recently-published book on young people in France. His response was to suggest that Cohn-Bendit take a dip in the pool, to which Cohn-Bendit riposted: 'That's the kind of answer you would get under a fascist régime.' The matter was smoothed over by way of a letter of apology, but Cohn-Bendit and the style of confrontation he represented would not go away so quickly.

Few would have made any connection between the Cohn-Bendit episode and the riots in Caen, yet between them they now read like a prefiguration of May. This perhaps makes it too easy now to mock the journalist Pierre Viansson-Ponté, who entitled an article in *Le Monde* of 15 March 'La France s'ennuie' ('France is bored'). The combination of material prosperity and governmental stability made any kind of social upheaval seem unlikely; to quote Capdevielle and Mouriaux, 'the events on May/June 1968 were all the harder to grasp because they had not been foreseen, and did not seem predictable'.[15]

Student discontent was not confined to conditions of life on campus; it also focused on the Vietnam war, an international rallying-point for the Left in 1968. The apparent stagnation of French – indeed European – social and political life meant that the Maoist and Trotskyist Left turned their attention much more towards the Third World. The Chinese Cultural Revolution, ingenuously taken at face-value, Cuba and Vietnam seen as twin Davids defying the American Goliath, and the liberation struggles in Central and South America were personified respectively by Mao Zedong, Fidel Castro, Ho Chi Minh and Ernesto 'Che' Guevara. The resulting cocktail of ideology and iconography provided an imaginative dimension sadly lacking in the France of de Gaulle and the established Left.

On 21 March, a Left-wing commando attacked the American Express building in Paris in protest against the Vietnam war. Among the six arrested was Xavier Langlade, a student at Nanterre, where the following day a meeting was held to decide how to respond. Cohn-Bendit moved the occupation of the administrative block, which towered over the campus and happened to be open and unguarded at the time. The students took over the *salle de conseil*, where the equivalent of the Senate or governing body met, and remained in occupation until 1:30 a.m., deciding to transform 29 March into a 'day of anti-imperialist debate and struggle'.

In the light of what was to follow, the occupation of 22 March seems very small beer indeed, but its importance at the time was considerable. For students – traditionally regarded as a docile if hedonistic mass – to occupy the major site of symbolic power in their institution was unprecedented in France, and the combined action of the Trotskyists in the JCR and the anarchist grouping around Cohn-Bendit decisively outflanked the established Left of the UEC.[16] It was the anarchists who ironically dubbed this heterodox combination the '*Mouvement du 22 mars*/22 March movement', in reference to the JCR's veneration for Castro's Cuban 'Movement of 26 July'.[17] Ironic or not, the term – and the group to which it referred – soon became a byword.

Because the May events so dramatically challenged established political iconography and discourse, they began literally before they happened to produce iconographies and discourses of their own – drawing on what already existed in France (as with the '*La chienlit, c'est lui!*' poster referred to earlier or the universal execration of the PCF) or elsewhere (as with the countless posters of Che Guevara or Mao Zedong), but supplementing it with a myth-making dynamic that undoubtedly accounts for their continuing fascination. Even those who have pronounced themselves bored with 'May', such as Serge July in *Libération*'s tenth-anniversary issue or the student demonstrators who in 1986 chanted '*68 c'est vieux, 86 c'est mieux*' ('68 is old, 86 is better'), express boredom with a set of names, slogans, above all images rather than with a political programme. The late 1960s were the period when Marshall MacLuhan could proclaim that 'the medium is the message', when Normal Mailer arranged to have a BBC film crew in attendance for his arrest on the 21 October 1967 anti-war demonstration, when television coverage of the bombing of Vietnam brought the war, and revulsion against it, into the sitting-rooms of Middle America. We shall see that the instantaneity of media coverage played its part in the May mythmaking too, but the example of Nanterre shows that process was well under way before television and radio took an interest. Cohn-Bendit and the 22 March Movement became well-known precisely because they were so unlike conventional student (or other) political figures and movements. Cohn-Bendit had never belonged to the UEC or any other organised grouping; the 22 March Movement brought together in unity of action Trotskyists belonging to what sought to be a highly-organised revolutionary vanguard party and anarchists for whom the form and style of action was often at least as important as any specific demands. These very different groups were united – at least at Nanterre – by their two-fisted contempt for the outmoded authoritarianism of de Gaulle on the one hand and the PCF on the other.

This rejection of established political styles and organisations was further emphasised by the virtual collapse of the UNEF, reduced to a battleground between rival Leftist groups. In April 1968 it was dominated by an uneasy coalition between the student wing of the PSU and the Trotskyists of the FER. The presidency was due to pass to PSU member Jacques Sauvageot at a meeting on 13 April, but after an attack by neo-fascists this broke up amid recriminations before Sauvageot's nomination could be confirmed. None of the wings of the UNEF – professional revolutionaries in training – had much time for Cohn-Bendit, seen as an irresponsible amateur; yet within three weeks Sauvageot and Cohn-Bendit were to be thrown together as allies by the force of, precisely, events. Joffrin points out that 'the curtain of May rose on this reversal of the balance of power between the troublemakers of Nanterre and experienced student politicians'.[18] Pierre Juquin, a member of the PCF's central committee, went to Nanterre on 26 April to denounce those whom he described as '*les agitateurs-fils à papa*/agitators with rich daddies', and was literally chased off the campus. Twenty years later almost to the day, the same Pierre Juquin was to stand against Mitterrand

and the PCF candidate (André Lajoinie) in the presidential elections, on a 'New Left' programme drawing on support from Trotskyist groups and dissident ex-Communists seeking to sustain the ideas and ideals of May.

THE EVENTS OF MAY

On 1 May, the traditional trade union march from the Place de la République to the Place de la Bastille was given government permission for the first time for fourteen years. The following day, Nanterre's faculty of letters was closed and eight members of the 22 March Movement, including of course Cohn-Bendit, were summoned to appear before a disciplinary committee on 6 May. A protest meeting called the following day at the Sorbonne was poorly attended, but that afternoon police invaded the courtyard, arresting 500 students. Alain Peyrefitte, the Education Minister, and Jean Roche, Rector of the Sorbonne, feared above all that the Sorbonne – France's oldest university, at the heart of Parisian student life – would be affected by the disturbances that had led to the closing of Nanterre. By sending in the police, who traditionally did not intervene on university territory, they ensured that this was precisely what would happen.

It took three hours to load all those arrested into police wagons and drive them away, and it was during this time that the extraordinary spontaneous energy that was to characterise May first erupted. Crowds began shouting slogans such as 'Free our comrades!', 'Stop repression' and the soon-to-be-notorious 'CRS–SS', to the astonishment of the arrested militants. The police responded with tear-gas and baton-charges of indiscriminate brutality but, instead of retreating, the students (already joined by other young people who were passing by) counter-attacked with cobblestones, building the first of May's barricades in the Place du Luxembourg.

Pent-up energy issuing in verbal as well as physical violence, a refusal to be cowed by authoritarian brutality, an eruption of solidarity among young people who did not even know one another – these key features of May had burst forth, and the government was ill-placed to deal with them, especially as the Prime Minister Georges Pompidou had left the previous day for a state visit to Iran and Afghanistan. Calls for an all-out strike in the universities were issued by the UNEF – suddenly at the centre of activity – and the major lecturers' union, the SNE-Sup, whose general secretary, Alain Geismar, was to be one of the three best-known faces of May along with Cohn-Bendit and Sauvageot.

The week of 6–10 May saw the student movement refuse any negotiations with the government unless those imprisoned were released, the

Sorbonne reopened and the Latin Quarter vacated by the police. Meetings, demonstrations, tracts, leaflets proliferated; May was the apotheosis of the roneo.[19] It was, however, the Latin Quarter that was the scene of the most savage pitched battles, culminating in the 'night of the barricades' of 10 May. Attention, if only because of the presence of film and television crews, has been concentrated on Paris during this period, but all France's university towns were the scenes of demonstrations and occupations, Nantes and Strasbourg among the most active.

Nowhere apart from Paris, however, had a 'night of the barricades', and if there is one moment in 'May' around which all its myth-hallowed liberating potential centres it is this. Negotiations had stalled on the government's refusal to free those students still in prison, and a large demonstration on the Left Bank found all the bridges across the Seine blocked by police. The call went out to 'occupy the (Latin) Quarter' – a territorial riposte to the police occupation of the Sorbonne – and at about 9 p.m. the first barricades were built. Branches and metal grilles from trees, cars (according to folklore often with the gleeful consent of their owners), paving-stones were piled up in a movement that spread like wildfire, yet in practical paramilitary terms was worthless. It was paradoxically in this very practical worthlessness that its symbolic value resided, as Joffrin shows:

> Against them [sc. the police], the barricades were the sign of revolt and fraternity. They had no military value. An armed battalion opening fire would have got rid of them in thirty seconds, with no need for tanks or cannon. They were thrown up in the Rue Gay-Lussac and around, with no preconceived plan or strategy, and often so close together that they might have penned their defenders in with no hope of retreat. One was even built at the entry of a cul-de-sac! In 1830 or 1848, the people of Paris could stand up to the army, resist their gunfire, break a cavalry charge. The barricade then was a technique; in May 68, it was a sign, at once a throwback to the nineteenth-century and conclusively modern. Nobody wanted civil war, but everybody wanted political victory. By reviving in a diluted form the memory of the Paris Commune, the barricade transformed the Gaullists into *Versaillais*. It rallied romantics, galvanised hotheads, caressed the republican unconscious. . . . In this battle for public opinion, it was a decisive weapon, putting history on the students' side.[20]

Other views of the barricades' symbolic and territorial value will be discussed in Chapter 3. For the moment, it is enough to note their extraordinary mobilising effect; the violence of the police caused widespread anger even among those not politically sympathetic to the Left, brought demonstrators together in fiercely euphoric solidarity and compelled the trade unions, hitherto disapprovingly silent, to become involved. Geismar's negotiations with Chalin (Roche's deputy) were broadcast live as they happened, though Chalin did not realise this while they were going on. Cohn-Bendit, officially banned from the Sorbonne for disciplinary reasons, nevertheless joined a student delegation to see Roche, who did not realise who he was until told to eject him by a furious telephone-call from Peyrefitte. The carnivalistic[21] aspect of May coexisted, on the night of the barricades, with its greatest savagery.

The two main unions, the CGT and the CFDT, met the next morning and decided on a general solidarity strike for the following Monday (13 May), by which time almost all the universities and many secondary schools were at a halt. Pompidou, back from Afghanistan on the Saturday evening, had appeared on television to grant all the students' demands, but that was clearly too little, too late. The thirteenth of May was the day when the movement became overtly political, for as Delale and Ragache say, 'Since the reopening of the Sorbonne did not put an end to the university crisis, the Gaullist régime itself was called into question.'[22] Two hundred thousand people (according to the police) or 800 000 (according to the unions) took part in a march through Paris led by union and student leaders, with professional politicians of the Left – Mitterrand, Rocard, Mendès-France, Waldeck Rochet – following behind. Cohn-Bendit, whose presence at the head of the march had angered the CGT, declared that evening: 'It was a real pleasure for me to lead a march with all that Stalinist filth in the rear'. Meanwhile, the Sorbonne was no sooner opened than occupied; the 'Nanterre effect' so feared by Roche was becoming a reality. Occupation was to be the keynote of the next few weeks, in factories and department-stores as well as school and university buildings, as the battle for political power and individual autonomy translated itself into a battle for the possession of (physical and symbolic) space. On 14 May, the workers at the Sud-Aviation factory near Nantes occupied their factory, sequestering their managing director and his assistants in their offices; the next day, workers at the Renault factory in Cléon (Normandy) followed suit. The sudden eruption of violence and the social tensions that underlay it were reinforced by the memory of 1936 for the older workers and solidarity with the students for the younger ones.

The occupation of the universities was characterised by a paradoxical blend of anarchistic liberalism and practical organisation: on the one hand, open discussions in amphitheatres and lecture-halls to which anybody was free to contribute, tracts, posters, graffiti representing a kaleidoscope of political styles and opinions; on the other, working parties democratically elected on a day-by-day basis to discuss and present reports on issues as varied as the fight against imperialism in Latin America and the redefinition of disciplines within the university, and a whole infrastructure of meals, crèches, dormitories (largely the responsibility of women). Factory occupations were more confrontationist (there were, after all, flesh-and-blood managers to deal with), less ideologically ambitious (questions of wages and conditions were dominant), but often no less festive, though cards, bowls and dancing were commoner than Maoist graffiti or the public recounting of dreams.

It was amid this questioning tumult that General de Gaulle left on a five-day state visit to Roumania on 14 May. It would have been difficult for him to do otherwise without admitting that his moral, if not his constitutional, authority was in doubt, but by announcing that he would not address the nation until 24 May he strengthened the feeling that he had become remote from its concerns. The shouts on the 13 May demonstration of 'Ten years are enough!' were to gain in volume through the month. Meanwhile, the main national theatre, the Odéon, was occupied on 15 May, and its director, Jean-Louis Barrault, expressed his sympathy with the students. Support for the movement was overwhelming in the intellectual and literary world; Louis Aragon, jeered by demonstrators because of his continuing support for the PCF, nevertheless proclaimed himself on their side, a group of writers led by Michel Butor occupied the offices of the Société des Gens de Lettres (the main writers' trade union), Jean-Luc Godard and others forced the closure of the Cannes Film Festival, Jean-Paul Sartre went to the Sorbonne to express his solidarity. Of greater symbolic importance than any of these was the strike at the huge Renault car factory at Boulogne-Billancourt, near Paris, which began on 16 May. 'Billancourt' was the unquestioned power-base of the CGT, and it was said that 'when Renault sneezes, France catches cold'; it was in keeping with the 'Alice-in-Wonderland' logic of May that it was only after France had caught cold that Renault finally decided to sneeze, but the impact of that sneeze was lost on nobody. The CGT remained resolutely hostile to any student-worker *rapprochement*, and a procession of students that marched from the Latin Quarter to Billancourt bearing the banner, 'The workers will take the torch of revolution from the fragile hands of the students', was turned away. Nevertheless, with younger workers going on strike and occupying throughout France in disregard of their union leaderships, there was little the latter could do but belatedly endorse the movement and try to assert their authority over it.

Cohn-Bendit (bearer of a German passport) was issued with a deportation order on 21 May, which was a highly counter-productive government move. There were large demonstrations in protest the following day and

Cohn-Bendit was to make a clandestine return to France (in one version smuggled in the boot of psychoanalyst Jacques Lacan's Jaguar!) before the end of the month, appearing at the Sorbonne in a wig and dark glasses which he removed to a tumultuous ovation. By the time de Gaulle addressed the nation on 24 May, France was paralysed, with more than eight million workers on strike, no public transport and precious little petrol. His speech was disastrously misconceived, a philosophical exposition of the need for 'participation' coupled with a proposal for a referendum that would effectively have been a vote of confidence in him. The combination of distant conceptual meditation and the reassertion of personal authority was exactly what strikers and students did not want to hear. The historian Adrien Dansette relates that throughout Paris people were saying, 'He's waited three weeks before announcing in five minutes that he's going to try in a month to do what he hasn't managed to achieve in ten years.'[23] That evening's demonstrations, inaugurated to chants of 'Adieu, de Gaulle!', were the most violent yet, bringing two deaths (one in Paris, one in Lyon) and what passed into folklore as the 'burning of the Bourse' (the Paris Stock Exchange), but was in fact only a minor local conflagration. The euphoria of the 'student commune' and the early days of factory occupation was giving place to a harder-edged sense of political conflict.

This was illustrated by the negotiations that opened on 25 May at the Labour Ministry in the Rue de Grenelle between the trade unions and a government team led by Pompidou and a dynamic young employment minister – Jacques Chirac, later to become (twice) Prime Minister. These went on throughout the weekend and at 7.15 a.m. on Monday, 27 May yielded a joint series of proposals, including an increase of three francs in the basic hourly minimum wage, a phased increase of 10 per cent in private-sector salaries with parallel examination of those in the public sector, a progressive return to the 40-hour week (which had been a casualty of expansion and restructuring), an advance of 50 per cent to those who had lost money while on strike, and perhaps most important of all, the nationally-agreed right to trade-union recognition and representation in individual firms.[24] This package was put to mass factory meetings and everywhere rejected; Georges Séguy of the CGT was jeered at a gathering of 10 000 workers at Billancourt, with shouts of 'A government of the people!' that unmistakably evoked 1936. It seemed as if the régime had played its last card, yet who or what was to take its place? For the next four days, France effectively had no national government, and a city such as Nantes was run for the last week in May by strike committees rather than by regional and municipal authorities. 'Almost all the French, who had been living for three weeks in an atmosphere of total unpredictability, had the impression that

"now everything was possible."'[25] This phrase evokes the title of a celebrated article by the Left-wing Socialist Marceau Pivert at the height of the
strikes and occupations of 1936, as well as the now still more celebrated
neo-surrealist Latin Quarter graffiti such as 'Take your desires for reality'
or 'Power to the imagination'. It was also, and at the same time, a profoundly disturbing and even frightening prospect for many, especially
given the apparent outflanking of politicians of the established Left.

ENTER THE POLITICIANS

These now for the first time moved towards the centre of the stage under the
aegis of the Socialists Pierre Mendès-France and François Mitterrand, less
reviled by the students than the PCF. Mendès's moral credibility was
particularly high because he had consistently declared his opposition to the
Gaullist régime and the personal centralisation of power under the Fifth
Republic, whereas Mitterrand had run against de Gaulle in 1965. Mendès
attended a meeting organised by the UNEF and backed by the CFDT at the
Charlety sports stadium (to the south of the Latin Quarter) on the evening
of 27 May, important as the first major assembly of the non-Communist,
non-CGT Left. Although he did not speak, his presence was highly significant for, as Cohn-Bendit says, "'All these forces brought together in search
of a political way forward were our only chance, and that chance was called
Mendès.'"[26]

He also said, more presciently: "'We're all working for François
Mitterrand"',[27] as though one were the (distant?) chance, the other (always
more of a tactician) the political reality. Mitterrand issued a statement on
28 May affirming that since 3 May there had been no real French state and
calling for an interim government pending presidential elections. He declared himself prepared to lead such a government while acknowledging
the possible rival claim of Mendès, but was unambiguous about his inten-
tion of standing in any presidential election. This proclamation drew a hail
of criticism, for it seemed that Mitterrand – a 'respectable' politician
echoing the street-cry that 'ten years is enough' – was further jeopardising
the fragile legitimacy of the Fifth Republic by preempting the resignation of
its head of state.[28] The PCF leader Waldeck Rochet, later that day, called for
Communist participation in any such government, doubtless hoping that
this would be enough to satisfy the workers who had rejected the economic
(not to say economistic) proposals of Grenelle.

The régime's survival now seemed all but inconceivable. The movement
had gone far beyond its university beginnings to bring together students,

workers (independently or through their unions) and all the political parties of the Left to call for de Gaulle's immediate departure – though that is virtually all they would have agreed on. The next day (29 May), he duly departed, though for a matter of hours only, in what was variously the acting-out of terminal political and personal breakdown, the greatest *coup de théâtre* in French history since Napoleon's return from Elba – or, paradoxically, both. At 11.45 that morning, de Gaulle left the Élysée Palace by helicopter with his wife – it was thought, to rest for a few hours at his country house at Colombey. At 2 p.m., the news broke that he was not there. For two hours, his whereabouts were unknown; the possibility that he had committed suicide was briefly envisaged at a meeting of senior ministers, and Jean Thibaudeau in *Mai 68 en France* mentions press speculation that 'he might have gone for a walk alone, to think, in a forest'.[29] The mythical dimension of both these actions, like what was to follow, suggests the demiurge rather than the practical politician. The latter title had uncontestably passed to Pompidou, who with admirable *sang-froid*, announced that he would make an announcement on television the following day, without having the slightest idea what he would say. The rumour spread throughout France that he had retreated to Colombey to prepare the announcement of his resignation.

Meanwhile, he was lunching (an omelette and two coffees) with General Massu, commander of the French forces in Germany, in Baden-Baden, only a few miles from the French border. Massu was to claim[30] that de Gaulle had arrived profoundly demoralised, blaming the Communists for paralysing the country and declaring himself on the brink of resignation; Massu's rousing reassurance supposedly caused him to change his mind within an hour. The possibility of military intervention seems not to have been mentioned, but perhaps it did not need to be. The very destination of de Gaulle's 'mystery tour', when it became known later that afternoon, could not but have suggested that threat to a society already poised between exhilaration and fear.

Pompidou's account substantially endorses Massu's, though one may suspect a certain *parti pris* from one who had been left in such a constitutionally and politically untenable position at the height of the crisis that he had decided to resign the Premiership before de Gaulle removed him. He maintains that twice in the days immediately following the events de Gaulle said to him: '"For the first time in my life, I had a moment of weakness. I'm not proud of myself."'[31] De Gaulle's mythological identification of himself with the French nation makes it plausible that he felt an almost unbearable sense of betrayal, and on a more prosaic level the fact that he was 78 years old doubly reinforces the 'Massu/Pompidou hypothesis'. Having scarcely slept since his return from Roumania, he was physically and mentally exhausted, and the continuous public derision to which he had been exposed made it plain how remote he seemed, to the younger French, at any rate.

For many others, however, including Michel Jobert (at the time Pompidou's senior adviser) and de Gaulle's son-in-law Alain de Boissieu, his departure and return were part of what was to be a brilliantly successful strategy. Since his disastrous speech of 24 May the situation had paradoxically turned to his advantage, for the scent of political crisis, at which he was a past master, was in the air. His biographer Jean Lacouture astutely observes: 'If the move from the lyrical towards the economic was made at Grenelle, the shift from the mythical to the political came about at Charlety.'[32] The dreaded *insaissisable*, from being unlocalisably omnipresent, might soon be nowhere to be found. What better strategy, then, than to threaten his miscreant people with what Lacouture calls 'that version of Hell invented by modern theologians embarrassed by the giant cauldron that the Middle Ages promised sinners – the deprivation of the father'?[33]

The journey to Baden then comes to seem a masterstroke of rhetorical reversal, de Gaulle asserting his command by turning the 'shift from the mythical to the political' back upon itself and reminding everybody from his Prime Minister downwards that in his France at least the political had always been, and was now more than ever, inhabited by the mythical. He said in his speech the following day that he had considered 'every possibility, without exception', and Lacouture adds: 'every possibility, and perhaps at each and every moment'.[34] At a time when it seemed that 'everything was possible', including 'taking one's desires for reality' – at a time characterised by the living-out of contradictions in language – such a coexistence of incompossibles even at the vacillating heart of power might appear almost natural.

DE GAULLE STRIKES BACK

On 30 May at 4:30 p.m., de Gaulle addressed the French people for the second time in less than a week, on radio, with sound but not visual television transmission. Much of the ORTF was on strike (initially as a protest against government interference in their coverage of the student movement), so this may have been a shrewd insurance against the indignity of being cut off in mid-broadcast. But it also acted as a powerful reminder of another de Gaulle radio broadcast many years before – the 18 June Appeal of 1940, a call from temporary exile in London to resist the German invader. Philippe Alfonsi, in Maurice Dugowson's 1985 television programme *Paris, histoire d'un jour/Paris, the story of one day*, introduced the speech by saying, 'Here is how to turn round a country in four and a half minutes'; Joffrin describes it as 'a political masterpiece',[35] and it is difficult to disagree. The voice was confident, far more so than on 24 May, the speech itself a devastating blend of self-revelation ('I have considered every possibility, without exception'), self-assertion ('I shall not step down; I have a mandate from the people, and I shall carry it out'), cunningly-fostered paranoia ('the intimidation, poison and tyranny of organised groups'), the threat of stronger government intervention ('If this situation continues I shall have to . . . use other methods than immediate national elections'), brandishing of the 'Red peril' ('the power that imposed itself at a time of national despair . . . would be that of totalitarian Communism'), and a rousing final flourish of confidence in the French nation ('The Republic will not abdicate, the people will rally. Progress, peace and independence will triumph along with liberty'). He seized the short-term political initiative by announcing the dissolution of the National Assembly and elections for the end of the following month. Bertolt Brecht had ironically asked after the violent suppression of the 1953 riots in East Berlin: 'If the government does not like the people, why don't they dissolve it and elect another?' De Gaulle's speech came close to doing precisely that.

Its resonance – vocal and mythical – was one major reason, its invocation of a possible military intervention another. The violence hitherto, though spectacular, had been largely symbolic, and the lack of petrol meant that there were comparatively few deaths in France in May 1968.[36] A demonstrator interviewed on 24 May said 'They are fighting in Vietnam, they are fighting in Bolivia, so we can fight here',[37] but Hamon and Rotman are more judicious when they say of the 10 May 'night of the barricades': 'All night, they played at war. On both sides, though nothing was said, everybody knew that the ultimate limit would not be reached – the point of intentional killing.'[38] De Gaulle's repeated cavernous references to the Constitution acted as a reminder that as President he was supreme commander of the armed forces, and his call to 'civic action' and menacing allusion to 'other methods than immediate national elections' suggested that he would not hesitate to use his powers. The workers had received what by normal standards would have been thought an extremely favourable offer, the students were suffering from advanced battle fatigue and difficulty in agreeing on how and even whether to adopt a political strategy, and there was a growing sense of weariness with the climate of emergency and the paralysis of national life. De Gaulle's speech came just before the

Whitsun weekend holiday, which, with no petrol available, many Parisians must have felt doomed to spend trapped in their paralysed city.

The did not happen, for the evening of 30 May saw the biggest of all the demonstrations of the events – in support of de Gaulle. The Right-wing daily *La Nation* put the number who marched down the Champs-Élysées at a million, the police more prosaically at 300 000. François Mauriac and André Malraux showed that the literary world was not entirely behind the students and strikes; Malraux, as Minister of Culture, headed the procession along with ministers Michel Debré and Pierre Messmer. (Pompidou refused to attend, judging that his presence might seem provocative.) Many present were probably as apolitical as many of the student demonstrators had at first been, but along with the 'silent majority' there were uglier elements, rallied behind the régime by a promise of amnesty for OAS terrorists still in prison. Thus, along with cries of 'Come on, de Gaulle!' could be heard as a vicious echo of 'CRS–SS' 'Cohn-Bendit to Dachau!' Large demonstrations also took place in the provinces over the next few days. The 'movement' no longer had the field to itself. Petrol returned to the pumps just in time for the Whitsun exodus.

The UNEF called a demonstration on 1 June under the slogan: 'Elections = betrayal', but this stood little chance of winning mass support. The tone of demonstrations and occupations henceforth changed, becoming more acrimonious and beleaguered; the festive aspect of May turned out to be, as by some neo-pagan coincidence, coterminous with the calendar month. The tenth of June, on which date the electoral campaign began, brought the most celebrated death of the events – that of the school student Gilles Tautin, drowned when he jumped into a river at Flins (near Paris) to avoid charging police. The following day brought the last of the mass demonstrations and a third 'night of the barricades', as well as two deaths at Sochaux in Eastern France. The ORTF buildings had been reoccupied on 3 June; the Odéon and the Sorbonne were vacated on 14 and 16 June respectively. On 17 June, Renault returned to work on the basis of the Grenelle agreement, and other factories did likewise. On 30 June, the second round of parliamentary elections brought a crushing Gaullist victory. The 'parliament of the scared' (as de Gaulle himself dubbed it) had more than a hundred Right-wing gains from the Left (in an assembly 485 strong). The slogan 'It's only a beginning – let's continue the fight' was to be heard on Left-wing demonstrations for many years afterwards. What 'it' was a beginning of, and what it was or had been a 'fight' for, remained a matter for debate.

2 The Interpretations of the Crisis of May/June 1968

(by Philippe Bénéton and Jean Touchard, originally published in the Revue française des sciences politiques, *summer 1970; translated by Keith A. Reader)*

Subversive undertaking? Crisis of civilisation? The crisis of May/June 1968 has given rise to a multiplicity of explanations and mobilised any number of interpreters. Since they were so close to the events, many of these interpretations resemble lyrical pleading more than scientific study, whilst others, fewer in number, suggest the attitude of a prosecuting lawyer rather than that of an analyst. Almost always passionately written, they nonetheless reveal – even help to explain – a complex, heterogeneous crisis, in which each commentator can detect the best or the worst, find sources of justification or reasons for condemning/condemnation. Difficult to grasp or pin down, this crisis swept along with it all kinds of different elements and thus admits of the most varied interpretations: barbarian invasion or renewal of the spirit, poetic revolt or class-struggle, revolution of youth or spiritual crisis.

The explanations – all the way from a chance accident to a spiritual revolt – are to be found on different levels, covering the whole of the events or only part, and calling upon different disciplines: sociology, psychology, biology, psychoanalysis, and so on. Classifying them is a delicate operation, since they are not all equally ambitious. Some analysts are interested only in one aspect of the crisis, whereas others put forward overall explanations, brushing aside chronology to assimilate the university, social and political crises into one. We have still thought it possible to distinguish eight types of interpretation, on different levels and of unequal significance:

- an enterprise of subversion
- a crisis of the university
- a rush of blood to the head, a youthful revolt
- a spiritual revolt, a crisis of civilisation
- a class conflict, a new type of social movement
- a social conflict of a traditional kind
- a political crisis
- a chance combination of circumstances.[1]

Our ambition is simply to give a general view of these eight types of interpretation, letting those who put them forward speak for themselves and pointing out the problems they seem to us to present. We are well aware of the drawbacks of such an analytical approach, but it is surely more helpful (especially for non-French readers) to record as meticulously as possible what has been said or written by others[2] than to try to add to existing interpretations a new one – our own, and therefore correct . . .

1 AN ENTERPRISE OF SUBVERSION

Inevitably, the first and most tempting explanation is that of a plot. General de Gaulle, who was later to offer a broader interpretation of the crisis – we must not 'take a small view of a great matter'[3] – began by declaring on 30 May 1968: 'France . . . is threatened with a dictatorship. There are those who want to compel her to resign herself to a power imposed amid national despair, a power that would obviously be that of the victor, in other words of totalitarian communism.'[4]

Several months later, in March 1969, the President returned to the same explanation:

> For almost two months, work was systematically prevented everywhere. Because of this dreadful confusion, which for a great many people verged on despair, we saw its principal authors rise up against the Republic, temporarily escorted by a gaggle of dreamers, of ambitious or vindictive people, first to seize power, then to impose a crushing totalitarianism on the nation. We all know how this vast enterprise of destruction and subversion was thwarted, thanks to the cohesion of the régime and the massive confidence the people expressed when I appealed for it, first by marches and demonstrations, then by elections.[5]

In June 1968, M. Georges Pompidou, who had not yet had the time to analyse the crisis of youth as he was to do in San Francisco in February 1970,[6] stressed the responsibility of a 'totalitarian party':

> First of all, you will remember, professional subversive groups – *enragés*, hotheads, anarchists – led young people and students astray under the cloak of solidarity. And then the apparatus of a totalitarian party joined in, trying in its turn to take control of the streets, bringing economic activity to a halt, and, finally, openly demanding power.[7]

If the Prime Minister focused attention, for the purposes of the electoral campaign, on the attitude of the Communist Party, the Interior Minister was particularly eager to unmask revolutionary groups, whose 'true objective is the forcible overthrow of the government and the destruction of republican institutions and democracy':[8]

> For some years now several revolutionary parties – Trotskyist, Castrist or Maoist – have been organising in our country. These revolutionary movements – highly sectarian, activist, practising violence, each bringing together between 1000 and 3000 militants – have as their goal to seize political power. Any means to that end will do: insurrectional strikes, occupations of public services, street demonstrations, riots.
> These new revolutionary groups played a decisive role in the demonstrations and riots of last May.[9]

From one minister to the next, opinions differ. If M. Marcellin vigorously condemns agitators who exploit the young,[10] M. Edgar Faure authoritatively dismisses the conspiracy theory: 'The students' actions and agitation cannot be explained by the energy of a handful of leaders, nor by nihilism, nor even by a taste for violence. At the origin of this anger, there is a deep malaise.'[11] These inconsistent statements hardly elucidate the conspiracy theory.

Conspiracy – what conspiracy? It was doubtless politically adroit in May 1968, as it was electorally profitable in June, to speak to the French of a 'totalitarian enterprise' and to call up the spectre of communism before them, but it would scarcely need long analyses to prove that the PCF was quite foreign to any far-Left plot, that it refused to consider the situation as 'revolutionary' and that throughout the first phase of the crisis it played a resolutely moderating role.[12] After the National Assembly had been dissolved, it methodically embarked upon an electoral campaign that was to yield highly disappointing results. Without launching into a discussion that would go well beyond the bounds of this article, it seems better sense to maintain that the PCF 'objectively' helped in May 1968 to defend the régime of the Fifth Republic than to saddle it with the responsibility of a subversive enterprise.

If responsibility for the plot cannot rest with the PCF, it is obviously possible to impute it to Beijing, to Havana, to the CIA, or (as François Duprat does) to East Germany.[13] These different statements are interesting, but they are and remain hypotheses, with the major drawback of lending the various 'sects' – anarchists, Lambertist Trotskyists, Franckist Trotskyists, Moaists, PCF dissidents, and so on – a coherence that (appearances notwithstanding) they certainly did not have in May 1968 and that even since the end of the crisis has been fragile to say the least.[14] To be sure, the militants of the 22 March Movement, the JCR, the FER, the UJCml . . .

played, along with the militants of the majority tendency in the UNEF,[15] a decisive role in sparking off the crisis with their simple yet effective tactics – 'provocation' leading to 'repression', solidarity demonstrations, occupations of university buildings, the setting-up of action committees, general assemblies, and so on. But the origin of the 'infernal machine'[16] is still obscure, and does not account for the impact of the revolt in the student milieu, or the wider effect of the crisis. It is thus important to seek other types of explanation.

2   A CRISIS IN THE UNIVERSITY

Speaking of the University on 24 May 1968, General de Gaulle denounced 'the powerlessness of this great institution to adapt to the nation's modern requirements as well as to the role and the employment of the young'.[17] Thus indicted by the President, the University has since that date been the object of a great many analyses, most of them far from indulgent. But, if value-judgements and peremptory statements abound, it is much less common to come across an attempt at dispassionate interpretation[18] or so precise a testimony as Épistémon's on the Faculty of Letters at Nanterre.[19]

Among all these analyses, we can distinguish between those that stress the ossification of the university and those that emphasise the student's social marginality.

The ossified university

Since late spring 1968, denunciations of the 'Napoleonic university'[20] have been commonplace and a great many people have vigorously denounced 'stilted, inert structures in thrall to stifling centralisation'.[21] Centralisation means uniformity, paralysing control, no autonomy. It means both vertical rigidity – iron curtains between faculties and disciplines – and horizontal rigidity – complete separation between those with doctorates and those without in faculties of letters, between those with the *agrégation* and those without in law or medical faculties.

Two years before the May 1968 crisis, the trial of university structures had begun at a conference in Caen,[22] by lecturers most of whom came from science faculties. These lecturers debated at great length autonomy, 'multidisciplinarity', and the 'abolition of professorial chairs', and advocated the founding of universities in the full sense of the word, not simply groupings of faculties intended to admit vast numbers of students and all conforming to the same model. Concrete proposals were put forward after this conference, arousing great hostility in faculties of letters and law, but several papers aiming to make university structures more flexible had been prepared by the Education ministry. These texts were supposedly 'about to be published' in the spring of 1967; they were still supposedly 'about to be published' in April 1968.

Was the university then resistant to *any* change? So thought Michel Crozier, who applied to the university his analyses of the 'bureaucratic phenomenon':

> Such a system is naturally impervious to change. It can neither perceive nor adapt to new social demands. Changing the syllabus calls into question career prospects and the power of the teaching body. Changing working methods and relationships would unbalance the organisation, and any change in the organisation is blocked by the opposition of lecturers and the struggles between the different groups who divide up power.[23]

These statements seem too general to pass unquestioned. To be sure, the university suffered from its rigid structures, and administrative centralisation, institutional uniformity, and the corporate conservatism of all-too-many members of staff presented obstacles to change, but we should distinguish between, on the one hand, power relationships and the organisation of study and, on the other, the different faculty groupings.

A great many reforms had indeed taken place over the previous fifteen or so years. Law degrees had been restructured in 1954 and 1959, medicine in 1958 and 1961, science and letters in 1966 pharmacy in 1963, and so on. These reforms, whose scope varied from one discipline to the next, did not stem from an overall view of the university; they were basically concerned with the syllabus and the organisation of study and did not affect either university structures nor the power relationships within each faculty.

This inflexibility quite clearly favoured the development of *contestation* – not, it would seem, vertical inflexibility, which never greatly troubled the revolting students, so much as horizontal inflexibility, which helped to mobilise a great many junior lecturers on the students' side.[24] The support of these junior staff members undoubtedly boosted the *contestataire* movement in the occupied faculties, but it would be rash to conclude that the May explosion stemmed from a revolt against ill-adapted university structures.

It is worth noting that it was not in the most traditional institutions but in those such as the Faculty of Letters at Nanterre, open to innovation and liberally administered, that the movement started and was strongest. Nothing would thus be more misleading than to suppose some connection of cause and effect between the outdatedness of structures and the scale of *contestation.* That seems to be much more closely linked with the profound change in the student population over a number of years and the radical change in students' situation.

Students' 'social marginality'

Higher education's public has changed markedly over the past fifteen years. The number of students has increased particularly rapidly: 30 000 in 1900–1, 135 000 in 1950–1, 395 000 in 1965–6, 508 000 in 1967–8, 587 000 in 1968–9.[25] The number of students has quadrupled in fifteen years.

The problems posed by this spectacular increase are aggravated by uneven distribution. More than a third of French students [nearly 200 000] – are in faculties of letters, where the main subsequent career is teaching – not notoriously attractive to students nor offering a particularly wide range of openings.[26] Within faculties of letters, students, attracted by the prestige of human sciences more than by a career in teaching, register in large numbers in sociology and psychology departments, where prospects are highly uncertain.

Furthermore, as Raymond Boudon clearly shows, the social structure of the student population has changed considerably over the past fifteen years.

Imperceptibly between the pre-war period and 1950, quite abruptly since, we have gone from a "bourgeois" university to one dominated by the middle classes.[27]

These changes have important consequences:

Today, especially since 1950, the complicity or collaboration between society and the family on one hand, the university on the other, seems less and less secure. The clerk's or workman's son going up to university cannot as a rule expect from his family or social background advice on the kind of course to choose, and technical and economic development has increased the range of professional activities, of which there are now a whole range of types that were all but unknown only ten years ago (information technology, sociology, psychology, etc.). Today's typical student thus has to make a more difficult choice than his predecessor, and one for which he is less prepared by his social peer-group.[28]

So the student starts out on a little-known route, strewn with obstacles, where the drop-out or failure rate is high. A rough calculation shows that

a student starting at university has a slightly better than even chance of emerging with a qualification after an 'average' period of study. . . . This combination of factors means that a seemingly growing number of students are prey to anomie. Not only do they have only a vague picture of what will become of them when they leave, but the length and direction of their studies are largely indeterminate.[29]

Thus, while they may occupy the rank of 'heirs' to culture, the students of 1968 certainly do not enjoy that security. Difficulty in making choices, along with fear of failure, social regression or unemployment, account for students' anxiety about their professional future:

> A high risk of failure, marking time, or social regression for some, of difficulty in finding a job after four or five years' higher education for others – that is what faces university students, especially in letters and in sciences. The unchecked play of social forces has thus led to a considerable worsening of the student's situation in an ever-wealthier society, whose intelligentsia takes perhaps premature delight in analysing the woes bred by the opulence of industrial societies.[30]

All this widespread anxious questioning on career prospects,[31] examinations, professional activity, has been reinforced by a general condemnation of the bourgeois university and of bourgeois culture – a culture spread by heirs for heirs,[32] in which lecturers are capitalism's 'guard-dogs',[33] 'the wretchedness of the student world',[34] the demands for 'student power' or the 'student veto'. . . .

Some of these themes subsequently received official sanction. M. Edgar Faure lost few opportunities to echo Bourdieu's and Passeron's ideas, criticising syllabuses and methods of assessment 'unconsciously favourable to particular categories or groups',[35] and condemning 'the transmission of privileges which, despite appearances, the traditional system of competitive examinations simply continues ad infinitum'.[36] It is interesting to note that these ideas reached a very wide audience, and were endorsed by the minister, just when empirical studies were tending to question their validity. On the basis of a survey of the results of 6919 letters to students, Noëlle Bisseret concluded:

> The objective situation seems to be determinant, since for students in a comparable position the success-rate is similar, whatever social category they belong to. Likewise, in the first year at university (though perhaps not by the time of finals), the better-off students do not seem to be favoured by the cultural advantages they owe to their family surroundings, since their success-rate is no higher than that of others at the same level.[37]

Another survey, carried out at Toulouse on 'ten years of a student generation',[38] showed that lowly social origin was no bar to success in examinations. Indeed, proportionately more working-class students get as far as the CAPES or *agrégation*.

These surveys – to which can be added Christian Delage's on first-degree work (letters, science and law) at Orléans, which draws similar conclusions, – probably have only limited scope. They simply go to show that in any event in faculties of letters (the sociologists' favourite target, and for them an important example), and conceivably in the university as a whole, as Delage seems to suggest,[39] there is no social elimination by way of university examinations. The most that can be claimed is that this examination does not so much eliminate culture's orphans rather than its heirs (which the statistics disprove) as keep in higher education heirs unworthy of the privilege. This argument seems implausible if we bear in mind the high failure-rates of students from better-off groups.[40] It remains true that the material advantages of such students do make it possible for a number of them to remain at university despite repeated failures, and that more generally their cultural inheritance is an important advantage for them, but one that comes into play before university, at primary and secondary school.

Nevertheless, the notion that higher education's 'objective role is to endorse by way of examinations membership of the cultured class'[41] was generally accepted by *contestataire* students, and was the main theme of a great many manifestos or pamphlets denouncing class education and bourgeois culture.[42]

Whilst these themes are hardly adequate to account for the crisis, the condemnation of the culture spread by the university and sanctioned by examinations would surely not have reached such a wide audience if examinations had not caused students profound anxiety. This anxiety was perceptible throughout May and June, and it is surely no coincidence that the crisis erupted just when examinations were beginning. During the crisis, 'selection' was vehemently denounced and, from the first days the faculties were occupied, the problem of examinations took an important, perhaps even essential, place in discussions between students.[43] So can one explain the university crisis by a fear of failure and the hazards of social competition? Partial as it may be, such an explanation can be advanced, bearing in mind the problems of competition within the university. This competition is arduous (many are called, but few are chosen), shortlived (it lasts only a few years), and sometimes offers only disappointing prospects (a mediocre social position and problems in finding a job). Because there is no preliminary guidance or selection, the whole professional future of thousands of students is decided in a few years, and only a minority will reach the high social level they had all hoped for on entry. Thus, 'examination results have come to appear as verdicts without appeal on the social position of those concerned'.[44]

Such competition can certainly cause distress and arouse tension, the more so as today's students form an unstructured mass, a 'lonely crowd' as Riesman puts it, a demanding yet anxious group with neither power nor responsibility, a mass of young adults reduced to the rank of consumers (of textbooks, handouts, knowledge), a group marginal in twentieth-century society.[45]

Yet this situation is not unique to France, and it seems hard to maintain that the university crisis, any more than the ideology and the actions of Left-wing sects, was in any way radically different from those that erupted at the same time in many other countries. What was unique to France was that the May 1968 crisis spread with extraordinary speed to the rest of society. To explain this quite unforeseen 'infectiousness', we shall have to look at more general interpretations.

3   A RUSH OF BLOOD TO THE HEAD: A YOUTHFUL REVOLT

A number of interpretations emphasise the psychological or psychoanalytic dimension of the crisis. A pacified, 'peace-sick' society[46] suddenly went from boredom[47] to fever, compensating in a moment's utopian explosion for the rigidity of its structures, the hierarchy of its spaces, the anonymity of its institutions. The lonely crowd was replaced by the fraternal community, relationships of subordination by a mysticism of equality, learnt behaviour by creative spontaneity: it was a game, a festival, a joyous release.[48]

This is the first form this interpretation takes – the sudden rush of blood of a pacified society. The second stresses more the youthful aspect of the revolt, leading to a psychoanalytic explanation through the 'murder of the father'.

A 'rush of blood'

A 'rush of blood', a 'psychodrama', a 'tragi-comedy', a 'vast release':[49] these are Raymond Aron's terms to define a crisis whose analysis inspired him to make this remark: 'The most suitable interpretative methods for the recent crisis are those that seem the most undistinguished: G. Lebon's crowd psychology or the interpretation of Pareto'.[50]

On the most general level – the student revolts in the USA, in Germany, in France, outbursts of violence in developed countries – Raymond Aron advances two explanations:

One is quasi-biological or psychological, the other sociological. The more peaceful character of our collective life leads to a kind of repression of our aggressive drives. Even sexual liberation does not necessarily mean that desires are satisfied. Society, as Marcuse would say, remains oppressive or, to use Konrad Lorenz's terms, man, an aggressive animal, needs to express his aggression. The sociological explanation stresses alternation: people are apparently reduced to private individuals, without membership of a religious or political community, when all of a sudden, alone in their love of comfort and prosperity, they are gripped by passion. This may be a rush of blood with definite aims leading to political or social upheavals, or one without definite aims, such as now. Without a model that satisfies our aspirations, these rushes of blood are essentially negative, nihilistic or destructive.[51]

For Raymond Aron, this 'compensatory' phenomenon is especially clear in French society:

The French suffer from an over-rigid system and an over-authoritarian hierarchy. Why do they retain such ecstatic memories of the periods when they dash everything to the ground? In these periods of crisis, when the system collapses, they have the illusion of fraternity – an emotion they feel – and of equality – a living reality for them – before they once again submit to their hierarchical shackles. The French since 1789 have with hindsight magnified their revolutions, those great festivals during which they live out everything they lack in normal times and feel as if they were fulfilling their aspirations, even if only in a waking dream.[52]

At the level of the university, the problem is worsened by the large mass of students and the individual's psychological situation:

French students, particularly in Paris, are a lonely crowd. A great many of them suffer from loneliness and the lack of community life – the lack of contact not just with distant lecturers, true though that often is, but with their fellow-students. . . . This kind of youthful fraternity in a semi-delinquent community is an overcompensation for the isolation in which French students generally live.[53]

For Aron, whose attitude towards the May crisis resembles Tocqueville's towards the 1848 revolution,[54] the French of 1968 played at revolution as their 1848 ancestors played at the revolution of 1789. An American academic, Robert Masters, goes much further; comparing in all seriousness the young revolutionaries' behaviour to that of young monkeys, he stresses the 'biological roots of revolt'.[55]

Without stooping to the level of animal comparisons, can we speak of a compensatory phenomenon, a collective release? There is no shortage of arguments and eye-witness accounts to corroborate the idea of a psychodrama on the grand scale. Who was not struck by the atmosphere of revolt? – the game, the festival, the influence of the street, the liberation of the spoken word, the flood of slogans and images, the blossoming of utopian dreams.

The street. Marching, singing, demonstrating, occupying the street, being with one's fellows, getting away from the bourgeois areas, discovering solidarity, merging with a crowd: that was an elementary and powerful feeling shared by a great many students – especially on the great demonstration of 13 May – much as their parents' generation had discovered it at the time of the Popular Front.

The festival. René Pascal tells us: 'Then all at once everything changed. Extraordinary things happened. Without drums or trumpets, an astonishing crisis erupted, undoubtedly the most disconcerting the French had ever experienced. . . . For thirty days French society was in a festive trance.'[56]

The game. Épistémon tells us: 'It's true – we all played a little. What happened was in part unreal. . . '.[57]

The liberation of the spoken word. Father de Certeau declares: 'Last May, we took the word as the Bastille was taken in 1789.'[58] Less enthusiastically, Raymond Aron speaks of a 'marathon talking-shop'.

The movement's slogans[59] show the blossoming of utopian dreams,[60] general contestation and the temptation of nihilism, the cult of spontaneity and the refusal of any organisation, the 'clean sheet' and the desire to provoke. Trying to analyse this ideology, Jean-Marie Domenach wrote in *Esprit*:

> The movement's playful aspect can be understood from its lack of theoretical consistency. If one cannot play one's own 'character', one plays several. That is one way of not being too rapidly paralysed by ideas and institutions when you have no clear vision of the society you want to build. The movement is kaleidoscopic: from Saint-Just to Guevara, by way of Rimbaud, Bonnot and his band of robbers, Trotsky, André Breton, it brings together all the outcasts of revolution, all the traditions of political and poetic assault on the established order . . .
>
> But the key point is this: in the name of what is this critique of society carried out? We have made out the answer, and it is not a paltry one: in the name of the desire to live, to express oneself, to be free.[61]

Thus May appears as a moment of dream and of revolt, which made it possible to mark a break with everyday life, to go beyond differences of age, origin and ability in a lyrical illusion, to transcend in fraternal celebration hierarchies and divisions, in a word to free the imagination and evict the rational. It was a utopian parenthesis, an explosion of 'the powers of life and freedom'.[62]

'The sudden emergence of youth' – The 'murder of the father'

According to Edgar Morin, the May–June crisis shows 'the sudden emergence of youth into French society':

> We must ask ourselves, in all Marxist orthodoxy, whether the 'intelligentsia' that thinks it is carrying out the proletarian revolution of Marx and Lenin is not really doing something else – bringing about a kind of youthful sociological 1789 and the sudden emergence of youth as a socio-political force. This new contribution of the young has come about only thanks to Marxist ideas and instruments, which justify their aggression and give it a constructive direction as they confer ideological coherence upon an effervescence that is still in search of its shape and its real name.
>
>   What is certain is that at the moment the student vanguard is playing the part of an intelligentsia, showing the way to young people who have joined the movement in all walks of life.[63]

We shall not ask whether it is right for Edgar Morin to speak here of 'Marxist orthodoxy'. The most we can say is that the 'spontaneous solidarity' of which he speaks seems to have concerned not all young people, but only a fraction of them. The collaboration between students and young workers does not as a rule seem to have gone beyond a pious wish, and the best-placed observers all agree that young farm-workers remained almost entirely indifferent to the movement.[64]

The opinion polls carried out early in 1969 likewise seem to disprove the view that the May crisis was the massive uprising of single-minded youth. An IFOP survey presents 'a reassuring picture of reasonable young people'.[65] Of those questioned, 89 per cent describe themselves as very (35 per cent) or fairly (54 per cent) happy; 71 per cent believe that 'the best thing about France is freedom'. There are, to be sure, doubts to be raised about a survey carried out eight months after May and containing some highly ambiguous questions.[66] And what does it mean to describe oneself as 'fairly happy'?

Did May have roots in the unconscious for those who experienced it intensely? Yes, according to two psychoanalysts who, in their study of *L'Univers contestationnaire/The World of contestation*, see the Oedipus complex as the key explanation.[67]

This world is characterised, for the authors, by hostility to any form of authority, the wish for absolute equality, and the constant striving to create – all revealing a refusal of fatherhood ('This is not about overthrowing the father, but about doing away with the order of the father – fatherhood, descendence, the family and its offshoots').[68]

Whereas the revolutionary sets himself up as a rival to the father and tries to achieve something, 'the *contestataire*, in rejecting the father, rejects reality and wants to replace it with a narcissistic ideal that is by definition impossible, since the least attempt to bring it about at once moves it from the narcissistic realm to that of reality, which has to be contested. Everything must be possible, but nothing must be achieved: "Be realistic, demand the impossible"'.[69]

Whereas the revolutionary is constructive, the *contestataire* 'wants above all to destroy (to "smash the joint up"). His negative ambition is only hazily justified by a few vague ands often contradictory formulas. . . . If the revolutionary puts his Oedipal dynamism at the service of a social 'cause' where the end and the means correspond, the *contestataire* will use society as a pretext for reacting against his own family conflict.'[70]

Even if one is slightly allergic to the vocabulary of psychoanalysis and feels slightly awkward faced with the virtually obligatory invocation of the Oedipus complex, it seems undeniable that psychoanalytic considerations can account for some individual itineraries. May revealed an extraordinary amount about people, sometimes very different from might have been expected considering their political and ideological views. People's enthusiasm, reservations, or outright hostility to the movement corresponded only very roughly to preexisting divisions between left, centre, and right.

So if it seems to us risky to explain May in terms of a collective psychoanalysis, and if in any event this type of explanation would need to be combined with a good few others, it also seems that individual psychology could illuminate some aspects of the crisis. It might well be possible, and it would not be without interest, to discover for what intimate reasons this or that individual had this or that attitude. But might this not atomise our analysis, and lose sight of the deeper causes of the revolt?

4 A SPIRITUAL REVOLT – A CRISIS OF CIVILISATION

Explanation diverge, ranging from playing at revolution to spiritual revolt, but analyses are often similar. It is on the basis of the same factors – dream, rejection, affirmation of vitality, and so forth – that some interpreters deduce a general crisis of values or a spiritual uprising.

This interpretation can appear on one of two levels. May is seen either as a spiritual revolt against an unjust or absurd society, or as the symptom of a more widespread upheaval –a crisis of civilisation.

A spiritual revolt

On 28 May 1968, Maurice Clavel wrote in *Combat*:

> We must repeat for as long as we can that this revolution is first and foremost a spiritual one. The spirit is taking its revenge, and not before time. Hope is with us, in the hands of students and young workers. They are not asking for vast salaries; they want to change life, to use a phrase whose simplicity is as illuminating as it is disruptive. This is radiant and triumphant. We must no more be afraid of it than we are of the sacred.
>
> Nobody has died, yet the old kind of life has already become impossible.

Was there a spiritual uprising? What is the 'spirit'? What is at the origin of the insurrection?

According to the editor of *Esprit*, Jean-Marie Domenach, the movement rose up against a certain type of society:

> The movement's failure causes despair to those who threw themselves into it body and soul. But could it have succeeded politically when it rejected any form of organisation, old or new? Its political failure does not detract from its central inspiration – the attack on a repressive and absurd society. It did not stem from a social class or an oppressed people. Its target was less a régime than a so-called 'civilisation'.[71]

Discovering in the May 1968 movement the origins of *Esprit*, the inspiration of the 1930s and the struggle against 'institutionalised disorder', Jean-Marie Domenach wrote a few months earlier:

> Politically the movement failed and could not have done otherwise, since it proclaimed itself at once against society and against political parties, and had neither the will nor the time to organise itself. But the failure of the political illusion should not make us forget the deeper sense of the movement: it was aimed in the first place at a civilisation, and secondarily at a régime that embodies and exaggerates its failings. . . .
>
> Political ups and downs will not overcome such an uprising. What is under way is the invention of a way of life that will take years to emerge fully. Europe has finally given its first hesitant response to the fascination of Americanism, a response that has come from the people and not just

from a few intellectuals. Let us help to extend it towards other layers of society, so that Europe may arise from its torpor and rediscover its forgotten passion: to change life.[72]

In much the same way, Jacques Maritain sees the revolt as reflecting metaphysical disquiet and stemming from a bankruptcy of values:

It is not simply about badly-organised education, or the lack of practical openings, or the incompatibility between a soulless civilisation and the basic needs of human life revealing itself to young people of a sudden and rightly arousing their anger. A metaphysical disquiet – even if one is not equipped to perceive it as such – is making itself felt in the depths of people's minds, affecting the young most cruelly because they are not yet inured to lying to themselves. What I am talking about is the void, the utter lack of any absolute value or law grounded in truth, with which young people are confronted by the dominant intelligentsia and an education system that on the whole (despite a good many individual exceptions) blithely betrays its essential mission. Young people today have been systematically deprived of any reason to live.[73]

The idea of a spiritual crisis found another defender in Edgar Faure who, when he was Agriculture Minister in May 1968, told the farmers' unions:

The current 'events' reflect a crisis which is not solely educational, economic, or social. It is a spiritual crisis with its origins in the upheavals of our age. . . . These upheavals, notably those due to technological progress, present everyone with the problem of what life means and what kind of society we should have. At bottom, it is the same problem as the [Catholic] *aggorniamento.*

For a long time, membership of the human community was seen as an insurance premium. Now, it also has to entail an active founding element.[74]

Did the May events express spiritual hunger, the result of moral and metaphysical bankruptcy? There is no doubt that they tapped generous dreams and lofty aspirations. Some rose up against the so-called 'consumer society',[75] many Catholics saw a chance to put forward the values of the Gospel in everyday life,[76] a number of intellectuals took up their old longing for a cultural revolution,[77] but commentators on the student movement use the term 'spiritual revolt' much more often than the students themselves. There were certainly those who experienced May as the proof of a spiritual lack and the search for reasons to live, but a reading of published texts and eye-witness accounts hardly suggests that these problems concerned more than a small minority of students or made any impact on the working class.

This impression seems to be borne out by an IFOP survey[78] carried out among students in September 1968. Here are the questions and the answers:

Students and school students have been classified into three basic categories: (a) those who want not just to change the university, but to transform society radically, (b) those who are actively trying to reform the university, syllabuses and teaching methods, (c) those who basically just want to take their exams. Which of these attitudes is closest to yours?

(a) 12%   (b) 54%   (c) 31%   3% did not answer

Here are three explanations for the student troubles of May and June. Will you place them in order of importance?

Worry about the chance of finding a job corresponding to one's studies: 1st 56%   2nd 33%   3rd 8%.
Rejection of consumer society; 1st 7%   2nd 10%   3rd 80%.
The unadaptedness of universities – curricula, teaching methods and material resources – to today's cultural needs: 1st 35%   2nd 54%   3rd 8%.

It is true that this poll covers a representative sample of the student *population*, not of the student *movement*. Even so, if only 7 per cent of students see the rejection of consumer society as the main reason for the explosion, we can be sceptical about the importance of this as the major explanation of the crisis.

If May was a spiritual revolt, it seems to have remained at the level of instinctive affirmation. If it reflected a spiritual deficiency, that seems on the whole to have remained unconscious or unexpressed.

A crisis of civilisation

Was May typical of French society, or was it the symptom of a wider crisis? In an article written on Whit Sunday, *Esprit* had mentioned 'the first phase of the first post-marxist revolution in Western Europe',[79] and in the same issue Jean-Marie Domenach's conclusion was: 'It has now become possible to imagine a revolution affecting not just a régime or a type of property relation, but as Emmanuel Mounier wished when he founded this journal, a whole civilisation'.[80]

This theme was put forward with customary eloquence by André Malraux in June 1968:

May began with the events at the Sorbonne, about which it is pointless to say any more. The students' most legitimate demands do not conceal from us that their problem is an international one. It is already part of history, universities are closed in China, students are fighting in Japan, in revolt in Germany, Italy, Holland, and even on the other side of the Iron Curtain. They are in revolt in American universities – hardly antique Sorbonnes. They are in revolt in the University of Mexico City, where they have their own police and the federal police have never set foot. Students have always been unruly, but it would be ridiculous to suggest that their current unruliness is like that of the Middle Ages when it is much more like that in California. To be sure, we have to reform the Sorbonne, Nanterre, and perhaps the whole education system, especially with new audio-visual technology knocking on the door. But can we not see that a reform of education throughout the world has less to do with its reform in the narrow sense than with its replacement by something that is sometimes chaos but would often like to be fraternity? What the real students expect of us is hope; but standing next to hope is the most fascinating of negative feelings, our old friend nihilism with its black flag, putting its sole hope in destruction. We are facing not calls for reform, but one of the deepest crises our civilisation has known.[81]

At Strasbourg, at the Young Gaullists' conference (13 April 1969), Malraux returns to his theme:

But you have one particular enemy, against whom your fate is to be played out. This is the unprecedented abdication of the world's young people, from Mexico to Japan. This vast despair, this convulsive revolt that confuses its joltings with the continuity indispensable to action, is what I once called the lyrical illusion, but it is also a tragic form of abdication. The times of the Apocalypse lead only to their own destruction. Faced with a desertion that rages round the world like an intermittent blaze, what can you do? You can make yours a phrase that you have not forgotten: 'I shall not step down'.[82]

These breathless statements open wide perspectives for thought, but there has been so much talk since the end of the last century of a 'crisis of civilisation' that the very word 'civilisation' is today somewhat worn-out and Malraux's interpretation seems dazzling rather than precise.

Is the 'civilisation' of which Malraux speaks the same as that whose decadence was proclaimed by Nietzsche's contemporaries as they were discovering the 'illusions of progress';[83] the temptation of nihilism and the mobilising function of myth? Is it the same as that spoken of in 1926 by the young author of *La tentation de l'Occident/The temptation of the West* himself? If it is a universal crisis of civilisation, then what is a 'universal civilisation'? Is 'civilisation' for Malraux characterised by a particular type of economic or socio-cultural relationship? Is it not rather the eternally reborn civilisation of non-sense, non-being and the absence of hope, the civilisation that condemns those living in it to non-existence? Are Malraux's young Strasbourg audience the only ones to reject this 'civilisation'? Should we not ask somewhat more precise questions about the social dimension of the crisis?

5   A CLASS CONFLICT – A NEW KIND OF SOCIAL MOVEMENT

Alain Touraine, Professor of Sociology at Nanterre, detects in the May movement the germ of a new kind of conflict, characteristic of 'programmed' society:

> The May movement is a new form of the class struggle. More than any other action in the past few decades, it has laid bare, and thereby constituted, the basic conflict in our society. . . .
>
> The current conflict is not directly an economic one; it is not concerned with the opposition between those who make the profit and workers reduced by exploitation to a minimal standard of living . . . Students in France, like their counterparts in Berlin or Berkeley, are in struggle against apparatuses of integration, manipulation and aggression. It is these words, not 'exploitation', that best define what the conflict is about. The struggle is not against capitalism, but primarily against technocracy.[84]

This fight against technocratic power 'is not a direct struggle, for it principally attacks the identification of this power with economic rationality and social progress'.[85]

Before May, in France, intellectual or limited forms of *contestation* had called into question this or that aspect of the dominant social order. But the May movement, by its very existence, laid bare beyond the multiplicity of social, national and international problems the unity of a system of power and domination.[86]

Of course, this movement takes varied forms, and the term 'class conflict' 'is in no sense a complete definition of what was at once a revolt, a striving for revolution and a trade-union struggle',[87] but it is still 'the most important element of it and at the same time the least obvious in a historical perspective'.[88]

So it is that the May events set before us a new type of conflict, where what is at stake is less economic interests than the power to take decisions, culture and individuality, whose actors are no longer the bourgeoisie and the working class but new social categories:

> The main actor in May was not the working class, but the whole of those who might be called professionals, whether they actually have a profession or are still in training. Among these the most active were those who were most independent of the large organisations for which, directly or indirectly, they worked: students, ORTF journalists, laboratory technicians, researchers (publicly or privately employed), teachers, and so on. The new class struggle brings techno-bureaucrats directly into conflict with professionals.[89]

This interpretation is a forecast as much as an empirical analysis, so that it largely escapes contemporary criticism. But it can still not fail to raise a certain number of questions.

Alain Touraine cannot be said to define the new 'dominant power' with sufficient clarity, and his successive statements may leave the reader somewhat perplexed. For:

(i)   There would seem to be one single dominant power: 'May revealed . . . the unity of a system of power and domination'.[90]

(ii) This dominant power appears to be technocracy: 'technocracy is a ruling class',[91] 'at the service of large apparatuses of production'.[92] These apparatuses 'take in hand both the growth of the economy and the manipulation of society'.[93]

(iii) Political power has a clearly determined function: 'Political power does not administer the common welfare; it imposes, through institutions and their administrative organisation, the domination of a few over society as a whole'.[94]

(iv) But technocratic power does not automatically entail political power: 'the existence of a technocratic class certainly does not imply that class itself holds political power, reducing the State to a mere instrument of the ruling class. This schematic picture is no truer today than it was last century'.[95]

Besides all this, the appearance of a social movement – that of the 'professionals' – is far from proven. The May/June strikes were undoubtedly characterised by a new phenomenon, sensed by a number of shrewd observers – the adhesion of technicians and of management. But, without a detailed study of this extremely important tendency (one of the most important for political sociology), we cannot tell whether it was a general movement or one confined to firms and organisations with particular characteristics. Moreover, even if this tendency did appear widespread (which we beg leave to doubt), we should need to ask it more questions about itself. Was it a movement inspired by neo-corporate demands or by the discovery of new forms of solidarity? If the second, was it a (problematic) solidarity with the working class or a (scarcely more obvious) solidarity with the students in revolt? In short, was it a more or less passing convergence of demands, a solidarity in action – or the birth of a new social class, the 'professionals'?

To these questions Alain Touraine gives no answers.[96] His stimulating generalisations bring to mind ideas on the 'new working class' that were highly successful a few years back but remain unproven. It is striking to note that this work – written by a sociologist – give only the bare minimum of details on the economic and social situation of France in 1968.

6   A TRADITIONAL TYPE OF SOCIAL CONFLICT

A new form of social struggle – or a traditional type of conflict? If Touraine confers upon the workers' strikes the seal of novelty, other explanations go back to what is traditionally at stake in social conflicts – material demands – and account for the rapid spread of the crisis largely, if not solely, by the economic and social situation.

The economic and social situation

Historians recently have perhaps been too clever by half in uncovering the economic causes of political movements, but those who have written on May have certainly not followed that example. Yet an analysis of the economic and social situation just before the crisis broke would have a good deal to teach us.[97]

The French economy enjoyed twenty years of uninterrupted growth after the end of the Second World War. One result of this was that 22-year-olds in 1968 lived in an economic and material world very different from that of their counterparts in earlier generations. The difference between 1958 and 1968 is striking, whereas between 1928 and 1958 it is almost negligible.

But, after 1958's successful devaluation, the stabilisation plan launched in 1963, and the slow recovery starting in May 1965, things began to decline in July 1966, and 1967 was worse for the French economy than any other that decade. The decline in production and the slowing in the growth-rate were comparatively slight, but the employment situation was bad, and the unemployment curve kept on climbing regardless of other factors.

Depending on which set of figures one chooses, there is an 800 per cent variation in the number of unemployed at the beginning of 1968: in February 112 000 workers claiming benefit (four times more than in 1964)[98], in April 245 000 registered as seeking work, 370 000 if on top of this we include non-registered unemployed, and as many as 800 000 if we take into account what economists call participation rate – including women, young people and the elderly who are neither working nor seeking work but would do so if the situation were more favourable.

These figures may seem unimportant, bearing in mind that France has a working population of 20 million, but they are the highest the country has known for a long time. Worse still, half the unemployed were less than twenty-five years old, and official statements stressing the increase in gold and dollar holdings tended to give credibility to the idea that increased unemployment was the natural consequence of economic modernisation, growing productivity and the opening of frontiers. It is easy to understand that the people most affected seemed less than entirely convinced by these arguments.

France's economic situation was clearly not so serious as to be properly considered a cause of May. However, the steady and seemingly inexorable rise in unemployment, affecting above all the young, helped to maintain a general feeling of worry and uncertainty about prospects which, once the crisis had been sparked off in the universities, gave it a momentum that Pompidou's government did not appear to have foreseen.

Monopoly politics

The PCF did not seem to foresee May/June any more than the government, yet that does not prevent it from saying (with the benefit of hindsight) that the events were inevitable. Its (then) General Secretary put forward an explanation so simple as to be self-evident:

> There is nothing mysterious behind the unprecedentedly vast strike of May/June 1968; it is the result of the government's policy over the past ten years. The ruling classes have been cynically indifferent to the workers' most urgent needs, and the fruits of scientific and technical progress have been confiscated by a small oligarchy. The working class did not need to wait for things to happen in the Latin Quarter to show its dissatisfaction. Do we have to recall the miners' 35-day strike in 1963? Is it necessary to bring to mind the great days of 1967 – 1 February, 17 May, 13 December – or the full symbolic force of the CGT demonstration on 1 May 1968?[99]

The strikes and demonstrations of May and June are the first major conflict of accelerated capitalist concentration, the first major clash between the mass of workers by hand or by brain and monopoly power grappling with contradictions it cannot resolve.[100]

Thus, for the PCF, the strikes of May and June were different only in scale from earlier ones, and can be similarly explained as 'workers' legitimate demands' in the face of 'capitalist exploitation' and 'monopoly power'. This is an explanation (albeit within a long-established ideological system)[101] rooted in the economic and social situation and a traditional model of social conflict.

If for the PCF May was first and foremost a social crisis, other observers stress its political and institutional aspects.

7 A POLITICAL CRISIS

Institutional responsibility

The crisis erupted just when de Gaulle's popularity, after a slight decline, was back at its 1964–7 level, and that of Georges Pompidou, his Prime Minister, was steadily rising. In April 1968, 61 per cent of respondents (as against 53 per cent in January) pronounced themselves satisfied with the President, a similat proportion to the period between 1964 and 1967.[102] The Prime Minister's popularity rose from 43 per cent in December 1967 to 48 per cent in April 1968.[103]

It thus seems impossible to back up with serious arguments the notion (largely accepted in countries hostile to Gaullist foreign policy) that the main cause of May was de Gaulle's unpopularity and the discredit into which the Fifth Republic had fallen. But we should still ask ourselves whether certain specific features of the French political system, without actually sparking off the crisis, did not greatly help to amplify it and give it, within a few days, a dramatic character.

In *Le Figaro* (5 June 1968), Raymond Aron emphasised, from a Tocquevillian perspective, the responsibility of the Fifth Republic's institutions – exaggerated centralisation, the bypassing of Parliament, the weakness of intermediary institutions. 'The régime', he wrote, 'has done away with all its safety-valves'.[104] Returning to this idea a few weeks later, he wrote: 'Gaullism has taken to absurd lengths the way in which the slightest incident can call the whole régime into question'.[105]

Pierre Avril, who has done important and often critical work on the institutions of the Fifth Republic, mentions the disadvantages of the bipolar division of power between the President and the Prime Minister – all the more obvious since the Prime Minister had been out of France between 2 and 11 May and the president between 14 and 18 May:

> This bipolar system served to amplify the May crisis. It had probably helped to prepare the ground for it, in that the distribution of power within it desensitised it and made it unresponsive to public opinion.[106]

François Goguel is of quite a different opinion. Asking why the Fifth Republic overcame the crisis of May, he concludes:

> One final word on this period: only the institutions of the Fifth Republic made this possible, for there is no doubt that under the Third or the Fourth the government would have fallen apart at the seams within a week. These institutions enabled those in power to atone for their earlier mistakes, since they made it possible for them to endure where earlier institutions would have forced them to resign at once.[107]

We cannot be certain what would have happened in May 1968 if France had a different political régime, but we find it hard to accept Goguel's argument. Under the Third or Fourth Republic, which had survived initially much more serious crises (1934, 1947), the events at Nanterre would probably have led to a ministerial change. The crisis might have lasted longer, it might even have been worsened by a ministerial change, but it would not immediately have turned into a constitutional crisis. Under the Fifth Republic, without safety-valves or statesmen used to real responsibility, the crisis directly attacked a President who had overcome major problems in the past but himself described the students' revolt and its aftermath as 'impossible to grasp'. So it is no paradox to maintain that those Fifth Republic institutions that had proved themselves on the barricades of Algiers in 1960 or during the generals' putsch in 1961 thanks to the President's exceptionally authoritative response, turned out to be in 1968 one reason why an initially minor crisis took on such historic dimensions.

The lack of a left-wing alternative

If the crisis became so serious, one reason is that constitutional procedures offered no political way out, and that the idea of a left-wing government in power was devoid of credibility for most people.

It is worth briefly mentioning the analyses offered in 1965–6 by politicians and political scientists of the bipolarisation caused by the election of the President by universal suffrage. Maurice Duverger said in 1965: 'There is clearly a movement towards bipolarisation, which may be encouraged by institutional mechanisms. One of these is the election of the President by universal suffrage'.[108]

Frédéric Mauro wrote early in 1966: 'The presidential election favours a change in French political life, since it will compel France *de facto* to adopt the two-party system, as in Britain, the USA or even Germany'.[109] Other observers after the December 1965 election had been more sceptical about the 'dynamic of the presidential election', the 'spirit of December' and the renewal of the French left.[110] These analyses were scarcely proved wrong by May, for one attitude common to all its originators was the outright refusal of a political solution that would have given François Mitterrand, Guy Mollet or Waldeck Rochet governmental responsibility. May can thus be seen as an 'anti-December'.

More generally, in majority and opposition alike, May was characterised right to the end by an almost total political vacuum – the vaporisation, loss of contact or silence of all those forces that had previously been defined as political. It may thus well be that the general weakness of 'political forces' in 1968 France – apart from a PCF that condemned 'ultra-leftist adventurism' – can help to explain the scale and the peculiarities of the crisis.

8 A CHAIN OF CIRCUMSTANCES

After so many general explanations, we should now look at the role of chance, or, if we believe that that does not exist, the influence of events that seem neither necessary nor even rational.

It was certainly not necessary, and it was probably irrational, to found at Nanterre a university cut off from the outside world, in a narrow area, with almost non-existent transport.

The 'Fouchet reform' clearly had very positive aspects (such as the setting-up of new technological universities) as well as highly dubious ones (such as compelling Letters students to make a once-for-all choice of discipline in their first year), but it would have made sense to give universities better funding for this reform and to be quite clear about the transitional regulations for students who had begun their studies under the old system. There was no historical need for all reforms to have been seemingly put on ice while M. Peyrefitte was Education Minister.

Was it necessary or not to bring the police into the Sorbonne courtyard on 3 May? Opinions vary, and it may well be that if they had not intervened then the 'provocation–repression–solidarity' machinery would have been set in motion sooner or later. But it was surely neither rational nor necessary to arrest demonstrators as they left the Sorbonne that day.

Was it necessary for the Prime Minister to be out of France between 2 and 11 May? Or would his being in France have had the slightest impact on the turn of events? Perhaps it was necessary for the government to decide on the night of 10–11 May to storm the Latin Quarter barricades, but it was surely not necessary to precede this decision by a week of uncertainty and shilly-shallying.

If the government's policy between 3 and 10 May was obviously inspired by necessity, it is hard to see why the Prime Minister saw fit, the minute he returned to Paris, to announce an entirely different policy, which led directly to the occupation of university buildings.

Was it necessary for de Gaulle to go to Roumania and wait until 24 May before addressing the nation? But who can be sure that things would have turned out otherwise if he had spoken earlier, or differently?

Finally, there are many questions that can be asked about what would have happened to the May movement if the mass media, especially broadcasting, had not put the whole of France in tune with a few thousand students. What might have happened on the night of 10–11 May if radio and television had not helped to dramatise an initially small-scale demonstration and to maintain the illusion that negotiations were under way and an amnesty might be in sight?[11]

All these questions, and many more, have already been discussed and will be discussed over and over again. Nobody can say that if this or that had not happened the May crisis would never have been. But these things did happen, all of them, and this chain of circumstances may well help to explain May.

Explanations by individual events seem trivial compared to more ambitious ones, and by definition cannot be proven, but it would be wrong to neglect them entirely. It would be more wrong still to attribute to them a scope they cannot have. There is no need to refer to Pascal's comment about Cleopatra's nose to show that accidents of circumstance are an integral part of history, but in trying to understand a historical event it is pointless to spend long wondering what would have happened if *X* had been there instead of *Y* or if this or that had not occurred. Circumstances, in the widest sense, play their part in events, and they played a large part in 1968 – probably smaller than in 1936. But, if they can help to explain how things turned out, they cannot account for the scale and importance of May 1968.

At the end of this lengthy survey, there is only one self-evident conclusion – that, to account for events as complex as those of May 1968, no single explanation will do. Without falling into interpretative eclecticism, we have, it seems, to combine different types of explanation. But first we need to be clear about what it is we want to explain:

– Is it the education crisis – the sudden paralysis of all teaching establishments?

– Is it the social crisis – the strikes of manual and office workers and of managers?

– Is it the disturbances in other parts of society – the crisis in the professions, the troubles in the Catholic Church, the excitement of artists and writers, and so forth?

– Is it the political crisis – the crisis of the régime, the conduct of key politicians and administrators?

It would also be a good idea to distinguish between the different periods of the crisis. Are we trying to explain the role played in its early days by the 'avant-garde minorities' which were seen by most analysts as incapable of any effective action in mid-twentieth-century industrialised society, or rather the extraordinary infectiousness with which it spread in France and France alone?

Distinctions of level, distinctions of period – here we are on familiar, and usually safe, ground. . . . But does such a piecemeal analysis not run the risk of leaving the most important factors out of account? Must we consider 'May', not as a single crisis, but as a superimposed series? Must we simply abandon the attempt to give it a meaning? What meaning, and what here does 'meaning' mean?

To these fundamental questions we have been asking for two years (without always giving the same answers) we shall not try to provide replies today. Our view is that any reply will be only an act of faith or a more or less dubious hypothesis while our knowledge of the crisis is as incomplete and riddled with gaps as it is at the moment.

On the university crisis and the action of political sects, there is no shortage of information or comment. But these comments, almost all entirely confined to France, do not allow us to give a confident answer to a fundamental question: was the university crisis in France radically different from those that occurred at the same time in a great many foreign universities? Was it a crisis peculiar to France or one example of a general university crisis (even of a 'world education crisis')?[112] While events in the universities have been widely analysed, those in secondary schools have attracted much less attention; we are still very poorly informed about them.[113]

On the political crisis, there are a number of books that form part of the 'lived or secret history' genre.[114] These are not to be despised, but they have their limitations. On the social crisis, on the other hand, we have hardly any precise data. All that are available at the moment are a few statements of commitment,[115] a few hasty pieces of reporting[116] dealing with 'flashpoints' such as the regions around Grenoble or Nantes and Saint-Nazaire,[117] a scattering of monographs,[118] and a few interesting personal accounts from Christian militants active in the movement.[119] Until an article appeared in a recent number of this journal, [120] it was impossible to find out how many were on strike and where. We are still lacking an overall study of the origin and intensity of the strikes, their regional characteristics, or how they affected various industries and public services. To the basic question: 'Were the May–June 1968 strikes on the whole of a traditional kind or were they qualitatively different?', the only possible answers at the moment are impressionistic, influenced largely by individuals' own positions.

Perhaps, when all is said and done, we are asking the wrong question. Perhaps overall the strikes were traditional ones and perhaps here and there new types emerged. But even then we would need to ascribe precise meaning to terms such as 'overall', 'here and there', 'traditional', and 'new type'. Until extensive and detailed research on this has been carried out, we can confidently assert that 'interpretations' of May will remain highly approximate.

Another gap is that most commentators on the crisis have concentrated on activists who were at the forefront of the movement, saying little or nothing about those who followed. Yet when speaking of the 'spirit of May' it would be helpful to specify whether one is referring to Daniel Cohn-Bendit's friends or to the mass of students who joined the movement temporarily, to militant workers at Sud-Aviation or peaceful strikes in a family firm in Chambéry.

The universities were occupied by students whose motivations were very different. There were a small minority of revolutionary students, who by paralysing the university tried to smash capitalist society; a larger group of reformist students favourable to co-management, ready to spend hours on end preparing and discussing constitutional texts; students traumatised by an examination system that resembled a lottery when it worked badly and a crushing burden when it worked well; students eager to talk, pleased to sit on the same bench as their teachers and to talk with them; and last but not least a mass of students keen to show solidarity with the demonstrators. No slogan mobilised people more effectively than the first slogan of May:

'Free our friends!' These various motivations, and others, should be studied, with clear divisions between disciplines and institutions, so that the spotlight is not solely on Faculties of Letters in Paris.

Likewise, where lecturers are concerned, it would be no bad thing to draw up a typology of attitudes a little closer to reality than the 'black-and-white' division made by many journalists between 'liberals' and 'conservatives'. So too for strikers, government employees, and the development of public opinion, in Paris and in the provinces.[121]

Finally, questions need to be asked about how the crisis was perceived in France as a whole. Almost everything written about it refers only to Paris, almost totally ignoring the provinces.[122] There is one exception – Georges Chafford's book describing the 'storms of May' in the quiet town of Vendôme,[123] where we discover a world very different from that of Paris.

Quoting Jules Lemaître in 1990, 'You cannot govern against Paris', Albert Thibaudet was wont to retort: 'You can only govern against Paris'. If the author of *La République des professeurs/The teachers' republic* had been alive in 1968, he would surely not have failed to reemphasise that Paris is not France.

Gaps to fill, distinctions to draw, new interpretations to seek: the crisis of spring 1968 is still a field worth exploring.[124] Profuse rather than fertile, the 'literature of May' abounds in brilliant intuitions and dazzling generalisations, but overall it is short on concrete analysis and modest research.[125]

3 Other Interpretations of the Events

More than twenty years later, Bénéton and Touchard's article remains the standard guide to interpretations of May,[1] which reflects not only the comprehensiveness of their work, but also the comparative dearth of new interpretations since. The only qualitatively new such type of interpretation is that, variously associated with Régis Debray, Gilles Lipovetsky, and the philosophers Luc Ferry and Alain Renaut, which sees the events as a belated exercise in social modernisation prefiguring the resurgent individualism of the 1970s and 1980s rather than as in any meaningful sense an attempt at political revolution. Why, then, try to go beyond Bénéton and Touchard's work?

The first and most obvious reason is that its focus is necessarily restricted by its length. Reproductions as opposed to interpretations – autobiographical accounts, works of fiction, films and television programmes – fall outside its scope altogether. A great many interpretative texts apart from those mentioned by Capdevielle and Mouriaux are omitted, and there are times when this does affect the piece's balance; thus, scarcely any space is given to those accounts and interpretations that saw May as a revolutionary opportunity missed or betrayed.

Moreover, the plethora of texts marking first the tenth, then the twentieth anniversary now deserve scrutiny, even though with the exceptions mentioned in the previous paragraph they tend more towards (auto)biographical narration or reflection on cultural change in the intervening years than towards interpretation in the narrower sense. Finally, Bénéton and Touchard's thoroughness does not exempt them from methodological criticism. Bernard Lacroix has criticised them severely for relying exclusively on published statements of position with 'no desire to find out who people were or what they thought',[2] and thereby appropriating the events as philosophical text rather than contradictory sociological reality. The view of philosophy and sociology as being in 'competition for the legitimate interpretation of what takes place' clearly derives from Bourdieu[3] who, shall see, both foreshadowed and analysed the crisis in the universities. Lacroix thus disparages any univocal interpretation (tarred with the brush of philosophy), and his stress on the (sociologically constructed) diversity of individual trajectories reads in places like an unwritten entry from Elizabeth Salvaressi's *Mai en héritage/ The legacy of May*, as when he imagines a 'former Maoist *normalien* who became a part-time lecturer at Vincennes before trying his luck at film-making'.[4] Reproduction of the events, in other words, is at least as import-ant as interpretation of them; indeed, such interpretation can only be an interpretation of reproductions – of the spoken, written and broadcast texts through which alone May is now available to us.

To deal fully with the multiplicity of these would require far more time and space than I have here. I have therefore eliminated three types of text altogether – those not written and published in French, 'journalistic' ac-counts (those published in newspapers or magazines, though not learned journals, and not reproduced in book form), and the immense variety of graffiti and poster-images generated by the movement. The latter would have posed technical problems of reproduction, and the bibliography con-tains reference to a number of works that deal extensively with them. (I also discuss the production of these texts within my consideration of images of May). Within the still daunting corpus remaining, I have eliminated works that appeared to be little more than ephemeral accounts of the events (of which a great many were produced immediately afterwards), and concen-trated my attention on 'symptomatic' texts that cluster around specific lines – one might almost speak of 'genres' – of interpretation and reproduction. Finally, I have (with a very few exceptions) not attempted any synthesis between or comparison of Bénéton and Touchard's survey and my own, even where they bear on the same texts. Twenty years' distance and the constraints of space would have made that an impossibly cumbersome and self-defeating exercise.

The binary divisions between interpretation and reproduction, and within interpretation between the political and the cultural, are at once untenable and difficult to avoid as structuring principles. The interpenetration of the political and the cultural is illustrated by Pascal Ory when he speaks of 'the great culturalist movement that swept through the French Left – first revolutionary, then reformist, in the footsteps of May 68',[5] and elsewhere contrasts the cultural politics of the PCF and the Socialists:[6]

The PC, more Jacobin, granted pride of place to intellectuals and gave priority to a widened 'access to culture' – a notion whose definition was never contested. The PS, affected by the *gauchiste* legacy, tended rather to stress spontaneity, collective creativity, people's cultural self-organisation.[7]

THE EFFECTS OF MAY

1968, that is to say, placed culture firmly on the political agenda, in France
as throughout the Western world. Alfred Willener in *L'Image-Action de la
société ou de la politisation culturelle/Society's action picture: about cultural politicisation* (which a malign chance brought to my notice literally as
I was preparing my final typescript to go to press), vividly evokes the
cultural forms, such as free jazz and a revitalised Dada, characteristic of this
moment, along with the vocabulary of mutilation and division that burst
forth in May to describe the system whose rejection those forms articulated.
In a more narrowly political sense, the short-term effects of May in France
were, we have seen, negative – a panic-stricken backlash fuelled by the
simultaneous fear of disorder and tyranny. In the medium term, however,
May claimed at least two casualties, and major ones at that. Less than a year
after the events, de Gaulle had lost a referendum on decentralisation –
effectively a national vote of confidence – and been forced to step down in
favour, ironically, of the same Pompidou he had relieved of power after the
legislative elections. However magisterially he had orchestrated his final
coup de théâtre, his unconvincing performance on 24 May and the suggestion of panic in his journey to Baden-Baden had hinted at feet of clay, and
the events themselves had made it only too plain how out of touch with
younger people in particular he had become.

The other major casualty of May, electorally and in wider senses, was the
PCF. Ory's remark indicates how the Socialists were better attuned to the
libertarian cultural collectivism of the times than the Communists, whose
centralising Leninist stance was as unappealing there as in the more narrowly political domain. The Party's history since 1968 has been a paradoxical one of increased membership (a peak of 730 000 in 1980 compared with
380 000 in 1969) with severely diminished electoral support (20 per cent of
the votes in the 1969 legislative elections, falling to 11.32 per cent at the
first ballot in 1988) and a veritable haemorrhage of its intellectual members.
The rise in membership can be explained by the Party's (abortive) 'de-
Stalinisation' and electoral pact with the Socialists between the mid-1970s
and the early 1980s. Once the Socialists had established themselves as the
dominant Left-wing party, and even more so when the Communist ministers resigned from the government in 1984, the PCF, having been outflanked to its left in 1968 and to its right by Mitterrand's PS thereafter, was
perilously close to seeming irrelevant as well as outmoded.

THE SITUATIONISTS

The question of May's longer-term effects is in a sense what the remainder of this book sets out to answer. Pascal Ory speaks of 'a simultaneous aspiration to the maximum of liberty and the maximum of identity',[8] which would certainly account for the jettisoning of de Gaulle and the PCF and also gives a good idea of the flavour of French politico-cultural life in the intervening years.[9] If such an aspiration was to be found anywhere on the French Left before 1968, it was in the work of a grouping who would indignantly have scorned any association with the world of organised politics, the situationists. Guy Debord's *La société du spectacle/The society of the spectacle* denounces the 'spectacle' – 'a social relationship between people mediatised by images'[10] – that for him is 'the omnipresent affirmation of the choice *already made* in production and its corollary, consumption'.[11] Long before the designer nihilism of post-modernism and its cohorts, here was a recognition that late capitalist societies maintained their sway, not by material impoverishment or even spiritualised alienation, but by the ceaseless production of the *unreal* – an unreal inexorably bodied forth in the illusions of ideology, the meaninglessness of affluence, and the distance masquerading as proximity of mediatised politics. Debord's vehement insistence on the direct democracy of workers' councils – the only non-'spectacular' form of organisation – preechoes May, as even more strikingly does the following passage:

From the new signs of negation . . . now multiplying in the most economically advanced countries, we can already conclude that a new period has opened: after the first attempts at workers' subversion, *it is now capitalist abundance that has failed.* When the anti-union struggles of Western workers are put down primarily by the unions themselves, and when rebellious youth launches a first ill-defined protest which immediately implies a refusal of old-style professional politics, art and everyday life, those are the two faces of a new spontaneous struggle that begins as *criminal.*[12]

Bearing in mind that the Interior Minister, Christian Fouchet, was to describe those fighting the police as '*pègre*' (translated as 'scum', and a term with specific underworld connotations), Debord's prediction, bizarre though it might have seemed at the time, was uncannily close to the mark. Twenty years after May, in *Commentaires sur la société du spectacle/*

Commentaries on the society of the spectacle, Debord had dialectically refined his view of the spectacle from a binary one ('concentrated' and 'diffuse', May arguably marking the shift from a diffuse to a concentrated spectacle of authoritarian power), to a synthesis of the two into the 'integrated spectacle', motivated in France especially by 'the need to put an end to a revolutionary challenge whose appearance had come as a surprise'.[13] This leads into the tantalising assertion that 'nothing in the past twenty years has been shrouded in so many commissioned lies as the (hi)story of May 1968. Yet valuable lessons have been learnt from a few demystificatory studies on these days and their origin, but they remain a state secret.'[14] 'Conspiracy theory run riot', it is easy to say – indeed all but impossible not to – but Debord's coy paranoia has the merit of reminding us, tantalisingly, that publicly available utterances on the May events are almost certainly not the only ones in existence.

The other major situationist text, which appeared in the same year (1967), was Raoul Vaneigem's *Traité de savoir-vivre à l'usage des jeunes générations/The Revolution of everyday life*, whose emphasis is more hedonistic than Debord's ('True love is revolutionary praxis or it is nothing')[15] but which like him sees revolutionary potential in that very affluence that might seem to preclude it ('Who wants a world in which the guarantee that we shall not die of starvation entails the risk of dying of boredom?')[16] The notion that 'as the period of calculation and suspicion ushered in by capitalism and Stalinism draws to a close, it is challenged from within by the initial phase . . . of the era of play'[17] is of a piece with the Cohn-Bendit clownery that way so as to enrage Georges Marchais, and the extraordinary psychic energy so characteristic of May – a month in which the consumption of anti-depressants and their bourgeois equivalent, psychoanalysis, fell sharply – is crystallised in Vaneigem's euphoric assertion that 'the reconstruction of society will necessarily entail the simultaneous reconstruction of everyone's unconscious'.[18]

The reconstruction of the unconscious is one form of the situationists' key demand that time and space should be reappropriated. For Debord they are stolen by society and turned into merchandise like everything else, while Vaneigem tells us that 'time has to be caught on the wing, in the present – but the present has yet to be constructed'.[19] Such a Dionysian utterance looks back to Nietzsche as surely as it does forward to May and the ecstasy of those occupations and barricades through which people reappropriated time and space not just in the factories and universities, but in society itself. The Strasbourg brochure *De la misère en milieu étudiant* captures the specific ambiguity of students' relationship to time in describing them as 'creatures divided between a clearly defined present and a clearly defined future state, the boundary between which will be mechanically crossed'.[20] Robert Merle has one of his characters (Ménéstrel) say in *Derrière la vitre/Behind the glass pane* that 'being a student is nothing, it's not a social class, it's not a job, it's not even a present, it's a state defined only by the future for which it prepares you'.[21] In a France where both that future and the quality of the preparation for it were increasingly called into doubt, the Strasbourg brochure struck an obvious chord.

In other respects, such as its dismissal of Mao's China ('the most gigantic bureaucracy of modern times'),[22] *De la misère* strikes an atypical, but now percipient, note. Its call for a 'fusion of student youth and advanced workers'[23] appears utopian in the light of what happened or failed to happen, but the situationists were virtually the only grouping to recognise such a possibility before the events started. Even once they were under way, the Maoists of the UJCml, like many Trotskyist groups, either disowned the student movement altogether or considered it merely a subordinate cog in the working-class machine; workerism (doubtless to Georges Marchais's chagrin) was not the exclusive property of the PCF.[24]

To quantify the situationists' influence in May is extremely difficult. They were poorly received in the occupied Sorbonne, where their distaste for Leninist organisational methods and insistence that the bourgeois university needed to be destroyed rather than reformed antagonised both the 'trainee revolutionaries' of the Leninist groupings and the mass of participant students. Nor were their calls for the direct democracy of workers' councils widely heeded in the occupied factories. Yet their idea of revolution as festival or carnival has never come so close to realisation as in May. To quote Pascal Dumontier:

> The situationists' conception of *play* is in no sense a gratuitous one. Theoretically, it is a way of breaking with the alienation of everyday life; practically, it develops the tactical and strategic sense necessary to the revolutionary struggle. From this point of view, May 68, with its original slogans, its outbursts of spontaneity and its extremist demands, is indeed the 'revolutionary fête' of the situationists. In the light of their ideas, it is easier to understand the most baffling aspects of the May movement.[25]

The situationists, in other words, 'read' May before it happened, a paradox piquantly in accord with their resolutely anti-commonsensical logic. Less than four years later, the Situationist International had wound itself up, feeling its specific utility past and exhausted by the attempt to find non-organisational forms of organisation. Its end, like its ideas, strikingly mirrors those of May.

COHN-BENDIT

The movement closest to the situationists, in its rejection of hierarchies and stress on direct democracy, was the 22 March Movement, so that it makes sense now to turn to Daniel and Gabriel Cohn-Bendit's *Le Gauchisme: remède à la maladie sénile du Communisme* – literally, *Ultra-Leftism: a remedy for the senility of Communism*, in ironic inversion of Lenin's *Left-Wing Communism – an infantile disorder*, but bowdlerised in its English translation as *Obsolete Communism – the Left-wing alternative*. This begins with a vehement denunciation of the conditions of its own possibility, for 'all they [sc. publishers] want is something they can sell – a revolutionary gadget with marketable qualities'.[26] For a text written in five weeks flat after the events finished, this is a very shrewd foreshadowing of the commercialisation of May that has continued more or less unabated ever since (and of which this book itself forms a part). Cohn-Bendit's[27] approach is more historical and less aphoristic than that of Debord or Vaneigem, concerned to show how May 'represented a return to a revolutionary tradition these parties [sc. the established Left] have betrayed'.[28] That tradition is one of spontaneous direct democracy, given here a more overtly Marxist cast than with the situationists. The Paris Commune, the anarchist currents in the Russian Revolution, the occupations of 1936, are invoked as precedents in the writing of an alternative history that is explicitly Marxist and anti-Communist. 'Inasmuch as the struggle against capitalism and the State is a struggle for freedom and self-government, its objectives can clearly not be achieved with the help of organisations whose very structure is designed to thwart them';[29] paramount among those organisations were the PCF and its industrial arm, the CGT – the 'Stalinist filth' denounced by Cohn-Bendit on 13 May. Nor are the Trotskyists, despite having been close allies of the 22 March Movement, exempt. The bureaucratic perversion of Marxism is represented as the work of Lenin and Trotsky as much as that of Stalin, for 'the workers could have managed without a Party, just as they do in their everyday life'.[30] The party (with a large or a small 'p'), for Cohn-Bendit as for the situationists, is as much the enemy of revolution as capitalism is.

This comes close to implying that the Marxist word became corrupted the minute it became organisational flesh – an intentionally theological formulation. Cohn-Bendit stresses how 'the movement succeeded in liberating language from its . . . strait-jacket';[31] the original French has *la parole*, which deriving from *parler*/to speak has much clearer overtones of the spoken as against the written word. We shall see that the Jesuit writer Michel de Certeau and others emphasise May as the liberation or capture of *la parole*, to be understood at once as 'the word' and as 'speech'. The

Catholic Bishop of Arras even went so far as to refer to the events – which came to a close at Whitsun, the time of speaking in tongues – as the irruption of the Holy Spirit into human affairs. This is not to try to recuperate Cohn-Bendit as a bearer of divine witness (however 'charismatic' in the secular sense he may have been), but rather to suggest some of the overtones and implications of May seen as liberation of *la parole*. Speech, in Western thought, has traditionally been conceived as anterior to writing ('In the beginning was the Word, and the Word was with God' – thus, precisely, the condition of possibility of sacred books and of the written book-as-sacred). The work of Jacques Derrida has undercut this originary duality, seeing the processes of postponement, spacing, deferral that characterise writing as inherent in language, so that the primacy of speech over writing comes to appear a metaphysical illusion. In that case, the liberation of *la parole* will itself be a metaphysical illusion of infinite regress towards a moment of (spoken?) originary plenitude.

This may seem irrelevant to Cohn-Bendit's denunciation of the perverters of revolution, but if that revolution – in May so often closely associated with *la parole* – is seen as a moment of originary plenitude corrupted once 'written' into organised political practice, the analogy will, I hope, become plain. It may be objected that 'revolution' is forward- rather than backward-looking, destination rather than departure-point; but the term also has implications of turning full circle, much as the Marxist dialectic implies the end (already) in the beginning. Its seemingly omnipresent use throughout May – even the young Gaullists were to call for a 'peaceful revolution' – suggests a timeless state of being rather than a historical process with a beginning and an end. May as moment of (revolutionary) speech or pure origin thus preexists the countless writings of May – histories, accounts, interpretations – that are our concern here.

Except, of course, that it does not, or not in any straightforward way. The situationists – like Bourdieu (see pp. 89–90), like Godard (see pp. 145–8) – in a sense read the events before they occurred, and in another sense each (re)writing of them alters the moment of which it (as it were) speaks, by the reading it gives or the testimonies it brings. The 'originary plenitude' of May's *parole* was in any event always-already complicated by the proliferation of written texts (banners, tracts, posters, graffiti), so that it has always been recoverable only through – has perhaps always been subordinate to – the process of writing. (A Parisian friend of mine, in 1988: 'May 68 was an extraordinary moment for me, but I couldn't begin to say why or how.')

Cohn-Bendit's assertion that 'my book is but an echo of the great dialogue that was begun in the forum of the Latin Quarter'[32] is thus on one level slightly disingenuous, for a writing of/on events is not the same thing as an 'echo' of them. His fierce rejection of established political forms of action and insistence that 'if a revolutionary movement is to succeed, no form of organisation whatever must be allowed to dam its spontaneous flow'[33] would certainly not have been shared by all the participants in the aforementioned dialogue (which may be presumed to have had at least two sides). The paradox 'that those who shun the limelight should be singled out for the full glare of publicity'[34] is difficult to dispel with the would-be performative assertion that 'their [sc. capitalists'] cash will be used for the next round of Molotov cocktails'.[35] The contradiction between *Obsolete Communism*'s revolutionary stance and its marketing as part of the 'Cohn-Bendit phenomenon' indicates how factors other than the *bête noire* of political bureaucracy, such as large-scale media exploitation, were to affect attempts to retain and develop – to rewrite – the ideas and lessons of May.

TROTSKYIST ANALYSES

Cohn-Bendit became a 'star' as the most prominent individual exponent of *gauchisme* – a term that had first been used only in 1962, and then pejoratively, to denote what the *Larousse Lexis* dictionary defines as 'the attitude of those who advocate extreme political solutions and immediate revolutionary actions'. That definition's stress on rapidity and extremism of method, rather than on specificity of analysis, suggests why *gauchisme* was so volatile and heterogeneous a phenomenon. Évelyne Pisier describes it as an 'anti-economist and anti-historicist critique of Marxism',[36] which suggests why it was above all the PCF – tribune for economic demands and self-proclaimed vehicle of history – that the *gauchistes* loved to hate. Such a description, however, does not apply equally to all the groups stigmatised as *gauchiste* by the PCF (which returned their hatred with symbiotic vigour). The various Trotskyist groups, mostly composed of defectors or expulsees from the PCF/UEC, saw themselves not as critics of Marxism, but as the true guardians of the Marxist-Leninist tradition. By far the most influential Trotskyist group in May was the JCR, which provided most of the stewards for the marches and demonstrations. Three of its leading figures, Daniel Bensaïd, Alain Krivine (now General Secretary of its successor, the Ligue Communiste Révolutionnaire) and Henri Weber, gave their interpretation of the events in *Mai 1968 – une répétition générale/May 1968 – a dress rehearsal*.

For Bensaïd, Krivine and Weber, May was a revolutionary opportunity less betrayed (as the Russian Revolution had been for Trotsky) than forfeited for lack of a sufficiently strong vanguard party. The attraction of *gauchisme* is accounted for by the failure of Communism in the USSR and increasing interest in the Third World, but 'because they did not find in place and equipped with a programme the revolutionary party in which they could struggle against the structure of capitalist society, the students gave themselves over to "globalism" and "maximalism"'[37] – a vocabulary of Leninist organisation far removed from that of the situationists or the 22 March Movement. Yet the approach of Bensaïd *et al*, is refreshingly free from the self-righteous puritanism of the PCF or many of the Maoist groups, fondly evoking the mood in restaurants where 'people spoke to one another from table to table, drank together, fraternised'.[38] Likewise, the immense symbolic richness of the movement is here fully recognised, for 'the pseudo-insurrectional demonstrations, the forests of red flags, the barricades, the university occupations – all these inspired borrowings from working-class tradition came to form a semantic whole whose aim was to make the student message audible'.[39] The students, that is to say, did not so much play futile revolutionary games, as the PCF would have it, as update and amplify a gamut of images and symbols that had been languishing under the drab yoke of Stalinism. Thus it was that, for the workers, 'the myth of the student-as-poof was replaced by the myth of the strong-arm student, fearless and beyond reproach'.[40]

For these myths to become political as well as cultural reality, however, political leadership was required, and it was this that for the Trotskyists was lacking, constituting 'the Achilles' heel of the powerful May movement, whereas "objectively" everything was possible'.[41] This last phrase, as we have seen, refers to Marceau Pivert, whose political conceptions – 'a slightly nebulous mixture . . . of a good dose of anarchism, a little Blanquist insurrectionary socialism, a dash of Trotskyism and ultra-pacifism'[42] – strikingly pre-echo those of 1968. More than 'a dash of Trotskyism', alas, would have been required – in 1968 as in 1936 – for the revolutionary transformation sought by Bensaïd *et al.* to come about, and the lesson they drew from May was thus to work towards the building of a vanguard party that would unlock the possibility of 'an unprecedented kind of power'.[43]

The Trotskyist analysis of May is virtually the only one – on the Left at all events – to have survived the intervening period in by and large identical form. Henri Weber, we shall see in Chapter 5, is now a Socialist Party member and adviser to Laurent Fabius, but Bensaïd and Krivine, in *Mai si! – 1968–1988: rebelles et repentis/May – oh yes! – 1968–1988: rebels and penitents*, maintain that the gathering of the non-Communist Left at Charlety signalled a genuine, albeit ambiguous, revolutionary opportunity – 'not the great moment of Revolution with a capital R, but the overthrowing of the régime by strikes and extra-parliamentary mobilisation',[44] Charlety for them remains the pregnant moment of May, whose 'symbolic scope is greater than its immediate impact, for it carried within it the tumultuous relationships of unity and disunity on the Left over the following decade'.[45] The major beneficiary of those relationships has undoubtedly been the PS, whose long-term ascendancy has led to the view, shared by many *soixante-huitards*,[46] that class struggle and revolution are outmoded concepts in a France where social-democratic consensus prevails. The Trotskyist analysis (in this respect at least virtually the only surviving Marxist one) views this consensus, however longlived, as fundamentally precarious, a papering over the cracks endemic to capitalism. Thus, 'the student and worker struggles of the winter of 1986–7, the nerve-racking stock-market crash and the affirmation that something else is possible were enough to disturb this resigned attitude and call that good conscience into question'.[47]

Not 'everything is possible', but 'something else is possible' – a something else whose possibility, like its definition, depends upon the organisation work of the vanguard party. . . . André Barjonet, who resigned from his post in charge of the CGT's economic and social study section in May at the same time as leaving the PCF for the PSU, could hardly be described as a Trotskyist; yet his pamphlet on the events bore the classically Trotskyist title *La Révolution trahie de 1968/The revolution betrayed in 1968*, and his presence at Charlety, described by the CGT as 'an anti-worker meeting', was the clearest possible indication of his distance from his former employer. For Barjonet as for Bensaïd *et al.*, May was an objectively revolutionary situation though, unlike the Trotskyists, he is extremely critical of Leninist party discipline. He criticises the CGT and the PCF for ignoring the fact that 'the students might also have *their word to say*'[48] – again, a stress on the plurality of discourses repressed by the political establishment – and is particularly scathing about Georges Séguy's dismissal of calls for 'workers' control' as a 'hollow formula'. For Barjonet, 'without becoming utopian, it was possible to define then and there a minimum degree of workers' control and power in each firm'.[49] It is here, not in any theoretically-defined bureaucracy, that he locates the betrayal of the revolution, calling rather like a shopfloor Cohn-Bendit for a return to Marx and Engels and a plurality of revolutionary parties.

THE DIFFERENT BRANDS OF MAOIST

There is nothing particularly remarkable in Barjonet's analysis as such. What is remarkable is that it should have been produced by a leading theoretician of an organisation whose basic conservatism was so tellingly shown up in May, and that in a matter of weeks it had sold 20 000 copies. Its pluralism and anti-Leninism did not find favour with other groups on the Left; we have seen that they conflict with the Trotskyist tradition, and the PCMLF's Jacques Jurquet, in *Le Printemps révolutionnaire de 1968 – essai d'analyse marxiste-léniniste/The revolutionary spring of 1968 – an attempt at a Marxist-Leninist analysis*, explicitly takes him to task for wallowing in 'the nauseating swamps of bourgeois ideology'.[50] Jurquet's brand of Maoism, which saw Stalin and 'Chairman Mao' as the only true heirs of Marx and Lenin and preached a ferociously anti-revisionist line, is similar to that lampooned by Godard in *La Chinoise* (see p. 146). ('The fire is lit! Managing directors and government ministers, you will not succeed in putting it out, even with the cooperation of your most expert and diligent firemen, the revisionist traitors').[51]

Aside from the easy mockery to which it lends itself, Jurquet's rhetoric is noteworthy for its ambition towards scientificity. Marxism's founding claim is to be a science of social relations, but this had been somewhat lost sight of in the PCF's electoral pragmatism until it was strenuously reiterated in the mid-1960s by the Mao-influenced philosopher Louis Althusser. Groupings such as the UJCml and the PCMLF attached the utmost importance to scientific rigour and the correct theoretical line, seen as an absolute precondition for effective political action rather than as a rationalisation of or metatextual commentary upon it. Thus, Cohn-Bendit is denounced by Jurquet as anything but a scientific Socialist, because of his 'great ideological confusion not exempt from anarchist tendencies'[52] – a reproach he would undoubtedly have taken for a compliment – and the PCF and its *gauchiste* critics are simultaneously dismissed in a triumphant theoretical recovery of the term 'Stalinist' ('What a curious conjuring trick it is to class as "Stalinists" the very men who have comprehensively rejected Stalin's teachings.')[53]

Such purism sat ill with the other dominant current in 1968 Maoism, best illustrated in fundamental writings by Serge July, Alain Geismar and Erlyne Morane (*Vers la guerre civile/Towards civil war*) and André Glucksmann (*Stratégie et révolution en France/Revolutionary strategy in France*). This, as the works' titles illustrate, saw violent revolution as imminent ('the horizon of France in 1970 or 1972 is revolution'),[54] and concentrated its analysis upon planning to achieve it. The self-emancipation figured by the mass movement of May, the destruction of the almost superstitious hierarchical respect that had dominated French society hitherto, the revolutionary developments in the Third World, were the harbingers of the 'great moment of Revolution with a capital R' later to be disavowed by the less

apocalyptic Trotskyists. The latter were criticised by July *et al.* for clinging
to their identity as bourgeois intellectuals rather than placing themselves at
the service of the masses, and – a specific symptom of that fundamental
error – seeing the question of organisation as a straight choice between
spontaneous action (in the long run doomed to failure) and the Leninist
vanguard party. For (this brand of) Maoists, new types of mass organisation
would arise in the course of struggle, so July *et al.*'s riposte to Bensaïd *et
al.* was that 'the cycle that goes by way of Charlety is not the future of the
revolution, and the cycle that leads from the anti-authoritarian revolt to
Flins [site of the bitterest working-class struggles and the death of Gilles
Tautin] is not the revolution's dress rehearsal, but its point of departure'.[55]

Vers le guerre civile is remarkable less for its political prognosis (all but
completely falsified by history) than for the subtlety and richness of its
cultural analysis, which draws extensively upon major concepts in structuralist and post-structuralist thought. The chain of struggles that began in
1968 is viewed as 'the first phase of a text which in realising – in *writing* –
itself brings with it other formulations as it grasps the truth of the enemy
and the truth of the fight'.[56] A text, that is to say, which in Derridean terms
differs/defers its closure with each addition to it, though that is a decep-
tively sedentary, 'easy' formulation; additions to the revolutionary text are
likely to be sentences, precisely, of death, 'the truth of the enemy and the
truth of the fight' appropriately hellfire–and–brimstone denominations for
the dialectical adversary to be engaged with in a combat that goes beyond
the verbal on which it nevertheless depends ('in the context of organised
repression, exemplary action bursts forth like a forbidden word').[57] Lacanian
psychoanalytic formulations of the role of desire and demand in the constitution of the subject are also prominent, so that 'to occupy a firm is to put
oneself in the position of a subject'.[58] This has a complex relation to the
vocabulary of emancipation that characterises so many first-hand accounts
of May. To be a subject is not (no longer) to be an object, but nor is it to
attain (unrealisable) total freedom. It can best be understood here as a form
of relative autonomy – autonomy compared to the subservence of the
dominated object, relative compared to the overarching domination of the
symbolic order that here takes the form of the class struggle. The illusion of
total freedom is, precisely, an illusion, which is not to pass moral judgement
upon it but to stress the importance of recognising its place in the realm of
ideology and the order of the imaginary. That place is dialectically determined, for (in a phrase evocative of Sartre) 'the revolutionary process and
the worker-becoming-subject give rise to each other'.[59]

In the light of all that has been said about their symbolic or, perhaps
better, allegorical, importance, the barricades would seem to have been the

privileged place for the dialectic of subjectivity in May. 'Allegory' is here contrasted to 'symbol', following Paul de Man, as less unproblematic and totalising. '(Allegory) suggests a *disjunction* [my italics] between the way in which the world appears in reality and the way it appears in language' (P. de Man, *Blindness and Insight* [London: Methuen, 1983], p. 191 – a disjunction endlessly enacted and reformulated in May). July, Geismar and Morane recognise this dialectically in saying that 'the barricades are the order of desire, negotiation is that of demand'.[60] The present tense dehistoricises their analysis, and makes it plain that it refers (performatively?) to barricades yet unbuilt and negotiations still to be carried out ('It's only a beginning, let's continue the struggle'). The two orders, following Lacan, are counterposed as necessarily complementary, so that the PCF's 'unwillingness for a real struggle'[61] appears as its cleaving to the order of demand into which that of desire was to burst, inaugurating a multiple Oedipal drama of rejection and assertion on the barricades and in the occupied institutions. Yet to elevate that order of desire (linked with the pleasure principle) to a position of dominance, as the situationists and the 22 March Movement did, is for July, Geismar and Morane to make an error no less fatal than that they impute to the PCF. The barricades of 24 May are described as 'the pulsion of the death drive; each new barricade repeats, mimes, ceremonialises the first phase and thereby condemns any positive revolutionary development'.[62] That pulsion, for Freud, issues in repetition leading to extinction, much as the barricades did in the movement's final phases. The negotiatory order of demand can be neither ignored nor given sole priority.

July *et al.* thus provide a sophisticated theoretical justification for their view that 'the keystone of revolution in France (is) the revolutionary fusion of the most advanced elements among intellectual and manual workers'.[63] Their text seems to invite us to see 'intellectual workers' (= the student movement) as representing the order of desire and 'manual workers' that of demand; yet that replicates the very division between mental and manual labour that the Maoist Left in particular wanted to do away with. When workers not only occupied their factories, but sometimes came to the Odéon to tell of their previous night's dreams,[64] as when students 'took their desires for reality' by manually constructing barricades, it might have seemed that that division was at least beginning to undermine itself. That, however, would have been to take for reality the desire for that 'revolutionary fusion' sought by July, Geismar and Morane in and through new forms of struggle.

André Glucksmann – a graduate of the prestigious École Normale Supérieure, which was to be a stronghold of Maoism throughout the late

1960s and early 1970s – agrees with July *et al*. in rejecting the model of a single vanguard party, seeing in the May movement 'a "party" in the very broad sense in which Marx sometimes used the term'.[65] Parliamentary opposition to Gaullism is deemed to have proved itself powerless in the June elections, which Glucksmann regards as complementary antithesis to May rather than its baffling contradiction ('May laid bare what people had tried to ignore – a daring France, the harbinger of a social revolution. June rediscovered a much more bourgeois, traditional, conservative country.')[66] The way out of this apparent impasse lies, ineluctably, through violence, for Glucksmann, initiated in May by the bourgeois state and replicated by the students only in the most refined symbolic form – 'how can an action whose "violence" is confined to disrupting traffic in five Parisian streets cause the state to totter and society to be turned upside down?'[67] Glucksmann's question is productively ambiguous – less dismissive than it may appear, for such limited action did after all cause the state to totter and society to be turned upside down, but emphasising that these disturbances were but momentary and implying that further, probably deadly violence will be necessary for real change to occur.[68]

For Glucksmann as for July *et al*, that violence is inextricably linked with language ('The movement of May awakened society in two ways: through violence and through language [*la parole*]').[69] Such a linkage may appear problematic outside a narrowly Leninist context, where language articulates the correct revolutionary programme and violence makes the word flesh, but the connection passes by way of the breaking-down of barriers, literal and metaphorical. Glucksmann speaks of the 'destruction of forms of linguistic segregation',[70] before asserting that the absence of a detailed revolutionary programme will not be a handicap, for workers will establish their own programmes in the course of their struggles.

That now reads like a pious hope, and perhaps one reason why non-Stalinist Maoism in France (ironically dubbed 'spontex', in a punning reference to its stress on spontaneity and a well-known make of absorbent sponge) no longer, in 1993, exists in any recognisable form. Its actions in the late 1960s and early 1970s, centring on the organisation La Gauche Prolétarienne (later Secours Rouge) and the newspaper *La Cause du peuple*, largely took the form of kidnappings and sequestrations that ran themselves into the ground when the masses, far from being fired to join in the 'new popular resistance', responded with indignation or boredom.[71] July is now proprietor of the daily newspaper *Libération* and a defender of the social market economy; Glucksmann was a leading 'new philosopher'[72] and has more recently rousingly defended the spiritually uplifting qualities of the nuclear deterrent.[73] This combination of political misjudgement and personal volte-face makes it particularly hard to evaluate their 1968 texts judiciously. Yet, aside from the conceptual interest of July *et al.*'s symbolic analysis, *Vers la guerre civile* and *Stratégie et révolution en France* sometimes suggest projective insights more accurate – albeit unwittingly so – than their apocalyptic titles might suggest. Thus, the Parti Socialiste (though not Marxist) is much more closely akin to the '"party" in the very broad sense of the term' spoken of by Glucksmann than the self-styled (Communist or Trotskyist) vanguard parties, and July *et al.*'s view that 'class struggles and their historical value are in contradiction with the dominant ideology of the French working-class movement'[74] suggest why it was that that ideology, linked with the PCF and the CGT, lost in May ground that it was never to recover. There is a curious irony too in Glucksmann's assertion that May was a movement directed against 'the depoliticisation of society by the state',[75] for much the same reproach has been directed against the recent consensualising approach of Mitterrand and the PS, whom the Glucksmann of the late 1980s and early 1990s supports. Political readings of 1968 inevitably run into historical ones.

The figure most prominently associated with French Maoism after 1968, Jean-Paul Sartre, was also the one who most vividly illustrated this interpenetration of the historical and the political. He might at the time have appeared an almost prehistoric figure, for he had abandoned literary production all but twenty years before and 'his' existentialism was felt to have been superseded philosophically by structuralism and its derivatives. These latter, however, with their dismissal of historicism – thus, too often, of history – and their undermining of the importance of purposive human action, seemed in many ways out of keeping with the *Zeitgeist* of May; a graffito in the occupied Sorbonne proclaimed 'Althusser-à-rien'/'Althusser is useless'. Thus it is that 'Maoists who had been pupils of Althusser found only the company of Sartre on the journey of political action',[76] which suggests a profoundly unmarxist division between political theory and practice. Althusser's continuing allegiance to the PCF, as against Sartre's refusal ever to join a political party of even vote, helps to account for this and for the fact that 'if 68 needed a philosophy, Sartre's was the only appropriate one: collectivist yet against apparatuses, individualist yet against bourgeois individualism'.[77]

Sartre's appearance at the occupied Sorbonne in May was thus something of a political and philosophical homecoming,[78] though cries of 'Sartre, make it snappy!' showed that the ultimate guru-in-spite-of-himself was as liable to questioning and disrespect as any other figure of authority at the time. Much of that questioning, fittingly, must have come from himself, for it is clear that the May events marked Sartre's final break with the PCF with which he had for so long sympathised. In an interview with the publishing-house Éditions John Didier in June, Sartre stated:

> The Communists have always maintained – *and up to now this has been true* [my italics] – that revolutionary movements claiming to be to the Left of the PCF helped to divide the working class and always wound up 'objectively' to the right of the Party. To discuss this view today is, I think, to state the problem wrongly. We have to ask ourselves, not whether we are to the right or the left of the PCF, but whether we are truly on the Left.[79]

The barricades and the street fighting, for Sartre, enacted the desire to escape from that seriality – the reduction of individual specificity to functional interchangeability – that he had long seen as the bane of Western bourgeois society. (Vaneigem's view that social organisation is nowadays the dominant form of social oppression has similarities with this.) May's violence was thus 'the expression not of a will to disorder, but of aspiration to a different kind of order',[80] though one that Sartre was quite clear could not come about overnight.[81] Students and workers would have to get to know each other better first, through working in each other's institutions. This heavily-idealised view rests, not just on the then-widespread enthusiasm for societies such as Cuba and China which were thought to be abolishing the divisions between mental and manual labour, but on the Sartrean stressing of action as constitutive of human essence ('People . . . never have anything to say to one another; they can only do things together').[82] That speech was a form of action, and action could have (a) language(s) of its own – both illustrated by May – is a consideration oddly disregarded by Sartre here.

It came into its own, however, in his political practice of the early 1970s. Although proclaiming himself not to be a Maoist, he lent the newspaper *La Cause du peuple* (banned in 1970) the protection of his name, selling it openly in Paris without ever receiving the ultimate confirmation of his good faith that arrest and trial would have provided. In 1972 he defended the Maoists' use of violence and (*contra* Lenin) their stress on spontaneous action as ways of progressing from the atomised society of the series to that, unified in purposive action, of the group:

> a *mass party*, along Maoist lines, must be constantly listening, drawing its slogans from the group and always striving to bring periods of seriality closer to periods of action. It will be in the first instance, so to speak, the memory of the masses (. . .) Wherever the masses move towards praxis, even on a local scale, they *are already* the people at the outset of its coming into being.[83]

Such apocalyptic essentialism was to run itself into the ground very quickly, but its consequences are less our concern here than its origins. If ever there had been a time when the anonymity of seriality transformed itself into the interpersonality of the group, it was May, and that is why it appears as so profoundly Sartrean a moment.

The PCF, unsurprisingly, produced a variety of interpretations of the events, beginning with Georges Marchais's 'manichean'[84] denunciation of *gauchisme*, which made so little mention of Gaullism that one might have wondered who the Party's real enemy was. A no less splenetic PCF rendering is Jacques Duclos's *Anarchistes d'hier et d'aujourd'hui: comment le gauchisme fait le jeu de la réaction/Anarchists yesterday and today: how gauchisme plays reaction's game*, which directly accuses the *gauchistes* of being 'teleguided' by the Gaullists. The PCF's change of tune after the factory occupations was clearly determined by tactical considerations, and much the same might be said of its increasingly favourable rewritings of the events since its jettisoning of the 'dictatorship of the proletariat' in 1976. This marked an effort at theoretical de-Stalinisation (and arguably de-Leninisation), in response to the changes in the French political and cultural climate – changes which were themselves, as Pascal Ory has suggested, largely the result of 1968. . . . No party putting itself forward as a serious alternative to Gaullism and post-Gaullism could afford to disregard the lessons of May, prominent among which was the diversity and plurality of alternative and oppositional social movements. Thus, from 1976 'the party tended to accept social movements as they came forward, and hence to lay claim to the heritage of May in its entirety, in a gesture of understanding if not of assimilation'.[85] The corollary of this is, to quote Claude Journès, that 'accepting May 68 was possible only through abandoning Leninism'.[86]

The very title of Waldeck Rochet's *Les Enseignements de mai–juin 1968/The Lessons of May and June 1968* shows that the PCF's leadership realised very soon after the events that they had important lessons to learn, culturally (May) and electorally (June). Waldeck indeed begins by asking why there had been such a massive electoral swing to the Right in June – a question ignored or marginalised by *gauchiste* commentators – before launching into some predictably disapproving remarks about the barricades ('These nights of disorder, which gained the student movement nothing, could not have caused the Gaullist régime the slightest anxiety').[87] We are clearly a long way from the excited symbolic richness of July *et al.* or the euphoric revolutionary purity of Cohn-Bendit. Perhaps the key word in the PCF's somewhat repetitive armoury of anti-*gauchiste* rhetoric is 'provocation', which makes a number of appearances here, backed by the historical antecedents of police infiltration of anarchist groups in the late nineteenth-century and the Reichstag fire. Any confrontational or non-constitutional type of action on the Left in the late 1960s and early 1970s was virtually certain to find itself branded by the PCF as 'provocation', calling forth as its inevitable consequence 'repression' that bred further provocation in its turn. Under the ferocious régime of Raymond Marcellin, Interior Minister after 1968 and notorious for his generous use of CRS manpower and deportation orders, such an analysis was not bereft of sense, but it was used with such knee-jerk regularity as to become a prime example of *la langue de bois* ('wooden language' – an idiomatic term of political platitudes).

The heroes of May, in Waldeck Rochet's account, are the workers, who returned to work victorious thanks to the Grenelle agreements; one of the villains is clearly Barjonet, compared, in a would-be insult, to Marceau Pivert. The choice before the movement is starkly articulated:

> either to conduct strike action to satisfy the essential demands of the workers while at the same time maintaining our political activity with a view to achieving necessary democratic changes in a framework of legality, or . . . to risk a trial of strength.[88]

The prospect of such a trial of strength, for Waldeck, was what underlay the electoral swing to the Right, motivated above all by fear of civil war. Given that if tanks had moved towards Paris from Germany they would have passed through the eastern working-class suburbs that have always been the PCF's bastions, that party might have been expected to have a certain vested interest in such an analysis. It seems clear that in May itself nobody was prepared to risk civil war (July, Geismar and Morane's title is prognosis not diagnosis), but the question of what form of resistance de Gaulle would have offered had the established Left simply taken power remains tantalisingly impossible to answer.

If the events reinforced the revolutionary optimism of the *gauchistes*, they all but deleted revolution from the PCF's agenda. The Communists' refusal to advocate a seizure of power ensured that, for if May had not been a revolutionary situation it was difficult to see what, in contemporary Western Europe, could be. The Party was obviously going to abide rigorously by the rules of the electoral game from now on, institutional patriotism being one of the lessons it had most clearly learnt from the events. This is reinforced by Waldeck's attempted reclamation of *La Marseillaise* (originally a revolutionary song) from the Gaullists who had bellowed it up and down the Champs-Élysées on 30 May ('the Communists indissolubly unite the strains of *La Marseillaise* and those of the *Internationale*').[89] It is not surprising that the book concludes with a reassertion of democratic centralism against what Waldeck calls, in a phrase that could have been drawn from Bourdieu's *La Distinction*, 'lordly aristocratic anarchism'.[90] The *fils à papa* may not have represented a threat, but they were none the less the enemy for that.

Just as Waldeck Rochet was the PCF's leading apparatchik, Louis Althusser was its leading intellectual. He remained silent on the events for the best part of a year, because of recurrent depressive illness but also perhaps because they had placed him in a peculiarly difficult position. His interest in the philosophical works of Mao Zedong (best exemplified in the essay 'Contradiction et Surdétermination/Contradiction and Overdetermination', in *Pour Marx/For Marx*) had been largely responsible for the popularity of Maoism in the French student world, especially that section of it that had been taught by him at the École Normale Supérieure. Yet he remained a loyal member of the PCF even after the groups most influenced by his work and teaching had left it or been expelled. It was not until 15 March 1969 – the date of his 'open letter' to the Left-wing Italian Communist Maria-Antonietta Macciocchi – that he attempted to deal publicly with the contradictions this must have entailed for him.

Althusser begins with a somewhat disparaging reference to the students ('Today, I still only have a few things on the "Student Movement". I am lacking the really *essential* material; *what, exactly, happened* in the working class and among the broad strata of (non-proletarian) employees who together made the portentous May general strike?')[91] The phrase 'general strike' is, we have seen, an example of 'PCF-speak', which Althusser goes on to qualify by describing the student movement as 'an extremely important phenomenon, but . . . *subordinated* to the economic class struggle of the nine million workers'.[92] If 'the relative order of importance of these two phenomena . . . has been *completely* reversed',[93] this is presumably because the student movement predated and touched off the general strike; but for Althusser that would be to fall into the trap of historicism, to suppose that the order in which events happened rather than their place in the social formation is what determines their importance. The 'real order' in which the PCF presented the events – the 'primacy of the general strike over the student actions'[94] – is thus a structural-synchronic rather than a chronological-diachronic (or even a moralistic-workerist) one.

Some of Althusser's pupils had arrived at far more extreme versions of this position in May; Robert Linhart, a philosophy student at the rue d'Ulm and leading theoretician of the UJCml, pronounced the student movement a time-wasting diversion and barricaded himself in his room, agonising over the correct theoretical line until he collapsed from exhaustion.[95] Althusser's own analysis is more in tune with the PCF's wish to recover for itself as much of May as possible, comparing the factory occupations to 1936 and saying that the students should have asked the workers to help them to organise an effective occupation of the Sorbonne. This may appear a bizarre suggestion given that the students had shown themselves perfectly capable of organising not one, but several occupations unaided; but it is entirely consistent with Althusser's position that he should advocate a student–worker fusion in which the students were clearly designated as the subordinate partners.

Such a fusion did not, however, take place. What occurred instead was an 'encounter', which was prevented from going further by student adventurism 'based more on a dream-experience than on an understanding of reality'.[96] This reads oddly from one who, as sometime analysand and assiduous advocate of Lacan, had better cause than most to understand how the 'dream-experience' can contribute, precisely, to an 'understanding of reality'; it is as if the repressed that here returns were the antique PCF distrust of psychoanalysis. The importance of the student movement lies not in the political but in the ideological sphere. ('N.B.: an ideological revolt is not, in and of itself, as the students too readily believe, a political revolution.')[97] Much as July *et al.* imply, without actually claiming, that the order of desire belongs with the barricades and the student movement and that of demand with negotiation and the workers, Althusser appears to ascribe the ideological sphere (on the whole) to the students and the political sphere (on the whole) to the workers. The workers, in his analysis, clearly have the advantage, but this is not the result of any *necessary* theoretical priority of the political over the ideological, for Althusser's own texts (notably 'Contradiction and Overdetermination') make it plain that for him the economic, the political and the ideological determine one another and one another's relative importance from moment to moment of the social formation. Such priority can therefore only be conjunctural, and it is always worth remembering that the conjuncture within which Althusser produced his analyses incorporated his role as the leading intellectual of the PCF.

This means that the students' ideological revolt cannot be dismissed out of hand; Althusser describes it as 'a true and proper mass movement, a petty-bourgeois one, to be sure, *but a mass one*'[98] from which Communist parties must learn the pressing need to reestablish contact with youth. How that might be achieved is barely suggested in this text, but more closely figured in the essay 'Idéologie et appareils idéologiques d'État/Ideology and ideological State apparatuses', written at much the same time as the letter to Macciocchi. This makes no overt reference either to the May events or to the PCF's relationship to youth, yet these constitute its hidden agenda, diagnostic and prognostic. The essay (which was highly influential in Anglo-American cultural and media studies in the 1970s) accords a more important space than most earlier Marxist theory to ideology, which 'interpellates individuals as subjects'[99] and is thus an inescapable part of any social formation. Language, culture and education therefore assume a central importance, manifested in the role of the 'ideological State apparatuses' (ISAs) – schools, universities, political parties, the family, institutions of communication and so forth – which are backed by, as they legitimise, the 'repressive State apparatus' of government, police and army.

Althusser's analysis in this essay has been much criticised for its supposed functionalist lumping together of virtually all institutions through which domination can be exercised, but my purpose here is not to evaluate it so much as to understand its relevance today. That ideological struggle, after all, had begun at the heart of a key ISA (the university), from which it had spread to challenge not only other ISAs – radio and television, trade unions, existing forms of political organisation – but the repressive state apparatus too, stopping short only of the army. Berating *fils à papa* and calling for a halt to provocation had in the circumstances scarcely been an adequate response. If the PCF were to win back the ground it had lost, a more imaginative politics in the cultural and superstructural realm – what Althusser here calls the ideological – would obviously be necessary. As we have seen, the Party was outflanked, here as elsewhere, by the Socialists; but this is no place to write its cultural obituary.

The historian Roger Martelli begins his *Mai 68* with the striking admission that on 13 May 1968 'I all at once discovered the PC and drew close to it.'[100] Even more strikingly, he remains at the time of writing a Party member, convinced that 'the whole of our time has remained marked both by [May's] irruption and by its relative failure'[101] – a contradiction that he tries to resolve by an appeal to the political history of the intervening years, embracing the triumph of the Left in 1981 but also its 'relative failure', at least in Communist terms, thereafter. The PCF is thus seen as the place from which the Left's changing fortunes – from May that wanted too much, to the Socialists who have tried for too little – can be 'correctly' understood and criticised.

Martelli criticises the *gauchiste* indictment of the 'consumer society' for failing to take questions of class into account, and the PCF for 'its continuing difficulty in thinking about individuals and the development of their place in society',[102] before concluding that:

> What May has left to us is its extraordinary cultural impact: its anti-authoritarian sensibility, a certain mood of impertinence, moral liberation, and concern . . . for structures and ideas.[103]

Yet none of these (except in a highly prescriptive sense 'concern for structures and ideas') can be said to have characterised the PCF before

May, nor in any durable sense since. Martelli's lessons of May are cogently drawn from a Communist perspective that their conclusions nevertheless implicitly undercut.

SOCIALIST PERSPECTIVES

Probably the best-known text on May from a point of view close to the Socialists is Régis Debray's *Modeste contribution aux discours et célébrations du dixième anniversaire/A modest contribution to the discourses and celebrations of the twentieth anniversary*, if only because substantial parts of it appeared in translation in *New Left Review*.[104] I shall deal with this in the following chapter, since it belongs more in the domain of cultural than of political analysis. Socialists and social democrats – until Charlety at least the most neglected if not despised political groupings in May – produced a number of analyses of the movement; it is perhaps fitting to begin with the most influential of their number, François Mitterrand.

Mitterrand, in *Ma part de vérité/My share of the truth*, makes clear his view that May could have not led to a revolution, while asserting that 'circumstances had rarely been so favourable to the coming together of the proletariat and the intellectuals'.[105] This for him was thwarted by the maximalist posturing of the students, with their wish to 'settle all their accounts at once – with de Gaulle, with capitalism, with the Communist Party, with social democracy, with the CGT, with the university'.[106] He contrasts the student leaders' 'simple and lively' interviews on television with the 'mixture of imitation Marxism [and] hotchpotch of confused ideas' with which they later expounded the reasons for their protest.[107] The student call for 'direct action' against the first round of the legislative elections is likewise mocked ('The Latin Quarter's polling stations have never been more peaceful places; our heroes were on holiday').[108] The tone here is markedly different to that of the PCF – less fulminatory, more understanding albeit patronisingly so, as befits the future Presidential *Tonton*/'Uncle'. There is perhaps a prefiguration of things to come in his suggestion that 'with memories such as theirs, this generation has it in its power to change the course of History',[109] for it is largely the generation of 1968, gravitating towards the Parti Socialiste rather than the PCF or other Leninist groups, who have been influential in the Socialist domination of French politics over the past ten years. From having been on his own admission in 1968 'the most hated man in France',[110] he was to become one of the best-loved, a living refutation of Sartre's (at the time understandable) assertion that 'the current leaders of the Left will represent nothing in ten years' time'.[111]

The most serious analysis of *gauchisme* from a social-democratic or reformist standpoint is provided by Max Gallo (later to be a Socialist minister) in *Gauchisme, réforme et révolution*. This concludes with a call for a broad socialist electoral alliance of a kind that 'might be able to turn revolutionary enthusiasm to its advantage'[112] – very similar, we have seen, to what Mitterrand, with his selective cannibalising of 'New Left' energies, was to undertake. The clear choice for socialists lies between 'being catalysts of the supposedly ineluctable *gauchiste* revolution and regulatory brakes helping to lead humankind slowly, through all the attendant risks, towards a socialism that has finally emerged from its primitive phase.'[113]

What is significant here is the placing of the PCF as 'omitted middle', perceived as having led itself into an impasse through its combination of revolutionary rhetoric and electoral political practice. His postscript, 'After Prague', sees the Russian invasion of August 1968 as the final discrediting of Soviet-style socialism for the mass of the French people. There is, for Gallo, no middle way between the species of French Fabianism he advocates and a far-Left putschism ruled out by the overwhelming likelihood of a military counter-coup. *Any* revolution is seen as '*gauchiste* and premature',[114] bearing the seeds of its own degeneration. Thus, 'the *gauchiste* urges of 1789–1799 may have given the Revolution its greatness, but they also led to Bonaparte'.[115] Bonaparte, of course, also led to that very de Gaulle against whom 1968's *gauchistes* rose in revolt; we seem not far here from a deterministically cyclic conception of history. Gallo's advocacy of regulatory, reformist socialism was about as unfashionable as it was possible to get in the France of 1968, yet at nearly a quarter-century's distance it is strikingly prophetic of the direction the French Left in government was eventually to take. 'Revolutionary enthusiasm', alas, seems to be one of the *gauchiste* babies thrown out with the Stalinist bathwater.

When Gilles Martinet wrote *La Conquête des pouvoirs/The Conquest of Power* he was a member of the PSU, though it would be difficult to claim that the book represents that party's 'line', since its determinedly non-Leninist approach meant that it did not have one. Martinet opens with the poignant assertion that Dubcek's reforms in Czechoslovakia, like the May events, figure a socialist democracy that 'has never existed, except in the idyllic and ephemeral forms that characterise the first phase of all great revolutions'.[116] It is clear for Martinet that May was such a 'first phase', and that its accomplishment could still be a long way off; he quotes a student's reply to a journalist who asked (on 24 May) if France was living through its 1917: 'Certainly not, we are only in 1905.'[117] Was Mitterrand's election in 1981 then to be the apotheosis of May? Martinet seems to suggest as much when he calls for 'the appearance of a new Socialist Party which, whereas the PCF has become a "party of resistance", can play the role of a "mass-movement party"'.[118] For Martinet, like Gallo, May should thus lead to the restructuring of the non-Communist Left rather than to any more (as with the Trotskyists) or less (as with the 22 March Movement) organised way forward. He acknowledges the attraction of direct democracy in a culture whose founding myths include the French Revolution and the Commune, but regards it as not viable in advanced industrial societies, where it readily becomes 'the screen for the tyranny of a "manipulative" minority'.[119]

Socialist democracy, however, 'is still to be invented',[120] so that Martinet's thought is more radical and innovative than Gallo's. His call for greater democratisation of economic and social planning found a ready audience in a Gaullist France that continued arrogantly to reaffirm the Jacobin tradition of government from the centre; the PSU's devolutionary and decentralisatory impetus owed much to the plurality of voices that made themselves heard in May.

That impetus, however, was – certainly for Michel Rocard, founder of the PSU and later Socialist Prime Minister – to become far more anti-Bolshevik than it was anti-Jacobin, and in that light Martinet's view that the PSU attempted to reconcile a traditional style of opposition (as in supporting a possible Mendès-France candidacy) with the call for soviets or workers' councils now reads ironically. To the question of whether May was a revolutionary situation, his response is predictably twofold: it was 'revolutionary in character',[121] thanks to the ideologies in which it was saturated, but the movement's lack of a programme and divisions on the established Left meant that it could not conceivably have seized power. The distinction between the ideological and the political sphere is clearly influenced by Althusser, who nonetheless comes in for criticism for failing to take his analyses to their logical conclusion – presumably by leaving the PCF. The Left intelligentsia are also taken to task for their 'sentimental populism strongly marked by cultural romanticism',[122] manifested by their transference of desire from the PCF (which almost compulsively attracts such Oedipal readings) on to the Third World, particularly Algeria and Cuba. New political forms, for Martinet, need to be sought within a European context – another respect in which *La Conquête des pouvoirs* is a strikingly 'pre-Mitterrandist' text.

Other social-democratic readings of May stress how it highlighted the need for radical modernisation of French society, whose social and political institutions lagged far behind its economic advance. Jean-Jacques Servan-Schreiber, who in the following year was to become General Secretary of the Parti radical-socialiste, criticised French society in *Le Réveil de la France/The Awakening of France* as still far too rigid and hierarchical,

closer to (then Francoist) Spain than to that Sweden so admired by progressive technocrats. For Servan-Schreiber, the time was ripe for a major
redistribution of political responsibilities, 'in which sense the situation is of
a revolutionary kind'.[123] This is scarcely a sense in which a Marx, a Krivine
or a Vaneigem would have used the term 'revolutionary', recuperated here
as little more than modish camouflage for a then-unfashionable stance.

Much of what Servan-Schreiber suggests is echoed more programmati-
cally in the pamphlet *Que faire de la révolution de mai?/What is to be done
with the May revolution?*, issued by the Club Jean Moulin. This, named
after the Resistance leader tortured to death in 1943, was one of the centre-
Left political clubs that were to be influential in the formation of the PS in
1971. It begins by endorsing the movement's criticism of the hierarchical
nature of French society – in a sense the 'lowest common denominator' of
all the Left readings of 1968 – before pointing out that it 'has not found its
language'.[124] The use of 'language' in the singular is noteworthy. May's
seizure of *la parole* had enabled it to find a variety of languages at once
exhilarating and bewildering, but precisely at the expense of 'its language'
as a single unified vocabulary. The language the pamphlet puts forward to
fill this gap is resolutely pragmatic, organisational and electoralist. Thus:

> the renewed France to which so many Frenchmen and Frenchwomen
> aspire can only be a France equipped with modern, dynamic local organ-
> isations that have found a way of reconciling the demands of democracy
> and those of efficiency.[125]

This is a very long way indeed from 'power to the imagination', but since
the Club Jean Moulin was composed largely of senior civil servants that is
perhaps not surprising. It might also help to explain why many of its
suggestions – for higher taxes on capital, greater delegated involvement in
cultural policy, more autonomy to the universities – were to form part of the
Socialists' programme in government. That programme was launched with
a series of 'revolutionary' verbal flourishes which clearly owed much to
May – Mitterrand's desire to 'finish with capitalism', Jack Lang's proclamation that the French had 'passed from darkness to light' – but in its
execution turned out to be (and not only for reasons of financial *force
majeure*) reformist much along the lines laid down in the pamphlet.

THE WORKING-CLASS MOVEMENT

After the Communists and the (various species of) Socialists, the third set
of discourses on the established Left I shall consider are those of the
working-class movement, within and outside the trade unions. Denis Barbet

contrasts the vocabulary of the CGT, which saw the events along PCF lines as primarily a class conflict, with that of the CFDT, for whom they were a social crisis producing and produced by 'new forces'. This contrast is most strikingly illustrated by divergent responses to the presence of the anarchist black flag on many of the demonstrations. For Georges Séguy (then General Secretary of the CGT) this is stigmatised as the 'mournful black flag of anarchy', whereas the CFDT militant Detraz hails it joyfully as 'the resurgence of an ideal of liberty'.[126] Differences – at once historical, analytical and organisational – again coalesce around the political language of the symbol.

This is a phenomenon analysed at greater length in *Grèves revendicatives ou grèves politiques?/Strikes for higher wages or political strikes?*, the work of a CNRS research team. The movement from non-political to political demands is here seen discursively as, following Julia Kristeva, a movement from the 'symbol' constituted as a self-contained whole to the 'sign' which literally only makes sense as part of a network of differential relations. The demand for a shorter working week can symbolise workers' disaffection outside any broader context, but only inscribed within a differential signifying system (of which a political programme is an example, though not the only kind) can it become political. Thus:

> a social movement only *really* calls power into question once it becomes *utopian*. In other words, once a demand becomes a sign, it also becomes the privileged index of all other demands, and thereby a *slogan* or rallying-cry for whatever its words introduce into the realm of the political.[127]

This leads to the conclusion that 'the decomposition of the movement does not mean that it fell apart powerlessly; it merely shows that its production of a political sense was only a partial one'.[128] The problem with this formulation is that it is, so to speak, shadowed by that very unitary sense of 'sense' that the concepts of 'sign' and 'difference' work to dispel. If 'a political sense' is to imply a single agreed system of relations (which is to say a programme, electoral or not), then May's production of it was partial precisely because it was excessive, as witness the host of readings and prognoses being examined here. Yet that very excess and heterogeneity were constitutive of May as seizure of *la parole*. The problem of the passage from the linguistic to the political (and back again) is most acutely and perceptively posed here, but resolved less conclusively than the text implies.

Whatever the *gauchiste* attitude towards trade unions (the Maoists in particular dismissed them as hopelessly revisionist), the struggle for union rights was, Dubois *et al.* make clear, the major common point of workplace activity in May. The most important divergence was in a sense one of class:

> The predominance of economic and social demands in working-class firms, the sudden prominence of demands for workers' control and self-management in technical firms, sometimes leading to a calling into question of firms' structures and their relation to economic and political power – this was the major division in the demands of the movement.[129]

Those employees most likely to have been students, in other words, were also the most likely to make demands that acceded to the political status of the sign – a view that in many ways meshes with that of Alain Touraine, to be discussed in Chapter 4. This goes some way towards explaining the calculations behind the PCF's changing attitudes; if the 'blue-collar' electorate that had consistently provided the bulk of its support was advancing largely quantitative demands, it was obviously in the Party's interest to endorse those and to dismiss or decry attacks on the consumer society and other positions that found little echo among manual workers. That, however, ignored the authoritarian homogenisation of Gaullist society, whose component parts manifested structural similarities despite their functional differences ('But the technocracy and the bureaucracy that were the students' targets in educational institutions were or the workers called into question in their workplaces').[130] In this respect, at least, May – 'the in-between period of modernity', as Capdevielle and Mouriaux aptly describe it – was a revolt against the modernising as well as the archaic aspects of French society.

More anecdotal, less exhaustive views of the workers' movement are provided by Philippe Bauchard and Maurice Bruzek (*Le Syndicalisme à l'épreuve/Trade unionism put to the test*), Philippe Gavi (*Les Ouvriers: du tiercé à la révolution/The workers: from betting-shop to revolution*) and Jacques Frémontier (*La Forteresse ouvrière – Renault/Renault, the working-class fortress*). These construct an unsurprisingly contradictory picture of the manual working class late 1960s vintage – ready to take up arms but unwilling for their daughters to marry a black ('Why? – I don't know'),[131] fearful of a Left government because of the British experience under Wilson (!),[132] yet perceived by Gavi at any rate as ripe for revolution ('From the betting-shop, the journey is a long one, but the beginning of the trial has been blazed',[133] than which it would be difficult to find a sentence more calculated to raise PCF hackles). Bauchard and Bruzek's analysis is the most interesting, for they situate the 'workers' May' in the line of a long march undertaken by the French working class since the great miners' strikes of 1961 and 1963. In 1963, the Bishop of Arras supported the

strikers, the UNEF and the Lens football team sent them money, the
Internationale was spontaneously sung in cafés, there were rail and power
strikes in sympathy, and the strikers finally achieved a substantial part of
what they had been demanding. Perhaps because this strike was more
conventional and less euphoric than the occupations of 1936, it has been
much less often cited as a pre-text for May; but the actions and episodes just
mentioned suggest that 1963 and 1968 were not without points in common.

Frémontier's study is of interest because it focuses on one employer,
Renault (France's biggest firm), in Boulogne-Billancourt ('the only town in
France that has one name for the rich and one for the poor'[134] – a reference
to the factory being situated in the exclusive Parisian residential suburb that
likes to think of itself as Boulogne-sur-Seine). Frémontier, like Gavi,
interviewed a wide selection of workers about their participation in the May
events. He is scathing about *gauchiste* attacks on the consumer society,
which 'blithely evade the class struggle'[135] and give students and intellectuals an easy conscience by privileging their privileges. Frémontier finds
class consciousness at Renault stronger than in 1968, reinforced by the
tendency to proletarianisation of the lower middle class and the continuing
material inadequacies of the workers' lives. The text is punctuated by the
ironic (in the long term wearingly so) refrain: 'No, definitely, there is no
longer a working-class condition', which alludes to Simone Weil's *La
Condition ouvrière/The working-class condition*, an account of her experiences as a factory worker in 1935. Weil's text (published posthumously in
1951) had drawn widespread attention to the degrading conditions and
relations of powerless dependence experienced by many manual workers.
The 'thirty glorious years' might have improved these; they had hardly
eliminated them.

HOSTILE VIEWS OF THE EVENTS

May unsurprisingly produced many fewer hostile than favourable readings;
the movement's short-term political failure and the triumphant reassertion
of the Right were enough to see to that. Its unexpectedness nevertheless
gave rise to a good deal of speculation about what (outmoded Gaullism?
Malraux's 'crisis of civilisation'? 'Moscow gold'?) had caused the crisis,
couched in tones ranging from pained bafflement to righteous indignation.

The supreme example of the latter is Raymond Aron's *La Révolution
introuvable/The undiscoverable revolution*, which for Bénéton and Touchard
explains the events as a psychodrama or 'rush of blood to the head'. This
might seem to place it more appropriately in the category of socio-cultural

interpretation, but the work's title suggests that it has important political ramificiations too. It is in any event so much the best-known hostile text on May (Alain Renaut describes it as a '*livre maudit*/cursed book')[136] that it all but demands to be treated before the others.

One major reason for that is that Aron was virtually unique among the major French intellectuals of the time in his vehement opposition to the May movement. (I discount Malraux because of his membership of the government, notwithstanding which he displayed far more sympathy for the students than Aron.) The recent discrediting of Marxism and rehabilitation of electoral democracy has brought Aron's liberal views back into the centre ground of political debate. In the aftermath of May, however, his declaration that 'I lived through these weeks in the USA [where he was from 14 to 23 May] with suffering and in France with indignation'[137] made him a very marginal figure indeed.

Aron's view that Marxism is 'the opium of the intellectuals', expressed as early as *L'Opium des intellectuels* of 1955, accounts for his disdain for 'revolutionaries' who 'forget a century's history and ignore the constraints of business and the economy'.[138] On one level this is a curmudgeonly response to a movement that drew its energy precisely from its ignoring of constraints, as well as a justified reminder of how weak most French (and other) Marxist intellectuals have been on the economy to which they have accorded overdetermining pride of place. On another, it (like the rest of the book) simply disregards the working-class movement and the substantial economic as well as social gains it achieved. On yet another, it prepares the ground for Aron's major historical offensive – that what seemed new and exciting was but a 'semi-delinquent' and totally unconstructive reworking of themes and styles of action tediously familiar in France ('The student commune, the great letting-off of steam – this ill-defined palaver is typical of French society . . . the carnival has nothing to do with the building of a new social order').[139] Bakhtin notwithstanding, May is not the apotheosis of French revolutionary history, but its disorderly and degenerate epigone.

It follows from this that for Aron the 'university Bastille' supposedly stormed in May was the 'symbol of a pseudo-revolution, because student power and workers' power have nothing in common'.[140] (The 'allegorical Bastille' will be given a very different value in Michel de Certeau's *La Prise de la parole*). The PCF, in the early days of May at least, could not have put it better, appropriately since Aron's text constantly tries to settle accounts with his old adversary – sometimes by stealing its clothes. Thus, the Party is described as 'the victim of the PSU, trouble-makers and small groups – in other words, of intellectuals, which is a form of poetic jus-tice'.[141] The poetry of that justice lies not merely in the intellectuals victim-

ising the PCF rather than vice versa, but in the deployment against the Party
of terms drawn from its own rhetoric ('trouble-makers and small groups').
(The French has *'juste retour des choses'*, which has overtones of both
reversal and getting one's own back.)

Aron's invective against the student movement, by contrast, is grounded
in nothing more sophisticated than hardline liberal moralism. The last two
terms are for him strictly tautological, for 'the university, in liberal countries, can exist only by the moral code of liberalism'.[142] It is this assumption
that the established order has a monopoly of morality that lends his strictures that very air of mandarin arrogance against which, in a multiplicity of
ways, the movement was directed. The effective recognition of unofficial
gatherings of all the teaching staff and/or students is castigated as illegal, in
violation of the university's obligatory professional neutrality. His recommendations – for less centralisation, broader access and more practically
relevant or vocational courses – were to find echoes not only on the Right
in much subsequent French educational policy-making.

The events' unconstitutional immorality is for Aron but one symptom of
the Left intelligentsia's scorn alike for reality ('the contempt of so many
intellectuals for facts reached incredible proportions')[143] and – under the
cloak of criticism of bourgeois democracy – for the masses for whom they
profess concern:

> the spectacular return to the party of order which any self-respecting
> Left-wing intellectual explains as a reaction of fear, can also be ac-
> counted for in a manner less scornful of the French people. Becoming
> aware of conditions indispensable to the running of any society . . . they
> felt a need, at least as strong as their earlier revolutionary one, to come
> back to reality.[144]

A version of Freud in which the 'psychodrama' is resolved by the victory
of the hero – the reality principle – over the villain – the pleasure principle
– is implied here. That the pleasure principle could ever be anything other
than an infantile threat to civilisation, a 'collective delirium'[145] – that its
assertion could have durable political effects, to be manifested in the
downfall of de Gaulle and later of Stalinist Communism – never seems so
much as to occur to Aron. Yet it would be quite wrong to conclude from this
that he was an unconditional Gaullian loyalist. June's reassertion of the
status quo ante – the triumph of common sense – is also, more ambivalently,
read as another instance of how 'the French, terrified of themselves, have
regularly raised from its ruins a bureaucratic hierarchy'.[146] The target of his
invective reveals itself to be not merely a posturing Left-Bank cabal, but the
French people themselves, for 'in no other modern country, I believe, has

society shown itself so incapable of surviving on its own, without the State'.[147] May's anarchy would thus merely have prepared the ground for the imposition of a Stalinist hierarchy rather than the Gaullist one that was incomparably the lesser of two evils.

Aron's anti-statism is thus of a piece with his anti-Communism rather than running counter to it, in which respect he is a forerunner of the anti-statist 'New Right' of the 1970s and 1980s – more of a 'French Thatcher', certainly, than de Gaulle ever was. De Gaulle, despite his magisterial liquidation of the crisis ('A man speaks and the comedy is over'),[148] cannot escape responsibility for what happened. The driving paradox of Aron's political rhetoric (as of Thatcher's) is that the tones in which it denounces authoritarianism are themselves often loftily authoritarian.

It thus seems ironically fitting that Jacques Laurent's *Lettre ouverte aux étudiants/Open letter to the students* begins by turning Aron's condemnatory vocabulary against its author:

> When it comes to infantilism, Aron goes even further than Mauriac. For the latter, de Gaulle is a good father. For Aron, he is a bad one, but it seems self-evident that it is better to have a bad father than no father at all.[149]

No father, bad father, good father (or even Godfather) – the Right-wing rhetoric surrounding de Gaulle makes the Oedipal component of May even clearer than its Left-wing counterparts. Laurent's admonitions to the students for the rest are a weary (and wearisome) blend of applause for their showmanship and condescension towards their political and philosophical naivety ('If you were aiming not to make a revolution but to put on a show, you did the right thing in occupying the Odéon').[150] The movement's supposed intellectual mentors are viewed either, in the case of the structuralists, paranoically, as part of 'a plot against humanism that runs from Auguste Comte to Marx, from Taine to Lévi-Strauss or Lacan',[151] or in that of the more humanist Marxists – Marcuse, Lefebvre – as victims of conceptual weakness and bad faith:

(1) They aspire towards a new society that they do not attempt to define.

(2) They believe – especially Marcuse – in the need for a revolution to bring forth a free society, but make no attempt to clarify the means it will use.

(3) They want to remain within the Marxist church.[152]

This is not the place to discuss the influence of Marcuse (notably *One-Dimensional Man*) upon the May movement, an influence described by

Cohn-Bendit as much overrated. What is important is the amalgam of conspiracy theory and patronisation, here assigned respectively to opposing schools of philosophy which can be read by extension as representing different factions of the May movement itself (perhaps the Leninist and non-Leninist tendencies?). We have found that same amalgam in the vocabulary of de Gaulle himself. It is as if May were at once the ultimate threat to freedom and no threat at all.

Neither Aron nor Laurent offers any specifically political solution to the problems raised by May; that, as we have seen, tends to be the prerogative of those writing from the Left. Gaullism did not, however, have a monopoly on the political Right, as the election of Valéry Giscard d'Estaing to the Presidency in 1974 was to show. Giscard's more Atlanticist approach and modernising drive caused him to be regarded as the first 'post-Gaullist' President, so that *Des barricades ou des réformes?/Barricades or reforms?* by Alain Griotteray (then Vice-President of Giscard's Républicains Indépendants party) is in a sense prognosis as well as diagnosis. The archaism of Gaullist France is identified as the students' main target, and their movement is compared to a collective form of public confession (the spiritual aspect of the movement, as Bénéton and Touchard have shown, attracted much commentary). 'A certain form of revolutionary romanticism',[153] on the one hand, the provocation of the PCF (here again victim of its own rhetoric), on the other, are blamed for the course events took, so that once more naivety and conspiracy go hand in hand. Naivety, on Griotteray's reading, came close to being the dominant partner, for 'in May 1968 the Communists very nearly pulled off a revolution in spite of themselves'.[154]

The measures proposed (in a text that, arising out a Républicains Indépendants summer school, can be supposed to have had some influence on Giscard's presidency) include a major renewal of social and economic structures, a balance between technical and social progress, and a recognition of what is seen as 'realistic' in younger people's calls for autonomy and participation while dismissing their 'total misrecognition'[155] of what is actually possible. Caring capitalism with a technocratic face, coupled with a stress on the role of youth appropriate to a party whose leader was to become the second youngest French President,[156] are Griotteray's recommendations. This is scarcely exciting, even (or especially) in a world where 'the only colour that still stands out a little from red is the black of despair';[157] but it was sufficiently different from what the Gaullists appeared to be offering to make Giscard's rise to power understandable.

Different again – radically, even grotesquely so – is *Les Journées de mai 68 – les dessous d'une révolution/The Days of May 68 – the shady side of a revolution*, by the neo-Fascist ideologue François Duprat. This (as Bénéton and Touchard suggest) is steeped in a conspiracy theory made barely more plausible by the author's assassination with a car bomb ten years later. Duprat seeks to give his thesis intellectual respectability through an introduction and conclusion by the literary critic Maurice Bardèche, an active Fascist since the 1930s. Bardèche asserts that the consumer society offered students nothing – a theme echoed by neo-Fascist movements at the time of the events ('there are undoubted points in common between our movement and the strong student *contestation* of a society that has become incapable of defending fundamental values and providing structures for the future').[158] Fascism, in 1968 much as thirty years earlier, strove to reclaim the West's menaced spirituality against Communism and capitalism alike.

Duprat's narrative plunges straight into paranoia with its claim that the riots were organised by a small number of specialised agitators influenced by the violence of Black Power in the USA, and thereafter scarcely lets up for a moment. (I have to confess that it gave me more unalloyed pleasure in the reading than virtually any other book on the events.) Of the different currents, the 22 March Movement was merely a media invention, whilst the Maoists benefited from Chinese funds laundered through either Lausanne or Belgium; they were, however, 'bested' by the Trotskyists of the JCR, quite a feat since the latter had to make do with money from Hanoi. Masterminding the whole process – providing, as narratologists might say, the invisible metatext – was East Germany, seeking to provoke a hardening of NATO's line that would lead to concomitant hardening in the Eastern bloc and thereby help to preserve its unpopular régime.

The Popular Action Committees that sprang up on an area (in Paris, arrondissement) basis manufactured weapons as well as stealing them from the PCF's clandestine armoury. This assertion is irrefragably proven by a photograph of a police-wagon on fire, captioned 'A police-station in flames'. Duprat spikes his narration with a rhetoric of disorder as lavish as it is predictable ('in appalling confusion, the Left Bank's entire population of tramps, drug-addicts, professional unemployed, half-starved beatniks, and failures of every shape and kind set out towards the new 'Promised Land' [of the occupied Sorbonne])'.[159] Fear of the urban mob has been a staple of conservative rhetoric in France ever since the Revolution and its *sans-culottes*[160] and was certainly not far below the surface of de Gaulle's comminatory utterances on 30 May. Neo-Fascist groups, according to Duprat, joined the vast counter-demonstration that evening, though often ejected by stewards – a bizarre inversion of the PCF's attitude on 13 May. The 'death and resurrection of the régime'[161] – appositely religious terminology – was clearly preferable to the Bolshevik alternative.

Bardèche's conclusion touches new circle-squaring heights in denying that the movement was anti-Gaullist ('It was the *style* of the régime that was called into question, not the individuals'[162] – as if under Gaullism of all things the two could be distinguished), before concluding with a ringing call to give young people a purpose and treat them (seemingly regardless of gender) as men. As for democracy, while it may have yielded the least bad result in June, it is still but 'a new conditioning of the opium of the people'.[163]

Duprat's conspiracy theory is comical through its extravagant incoherence; that of Raymond Marcellin in *L'Ordre public et les groupes révolutionnaires/Public order and revolutionary groups* may be less preposterous, but his appointment as Interior Minister immediately after the events made it far more dangerous. He detects disturbing resemblances between the activity of *gauchistes* in France and that of Left-wing groups in Germany, Italy, Britain and the USA – a less florid variation on the 'international conspiracy' theme – and denounces the supposed corrupters of youth in terms not unworthy of Duprat ('These tremulous, touchy, anxious adolescents were to be recruited by men in search of power, who would indoctrinate, enthuse and then sacrifice them. There is no commerce more shameless or Machiavellian than this').[164]

Marcellin's crusade was to rid France of the 'revolutionary parties of Trotskyist, Castroist or Maoist inspiration that have been organising on our territory'.[165] The juxtaposition of three foreign names with the phrase 'organising on our territory' clearly suggests a species of ideological invasion or colonisation, implicitly ruling out the possibility that *bona fide* French citizens might of their own volition have set up such groups. Marcellin's trademark during his nearly six-year reign was the instantaneous deportation of any foreigner found taking part in a political demonstration, justified by an appeal to the 'strict political neutrality imposed on foreigners resident in France by an international rule applied in every country in the world'.[166] In few others, however, was it applied with such remorseless zest; Marcellin metaphorically flourishes the scalp of the Paris correspondent of the *New York Guardian*, deported for 'persistent' presence on demonstrations, as proof of his determination. The internationalisation of the new Left-wing politics in the 1960s, exemplified in the somewhat optimistic slogan 'Paris, Warsaw, Rome, Berlin – we shall fight and we shall win', was quite a new phenomenon, reflecting a refusal of American and Soviet social models alike and a recognition of common interests shared by student movements everywhere. Marcellin states that 250 of the 1000 people taken to the Beaujon detention centre in May were non-French citizens. In this sense he was right in perceiving the movement's internationalism as a threat to his severely nationalistic brand of Gaullism, though he does not escape the logical trap of implying that that threat is really no threat at all ('These revolutionaries are steeped in internationalism, but it is a vague, anarchic, inorganic internationalism').[167] His defence of the police – provoked physically and psychologically by the demonstrators, slanderously accused of using poison gas, unnerved by rumours that some of their number had disappeared or even been executed – brings almost as many tears to the eyes as the gas they undoubtedly did use, a use that of itself would seem to refute Marcellin's bland assertion that 'in general the conduct of the forces of order was exemplary'.[168]

PARIS AND THE PROVINCES

Virtually all the interpretations so far considered have treated May as a Parisian phenomenon. At the final session of the Paris conference 'Acteurs et terrains du mouvement social de 1968' ('Participants and contexts of the social movement of 1968'), a member of the panel commented that it had marked the beginning of the history of May in the provinces – after twenty years, it might have been thought, not before time. That conference heard papers on different aspects of the events in Alsace, Béarn (in south-western France), Brest (Brittany), the Somme (in the north-east) and Caen (Normandy), as well as a more general contribution from Danielle Tartakowsky which emphasised the extent and scale of the movement outside the Paris area (an average of twenty-five provincial demonstrations per day between 1 May and 13 June).

Yet this generalised neglect, which typifies the often stifling dominance of Paris over the remainder of the country, has not been universal. The situationists' coup in Strasbourg rapidly formed part of the 'pre-mythology' of May, and the movement in Western France – Caen and, above all, Nantes, at the Loire estuary near the southern tip of Brittany – had received a certain amount of attention. This part of France had been particularly marked by the post-war shift from an agricultural to a manufacturing economy, and by the accompanying process of industrial decentralisation, which 'meant . . . the speedy introduction of Fordism. All the recently-built factories were organised around the production line and cared only for output.'[169] The January strike at Saviem and the violent demonstrations that accompanied it were thus, we have seen, perceived as precursors of the May events; for Gérard Lange, 'those who see the 1960s as the years of powder can be in no possible doubt: Caen is a symbol, a reference-point, explicitly mentioned in the 22 March tract from Nanterre and the UNEF's press release of 6 May'.[170]

If Caen symbolises the thunderclouds, it is Nantes that represents the storm. There more than anywhere else, in a large port that is also the centre of an important farming hinterland and a major university city, the threefold collaboration between industrial workers, agricultural workers and students so ardently sought by the *gauchistes* became (some kind of) reality. The strike committees, rather than the elected local or appointed national authorities, effectively ran the city for much of May; but Adrien Dansette warns against 'drawing from an epithet the raw material of a legend',[171] pointing out that the committees ran the existing system (in itself, one would have thought, no mean feat) rather than instituting a new one. Dansette's stricture illustrates how quickly May, in an age of communications far less sophisticated than now, generated its myths; the title of Yannick Guin's *La Commune de Nantes/The Nantes Commune* (by analogy, clearly, with the Paris one) goes to reinforce that dimension.

Figures such as Juvénal Quillet (*gauchiste* activist in the students' union) and Alexandre Hébert (an anarchist prominent in union activity at the occupied Sud-Aviation factory) suggest a very distinctive local political culture – probably the indirect result of belated industrialisation and strong Catholic traditions, which between them would have lessened the influence of the PCF. The spiritual and symbolic dimension of the events was thus particularly in evidence. A nun publicly proclaimed that Jesus Christ was the first anarchist (and was promptly ordered to return to her convent); the main square, the Place Royale, was renamed the Place du Peuple (Square of the People); the secretary of the CGT's naval section asked the Prefect to demand the resignation of the very government that had appointed him; 300 workers came to a *méchoui* (spit-roasting of lamb) at the University's law department. Anecdotes such as these readily suggest why Nantes's 'curious mixture of Trotskyist, anarchist and situationist themes'[172] lent itself to becoming one of the great myths of May, for it was (or could claim to be) everything that the established Left had never been. Guin's reading is much more sanguine than Dansette's:

> In Paris, the revolt and the struggle were directed against a government: capitalist society was only verbally vilified. In Nantes, the struggle and the new institutions aimed at the direct overthrow of capitalist society. It was not a head-on battle so much as a movement towards abolition accompanied by the attempt to install effective workers' power.[173]

The organisation of food distribution by the central strike committee, according to an approximate principle of 'from each according to their ability, to each according to their means', like the takeover and running of social security offices and even newspapers by the trade unions, certainly came closer to a concrete vision of an alternative type of social organisation than anything achieved in Paris. Yet the movement declined, swiftly and violently, towards the end of the month, for much the same reasons as elsewhere – insufficient organisation and what Guin depressingly describes as the 'absence of a revolutionary Jansenism'.[174] That revolutionary Jansenism, which made membership of a preordained caste at once a necessary and a sufficient condition of 'salvation', had found its clearest expression in the Stalinist Communism against which the movement, in France as a whole, had represented so massive a reaction. It is almost as though the absence of such a tendency caused the 'Nantes commune' to fail for want of sufficiently defined opposition.

A cautionary tale to offset Guin's visionary zeal is to be found in Georges Chaffard's *Les Orages de mai – histoire exemplaire d'une élection/The storms of May – the exemplary story of an election*. The author (a foreign correspondent who had been reporting on the Vietnam peace talks in Paris) took himself off to Vendôme, a market town in the Loire valley, to cover the June electoral campaign. Vendôme's main industries included a printing-works (owned by the academic publishers Presses Universitaires de France) and a large dairy, both of which went on strike, albeit belatedly (20–21 May). It also had a Socialist mayor, to say nothing of one Communist and two extreme Left municipal councillors (out of 104). Even so, the response of the mayor's deputy to a request from the Communist that the council should stand in salute to the local working class speaks volumes:

> The global critique of society and other such pompous revolutionary formulas are not to be brought up or discussed in the deliberations of a modest local council running a town of 17 000 inhabitants, and a very politically moderate one at that. This whole business is deplorable![175]

The dairy was to return to work, after a negotiated settlement, within three days, so perhaps the Communist's homage would have been a trifle excessive. Chaffard also reports widespread disapproval of teachers going on strike and of the hoisting of a red flag over the town's war memorial. ('Red, for country people, symbolises urban disorder and even more collectivist communism, the one thing in the world which still most terrifies small farmers and village craftsmen.')[176] In the circumstances, it is not surprising that in the legislative elections the sitting member of parliament (Gérard Yvon, the Socialist mayor) was defeated by a candidate of the Centre, who presented himself as the 'man of dialogue' and blamed the government for the workers' discontent while maintaining that 'no country in the world can afford to indulge this kind of fantasy for long'.[177]

It is tempting, but facile, to dismiss reaction in Vendôme as qualitatively and quantitatively insignificant. It was a town only a hundred miles from Paris, with a fifteen-year tradition of Socialist rule and strong local PSU and CFDT organisation (a CFDT branch was set up at the dairy during the events). If such a comparatively central community could manifest such ambiguous and sometimes vehement reactions – from the deputy mayor's diatribe to the enthusiasm of some of the local clergy and the threats of some *gauchistes* to burn down the Giscardian candidate's house – culminating in a major electoral setback for the Left, the reasons were surely to be sought in the inequalities and divisions of the France against which the movement had risen, as much as in any supposed irresponsible extremism or rustic obtuseness. The two latter, after all, were but mirrored misrecognitions of each other within the abiding context of Gaullism.

4 Cultural Interpretations of the Events

[This was] a revolution more philosophical than political, more social than institutional, more exemplary than real, destroying everything without being destructive, destroying rather than the past the present without even seeking to give itself a future, utterly indifferent to any possible future, as though the time it sought to open were already beyond any such habitual determinations.[1]

This chapter will look at those readings of May that view it essentially as a cultural rather than a political phenomenon – whether, to follow Bénéton and Touchard's taxonomy, a crisis in the university or a wider 'crisis of civilisation'. The overwhelming majority of tenth- and (*a fortiori*) twentieth-anniversary interpretations on the events are of this kind, reflecting the piecemeal displacement of revolutionary politics by radical culture that has characterised the period since May. It is significant that the only twentieth-anniversary work to have been considered under the heading of political interpretation was Bensaïd and Krivine's *Mai si!*, a fact which emphasises the tenacity of Trotskyism as compared to other forms of *gauchiste* politics (Maoism, situationism . . .) that have all but ceased to exist.

Morin's reference to the word 'revolution' as 'polluted'[2] is but a particularly highly-coloured instance of how a term incessantly bandied about in May thereafter fell into decline, at any rate on the Left. Jean-Claude Guillebaud, specialist in Third World affairs for *Le Monde*, charted the course of this process in *Les Années orphelines/The Orphan Years* (1978), whose title clearly situates itself in the generational/Oedipal view of May that dominates the anniversary retrospectives. He begins by posing an ironic question to his hypothetical (ex-) revolutionary reader ('Have you put on weight, contracted a legal marriage and joined the CERES [a Leftist grouping within the Socialist Party] while waiting, from one congress to the next, for the magic day of an overall majority?'[3] Sartre, the previous year, had stated that he had not considered himself a Marxist for three or four years, and the litany of disappointments for the Left (which snatched defeat from the jaws of victory in the 1978 legislative elections) is a long one. The crushing of the Prague Spring, the revelations about Mao's China, the horror of the Khmer Rouge in Kampuchea were the most sensational of these, but more significant for political developments in France was the determinedly non-revolutionary turn of events in Western Europe. The struggle against the colonels' régime in Greece -- the "'Spanish Civil War" of the Nanterre generations'[4] – lost its interest after an elected government of the Right had replaced Papadopoulos. Even more significant was the dilution of the 1974 'Carnation Revolution' in Portugal, which led to the election of a fairly conventional centre-left government rather than to the more venturesome political forms hinted at in May. Guillebaud's dominant theme, already suggested in more aggressive form by Aron, is one that will recur in different guises throughout this and the following chapter – that the revolutionary political attitudes which held sway for a number of years after 1968 were a form of superstition verging on mass delirium ('Our conduct as militants for ten years smacked of religious activity').[5] The awakening from this is accounted for by France's emergence from three 'Manichean' periods – the war against Nazism, the colonial period and the Cold War's division of the world into two antagonistic blocs. The *gauchiste* Left were in no doubt about where they stood on the first two questions, but the plausibility of Guillebaud's thesis is somewhat undercut by the 'plague on both your houses' attitude often shown towards both sides in the Cold War. The search for an alternative mode of social organisation to capitalism or (Stalinist) Communism was indeed one of the mainsprings of *gauchisme*, so that its rise as well as its fall can be seen as part of the decline of Manicheism.

The important thing from our point of view is that, for Guillebaud, what presented itself as 'political' analysis and activity was 'really' something else – a complexly determined, but historically doomed, acting-out of generational conflicts and contradictions. May on this reading thus ceases to be a political phenomenon at all and can be left to the cultural analysts; except, of course, that culture is political as well as vice versa. 'The personal is political' (Kate Millett) makes sense via the omitted middle of culture, the sphere in which everyday life and politics articulate themselves to and through each other. Thus, for Guillebaud, May's possible saving grace was that 'a thousand struggles began on the real territory, that of life'.[6] That statement, with its privileging and hypostatisation of 'life', is no more politically innocent than any other.

CULTURAL INTERPRETATIONS: THE INSTITUTIONS OF CULTURE

Cultural analysis of May in particular will inevitably tend to focus on the universities, whose radical reorganisation and partial democratisation afterwards made them probably the sector of French society most durably affected by the events. Pierre Bourdieu and Jean-Claude Passeron had drawn attention to the potential crisis of the education system in *Les Héritiers/The Heirs* of 1964. Their assertion that group-centred methods of work had been unsuccessful because 'students, the products of a system that develops the tendency to be passive, cannot . . . miraculously create out of nothing new forms of integration'[7] seems in the light of May a trifle wide of the mark, but precisely thereby emphasises the events' surprise value, undercut elsewhere in the book. Thus, the paradox of a socially and culturally privileged minority embracing the values of the Left is for Bourdieu and Passeron really not a paradox at all:

> If we bear in mind that the cultural advantages generally associated with a bourgeois origin are magnified through living in Paris, we can see that bourgeois Parisian students, who combine all manner of privileges, are better placed than any others to show that casual detachment from their studies which is perceived as a sign of intellectual mastery, and likewise more inclined to bold political positions that give them the satisfaction of accepting the intellectual consensus in a manner all the worthier for seeming a deliberate choice.[8]

It is difficult not to hear, in this portrayal of a seigneurially outrageous radicalism that is but a disguised form of social conformity, a more intellectually sophisticated pre-echo of Georges Marchais's strictures on the leftism of the *fil(le)s à papa*. Bourdieu and Passeron's analysis nevertheless has the merit of suggesting how the roots of the 1968 crisis lay in the combination of privilege and overcrowding that characterised Parisian universities in particular. The reaction against mandarin authoritarianism and the demands for greater control over one's education is ascribed to the ideology of 'the permanent festival, through which a group can assert its integration through the fictional intensification of symbolic exchanges'.[9] The term 'permanent festival', with its simultaneous overtones of the Trotskyist 'permanent revolution' and the Bakhtinian 'carnival',[10] prefigures what was to follow in four years' time, just as May's extraordinary combination of fierce violence with almost complete lack of bloodshed can be understood as a 'fictional intensification of symbolic exchange' – the acting-out of the desire for revolution rather than of revolution itself.

Bourdieu returned to the pre-1968 university (this time without Passeron) with *Homo Academicus* of 1984. This does not present itself primarily as an 'interpretation of May', for Bourdieu is more concerned to establish as applicable to the university system itself his methods of sociological analysis. That these methods were constructed largely against that very system and the hierarchy of disciplines within it[11] suggests that Bourdieu's choice of the pre-May university is not an innocent one, manifesting as it does symbolic solidarity with the movement by turning its conceptual armoury against a common adversary.

Bourdieu takes as a given that May was primarily a crisis of the university system, latent in it for some considerable time before because of what he terms 'the logic of the field' – the rivalries between different types of academic from different social backgrounds, active in different fields and disciplines (some residual, some dominant, some emergent, to borrow terms from Raymond Williams),[12] and likely in consequence to espouse different cultural, ideological and political positions. The rivalry between (declining) philology and (emergent) linguistics is one instance he cites; British and American readers will recognise in the changing institutional importance of (say) classics on the one hand and media studies on the other a more home-grown instance.

For Bourdieu, this (sociologically-determined) disciplinary ferment broke the quasi-organic cycle whereby students graduated to lectureships and produced younger versions of themselves, so that May appears as a specific generational crisis within the university as well as within society at large. The tensions that arose as newer disciplines vied for legitimacy and older ones found themselves embattled were augmented by the increasing range of intellectual outlets outside the university, notably in the world of publishing.[13] Many of France's most prominent intellectuals have either not occupied university positions (Beauvoir, Debray, Lacan, Sartre), or occupied them belatedly and unconventionally, as with Roland Barthes whose first and last 'mainstream' academic post was at the Collège de France in 1976. The division Bourdieu establishes between 'university professors' – on the whole inclined to conservative social, religious and political views – and the more radical 'intellectuals' is thus less facetious than it may sound to a non-French audience. May saw the traditional university under attack from without as well as within, so that a response as extreme as that of the egregious Professor Deloffre – a Right-wing literary mandarin at the Sorbonne who bit a (woman) student demonstrator on the ankle in 1968 – is rooted in complex sociological factors as well as in individual psychopathology, for all the scorn such an interpretation would doubtless arouse in the Deloffres of this world.

For detailed documentation of the movement in the universities before and during May, Schnapp and Vidal-Nacquet's *Journal de la commune étudiante* remains an unrivalled source. The particular importance of Nanterre is argued in *Ces idées qui ont ébranlé la France/Those ideas that shook France*, by 'Épistémon' (Didier Anzieu). The liberal attitudes of the teaching staff, connected with their disciplinary distribution – one-third in the Faculty of Letters were in Human and Social Sciences, the highest proportion ever recorded in France – are adduced as important factors, along with the progressive approach to teaching and learning. Nanterre thus appears as the dialectical antithesis of the Sorbonne, flexible, innovatory, pedagogically open where the 'parent' institution was closed, reactionary, hierarchical, and thereby providing a model with which to oppose it.

Épistémon's view of Nanterre lays particular stress on its phantasmal aspects, as when he tells how students:

> cut all links with reality as well as rationality and launched themselves, without a psychoanalyst, into a vast collective session of free association of ideas, day and night. Imagination took power at Nanterre some two months before the Sorbonne.[14]

Beyond this amalgam of condescension towards utopianism and avant-garde civic pride, Épistémon/Anzieu has a specific intellectual axe to grind. This resides in his assertion that May was 'the death-certificate of structuralism'[15] – the term here understood as implying above all the unimportance of history:

> The main thing for Lévi-Strauss's study of myth, for Lacan's deciphering of the unconscious, for Althusser's questioning of the relationship between the work of economic production and that of thought, was structural organisation. History was an incidental detail, a vicissitude, the realm of the inessential. History, thus negated, negated its own negation and presented itself in May 1968 as indestructibly existent, on its own terms of conflict, destruction and movement beyond.[16]

This criticism is similar to those later made of Althusser by Anglo-American writers such as E.P. Thompson (*The Poverty of Theory*) and Tony Judt, who avers that 'the mass strike . . . posed a simple empirical threat to the Althusserian theorem which had supposedly abolished such acts of conscious mass volition in de Gaulle's France'.[17] The absurd rhetoric of Judt's claim that so resolutely ahistorical and anti-voluntarist a thinker could conceivably 'abolish' anything at all in de Gaulle's France (or anywhere else) should not blind us to the immense challenge the events posed to a system that, as Judt elsewhere and rightly says, 'excuses marxism from any obligation to offer an account of revolution'.[18] Yet the notion that 'May refuted structuralism', whatever the (necessarily contentious) definition of 'structuralism' upon which it rests, is surely too undialectical by half. That is, after all, a very important sense in which May was *also* about 'structural organisation' – not only in the universities and other social institutions, but in the domain of language seen by Lacan (and, following him, Althusser) as the inescapable horizon of all human activity. What is at stake in Épistémon's formulation is a binary alternative – either structural organisation or History with a capital H, either a univocal determinism verging on predestination or a process in which human beings can and do intervene towards a goal (chosen by what or whom?) – that does not appear tenable in those terms. It is relevant here to note the dominance of non- or anti-structuralist thinkers (Lefebvre, Ricoeur, Touraine . . .) at Nanterre, whereas Althusser and Lévi-Strauss, at the École Normale Supérieure and the Collège de France respectively, were in more established institutions. Bourdieu's 'logic of the field' would produce a symptomatic reading of Épistémon's *parti pris* here, suggesting a correlation between the age and prestige of an institution and its members' openness or otherwise to the human shaping of history perhaps just plausible enough to be misleading in the context of May.

For the École Normale – despite Althusser's equivocation, despite Robert Linhart's self-immurement – was a key institution throughout the events, its traditional openness to visitors enabling it to host numerous (especially Maoist) meetings and to act a refuge for weary participants in the night of the barricades in particular. The oldest Parisian academic institution (the Sorbonne) and the most prestigious were thus two of the major epicentres of the movement, along with two far newer buildings whose threadbare functionalist rigour seemed to complement the Sorbonne's baroque com-placency as the very expression of what the students yearned to overthrow. These were (of course) Nanterre and the somewhat neglected Sorbonne 'annex' in the rue Censier, from which it drew its name. Jacques Baynac's *Mai retrouvé/May rediscovered* fascinatingly documents the activity that went on there – less flamboyant than at Nanterre, less spectacular than at the Odéon or the Sorbonne, but productive through the commissions that were set up to examine a host of educational, social and political questions, and through its role as a base for foreign students, who held their own *Assemblée générale*/mass meeting there each day. Baynac also asserts that much closer student-worker links were forged at Censier than at the Sorbonne, disdain-fully viewed as a centre for radical tourism. The film-maker William Klein and the writer Jean Genet – both frequent visitors to the Sorbonne – were, Baynac proudly proclaims, turned away from Censier.

It was probably at Censier that the most far-reaching (which is also to say wildly utopian) reflection on the status and direction of the university took place. The tract 'Nous sommes en marche/We are on the march'[19] is the best example of this, stating as it does that 'there is no longer a student problem; the "student" is an outdated notion'.[20] The status of 'worker' – 'by hand or by brain', as the British Labour Party has it – is henceforth to apply to all, and knowledge no longer to be the privilege of a certain (in other respects, such as the insecurity of its future, underprivileged) caste:

> Any possessor of knowledge – practical or cultural – is obliged to 'return' as an *individual* what they have received by way of a social 'privilege', so that this knowledge shall no longer be a new privilege of the ruling class, which for all the good will and individual messianism in the world can only alienate and exploit workers as a whole.[21]

The manifest utopianism of this is to some extent offset by the fact that it sprang from a (relatively) prolonged day-to-day experience of thinking through the causes and consequences of the privilege-ridden French educational and social system. Censier may have been impossibilist, but it was not necessarily apocalyptic, for as Baynac says: 'The "great moment" is in books. Here, things were alive.'[22] This reads like an anti-intellectualism verging on the Poujadist,[23] and such attitudes were widespread enough in May. It also, however, powerfully suggests what Vaneigem's English translator calls 'revolution in everyday life', radical social change as process of (self-) transformation rather than as historical moment generated and dominated by a revolutionary hierarchy, and thereby contributes to the reclamation of time as well as space, so important for May. It is no accident that the movement at Censier was on the whole strongly anti-Leninist, nor that women's participation there seems to have been particularly strong, with the movement's first meetings for women only. A woman student says: '"I realised May was over when, after the 24th, a fellow tried to pick me up in a corridor. The old order was back – I was a "girl" again.'[24]

'Girls', however, seem to have remained 'girls' where the large-scale 'household tasks' of occupation were concerned. One Martine Olivier is credited with setting up the *ad hoc* refectory at Censier, which dispensed chicken as the staple diet and managed a record serving of 700 portions of sauerkraut. At Censier and elsewhere, gender remained more determinant than class; Adrien Dansette's statement that at the Sorbonne 'the honest task of cooking was carried out by prostitutes' (!)[25] finds an unwittingly apt complement in Épistémon's observation that at Nanterre, 'whether they liked it or not, the girls [sic] discovered household and domestic tasks they had hardly ever carried out at home'.[26] May clearly came nowhere near marking the end of the 'old world' of sexual politics.

The occupation of the two main art schools, the École des Beaux-Arts and the École des Arts Décoratifs, remains significant in popular perceptions of May because of the immense quantity of posters produced. The Beaux-Arts occupation was largely the work of the Salon de la jeune peinture (= 'young painters' group', the term 'salon' being used ironically), so that as at the École Normale Supérieure a prestigious institution's radical momentum was increased by those coming to it from outside. Silk-screen printing (as Gérard Fromanger points out 'not a well-known technique for painters, nor a noble one')[27] enabled 2000 to 3000 posters per day – commissioned by different occupying groups throughout France or discussed and voted on at open meetings – to be produced. These were not signed by those who had designed them, in defiance of the (bourgeois) ideology of artistic individualism. It was a rejection of that same ideology that led to what Fromanger calls 'the total fantasy of workerism; provided a drawing had been done by a worker, it was fantastic'.[28]

Meanwhile, not far away at 'Arts-déco' – as its name implies more orientated towards design – similar work was going on, but the relationship between the two institutions was in many ways a fraught one. 'Arts-déco', where 'anti-communism was very weak',[29] mistrusted what it saw as the sectarian Trotskyism of Beaux-Arts, who in their turn 'found Arts-déco's posters a little formalist, a little aesthetic'.[30] Bourdieu's 'logic of the field' suggests itself again; the more 'practical' institution, by educational and ideological orientation alike, yielded the more 'formalist' designs, the 'purer' – thus more prestigious – one produced work much closer to the Russian Bolsheviks' agitprop while embracing a more exclusivist politics. (François Miehe, the Communist president of 'Arts-déco's' mass meetings, claims to have been turned away from Beaux-Arts when he attempted to discuss poster-design with them.) It is impossible to determine here how valid these reciprocal criticisms were, though the reproach of 'formalism' would be difficult to level at the poster 'Arts-déco' were preparing when the CRS burst in ('we were making a poster "The OAS, the shambles [*chienlit*], is them." It was a bloke shitting, and his shit formed the letters OAS – classy, don't you think?').[31]

THE MEDIA IN MAY

Consideration of the art schools leads logically on to consideration of the importance of May for the media. Newspapers appeared much as usual (apart from in Nantes, where 'pirate' issues were produced by the unions in the week 24–31 May), but the medium through which most people got their news was the transistor radio, all but omnipresent on the barricades. The administrative and production staff of the ORTF voted overwhelmingly to strike on 17 May, though the journalists were authorised to continue; aside from the practical utility of this, they were, as Claude Frédéric points out in

Libérer l'ORTF/Freeing the ORTF, the least militant sector of the organisation. Unlike that popular Conservative bugbear the BBC, the ORTF had become notorious as a virtual instrument of government propaganda; so much of the written press was hostile to de Gaulle, whether on the 'old' colonialist Right (*L'Aurore*) or on the Left (*Le Monde, L'Humanité*), that he made quite brazen use of television in particular, whose directive and hierarchical structure came to be a mirror of the France rejected by the movement.

It is thus not surprising that no images of the 3 May student demonstrations were broadcast, nor that thenceforward the ORTF hierarchy did its level best to minimise if not suppress coverage of the events; the private stations Europe One and Radio Luxembourg were a precious source of information to students on the barricades. Even such a pillar of Gaullism as François Mauriac refused to take part in an interview because no mention has been made of the telegram he and others had signed calling for the imprisoned students to be released. When the leading current affairs broadcaster Léon Zitrone's programme was prevented from appearing on 16 May, it was the last straw. The proposal to strike was carried by 97 votes to 23 which, considering the number of government placemen in the organisation, was truly remarkable. A group of journalists visited the Sorbonne on 30 May, though according to Frédéric the students found their attitude far too legalistic. The strikes' major coup was 'Opération Jericho', in which large demonstrations wound their way round the ORTF headquarters for six successive days before the police intervened.

The return to work, like the decision to strike, was a belated one, not officially announced until 23 June. More representation of the personnel at all levels within the organisation, along with the implementation of the Grenelle agreement, was the strikers' major gain. Mitterrand seems to have been almost alone in attaching great importance to the ORTF's problems (doubtless a foretaste of the media manipulation at which as President he was to reveal a skill not unworthy of de Gaulle); in France as a whole there was 'little or no reaction'.[32] Yet the ORTF was not to survive the *après*-Gaullist years of Pompidou; one of Giscard's first actions as President was to break it down into seven independent companies, not that this dispelled the often-justified criticisms of both the quality and the objectivity of French television programmes in particular.

Films about the events will be dealt with in Chapter 5, but this is the appropriate place to look at how the film world and the major cinematic institutions responded to the events. An indication of how explosive the Gaullist régime's cultural authoritarianism could be had been provided by the 'Langlois affair' in February 1968. Henri Langlois, the co-founder and curator of the Paris Cinémathèque, was removed from his post by governmental decree, provoking an enraged reaction among film-makers and critics all round the world. Langlois's curatorial methods were doubtless eccentric (he had been alleged to store films in his bathtub), but the regime's arrogance was intolerable. Sixty or more directors immediately banned the showing of their films at the Cinémathèque, and large-scale demonstrations took place regularly outside the building (in the exclusive sixteenth arrondissement). Jeanne Moreau, Claude Chabrol, and François Truffaut were among the participants, as – symptomatically, inevitably – was Jean-Luc Godard. Langlois was reinstated on 22 April (albeit at the cost of considerable state subsidy to the Cinémathèque), after a campaign that prefigured May in the vehement outburst of resentment against governmental high-handedness and the strong-arm tactics used by the police against demonstrators. Mendès-France, addressing a meeting of support in Grenoble, said: 'The ORTF, the AFP and the universities must not become the servile instruments of those in power, helping them to impose their ideas, their politics and their law'[33] – an indication of how important the politics of culture were to become. More significant still, perhaps, was a taxi-driver's refusal to accept payment from Langlois, saying that '"what you are defending in your area is our problem too as taxi-drivers"'.[34] The community of interest may seem scarcely evident, but with hindsight the community of dissatisfaction is surely significant.

'Jump-cutting' (fittingly in this context) to May itself, it is thus predictable that the cinema world became a hive of *contestation*. Doctors, architects, even executives occupied the buildings of their major professional organisations, less to make demands of hierarchical superiors than to challenge the manner in which their activities were organised nationally. (The slogan 'Football to the footballers' has been cited as an example of the excesses of May at their most surreal, but a contributor to the 1988 Paris conference explained that it was in fact a protest against the mechanistic style of play favoured by the national manager, Boulogne, and a plea for greater individuality to be encouraged – football as microcosm indeed). The setting-up of the Estates General of the Cinema (EGC) on 17 May, instigated by the film technicians' union, involved producers, directors, students and critics, brought together in an awareness of the contradictory status of the cinema (especially in those days before truly mass French television) as popular entertainment ('commodity') and as medium for artistic experimentation and cultural critique. The negotiation of this contradiction proved to be itself contradictory, with the various projects put before the EGC agreeing on the need to abolish the Centre National de la Cinématographie (CNC) – the government's arm for film subsidy – but putting forward differing suggestions for what should take its place. These included the setting-up of a non-profit-related public sector (controlled by those working in it), the broadening of film education and the search for new venues for projection, and in the most 'utopian' proposal (number 4) the funding of the public sector by a national levy which would make admission to all screenings free.[35] The ECG were, unsurprisingly, not able to agree on a concrete programme for action, but they seem to have been among the very few organisations seriously to have debated the relationship of culture to the state, on the one hand, and the market and profit motive, on the other – the terms in which cultural debate, particularly in the Mitterrand era, was to be articulated. In this context it appears premonitory as well as ironic that Marin Karmitz, a film-maker of Maoist sympathies, and one of the advocates of the free-access policy at the EGC, is now France's leading film producer and distributor.

MORE GENERAL CULTURAL INTERPRETATIONS

May as cultural phenomenon goes far beyond its specific repercussions in the various cultural institutions we have considered. The very definition of an 'institution' is interrogated by René Lourau in *L'Analyse institutionnelle/ Institutional analysis*, which speaks of the 'transversal' relationship between institutions such as factories, schools and prisons. Structural comparison between very different types of institution was a major feature of French work in the human and social sciences from the mid-1960s; Foucault and Bourdieu are the most obvious examples. May brought such 'transversal' perceptions sharply to the fore of lived experience through shared forms of action both organisational (occupations, action committees) and verbal, as with the classic slogan *'Ce n'est qu'un début, continuons le combat!'*/'It's only a beginning, let's continue the fight!' What the 'fight' precisely is, what 'it' is the beginning of – what, even, 'it' might be – are all secondary in this utterance to its 'phatic' function, 'used to establish social contact and to express sociability rather than specific meaning' (*Collins English Dictionary*). The 'social contact' and 'sociability' articulated by the slogan are several degrees more complex than in a commonplace phatic utterance (such as 'How are you?'), implying in the stratified and anomic world of late Gaullist France a commonality of struggle against opponents and hierarchical 'superiors' ranging across very different kinds of institution.

Marxism, of course, had been arguing this for a very long time, but as Lourau points out, its dominant forms had tended to confine the institutional dimension, as well as the ideological one, to a 'superstructural ghetto'.[36] May can then be seen as the moment when the question (and the questioning) of institutions broke out of the ghetto, when 'transversal' relationships, invested by desire, became a passionate assertion of similarity-in-difference that spanned the personal and the political without reducing them to each other. The institutional analysis Lourau invokes is thus not far removed from its Freudian and post-Freudian counterparts ('Lack of knowledge about desire and lack of knowledge about what founds society perhaps share a common origin: there is a post-Freudian hypothesis').[37]

The convergence of desire and the societal is again figured in the title of Alain Touraine's *Le Mouvement de mai ou le communisme utopique/The May movement or utopian Communism*, which announces itself as the first sociological analysis of the events. The second part of the title is clearly a reference to Engels's *Socialism: utopian and scientific*, which counterposes the 'utopian' socialist writings of such as Fourier and Saint-Simon to the 'science' of Marxism. The dream of scientificity that impelled so much French Marxism had appeared, for the duration of May, to have met its utopian match. That could not last (Utopia, being literally 'no place', can scarcely exist in time either), but it was to persist as, precisely, an object of desire ambiguously complementary or contradictory to that scientificity against which it had reacted. The previously-mentioned tendency to subsume the political under the cultural in recent readings of May owes much to this persistence; Marx, Lenin and Mao had always-already been objects of desire before they were propaedeutics to revolution, and remain so in some measure even to May's some hostile or embarrassed commentators.

This is, once again, emphatically not to reduce the political to an epiphenomenon of the cultural, any more than Touraine's analysis does. He speaks of the movement as a struggle between 'drives' (the French *pulsion* has clear Freudian overtones as the translation of *Triebe*) and 'apparatuses'[38] but this cannot be collapsed into some archetypal battle between freedom-seeking individual and statist bureaucracy, as he makes clear when he imputes specifically political values to each of the three student leaders whose union was 'that, full of contradictions of the movement'.[39] Cohn-Bendit, that Rameau's Nephew for the late twentieth-century, is 'revolt'; Geismar, the chunky bulwark of academic trade unionism metamorphosed into gamekeeper-turned-poacher, represents 'uprising'; and Sauvageot, uncrowned king of the power-vacuum that was the UNEF, supplies 'political strength'.[40] Thus was to be found in microcosm within the student movement the 'revelation . . . of new social conflicts'[41] Touraine perceives in May.

Touraine's statement that the 'new social movement' 'reinvented, amid a crisis of social change, the class struggle'[42] foreshadows important polit-

ical developments over the following decades (so to speak, 'from Eurocom-
munism to post-modernism'), characterised by the shift away from manual
work and the growing importance of 'those who might be called profession-
alist'.[43] For these, in a formula reminiscent of Marcuse, 'awareness of
exploitation is replaced by awareness of repression and alienation',[44] an
analysis that aligns students with the 'professionals' they were presumably
to become. The rigidity of the university and the elitism of the state were
both challenged by Nanterre (where Touraine taught), whose 'vacuum,
disorganisation and lack of university "feeling" were important in that they
did away with the peculiarities and limits of the student experience'.[45]

May for Touraine was thus prophetic of new types of struggle, rather
than *per se* revolutionary ('the May movement is not to the Left of the PC,
but ahead of it; it belongs to the next generation').[46] Its utopianism was for
him its unity, for:

> Because . . . the function of Utopia was to rediscover unity beyond the
> opposition between social conflict and cultural crisis, it was the utopians
> who most clearly proclaimed and defined the objectives of the move-
> ment, whilst the first-named [= social actors] were at the forefront of its
> action and the second [= cultural militants] were responsible for its
> climate. The May movement is a utopian Communism.[47]

Utopia, in other words, reinscribes the horizon of desire into the political,
enabling civilisation to 'enjoy'[48] its discontents as well as to combat them
– a vision that is prevented from drifting off over the said horizon by the
solid ballast of Touraine's assertion that students are 'directly concerned, in
their capacity as workers, by economic and social choices'. These choices
were increasingly to involve questions of power and legitimacy, and thereby
also the whole status of education in culture challenged by the students.
Touraine's work is (as Bénéton and Touchard have suggested) open to
substantial criticism, but it was among the very first, and remains one of the
best, attempts to place the student movement and its desires in a wider
context. It is thus haunted by one, perhaps insoluble, contradiction: what
does it mean to contextualise Utopia?

Edgar Morin, Claude Lefort and Cornelius Castoriadis – the first-named
a former PCF member, the latter two co-founders of the Socialisme'ou
Barbarie [Socialism or Barbarism] group that in the 1950s and early 1960s
had prefigured many of the ideas of May – discuss a number of themes
broached by Touraine in their *Mai 68: la brèche suivi de Vingt ans après/
May 68: the breach followed by twenty years after.* Morin's notion of the
'student commune' has suggestive parallels with Touraine's 'utopian communism', much as the latter's disarticulation of May in political space and

time – 'not to the Left of the PC but ahead of it' – is echoed by Castoriadis's 'anticipated revolution'.[49]

Morin *et al.*'s analysis does, however, differ markedly from Touraine's in a number of ways. While for Touraine the student movement is understood as part of the wider shift of power toward the 'professionals', for Morin in particular the generational theme is an all-important one, expressed here in a prose whose periodic purpleness owes much to its having been written (for *Le Monde*) at the height of the events (between 15 May and 10 June):

> Like a revolution, it brings together individuals and groups in transports of generous fraternal communication. Like a revolution, it sometimes brought the worst out of people, but more often than not the best. I think of those children waiting for just one thing a whole Friday long – the freeing of their unknown comrades, whether students or not, French or foreign; those woman students walking out of the competitive examination into which they had put so much work, those militants dedicating themselves to the workers' cause.[50]

Morin (at a time when the orthodox 'adult' left was still very condescending towards it) saw the 'student commune' as 'perhaps a classic model for future changes in the West',[51] '*a kind of socio-youthful 1789* involving the emergence of youth as a social and political force'.[52] The historical reference back (reinforced by another to *The Battleship Potemkin* a couple of paragraphs later) serves to propel the analysis into a future that by definition cannot be precisely described. Ten years later, in the essay 'Mais'/'Mays', May retains its sphinx-like ambiguity (even though that sphinx might have begun taking on some of the features of François Mitterrand), baffling through its simultaneous 'enormity and insigificance'.[53] The political now clearly takes second place, in Morin's analysis, to the mythical and the psycho-affective:

> May can be considered as a moment of passage, a *Passover*, through which a whole repressed world of marginality, the unconscious, need and libido rushed.[54]

Twenty years on, in the essay 'Mai 68: complexité et ambiguité'/'May 68: complexity and ambiguity', historical distance has made it possible for Morin to distinguish the libertarian aspect of May ('counter-cultural') from its Marxist side ('militant'), and to situate in the period from 1973 and 1976 the point at which these ceased to function in tandem as critiques of existing bourgeois society. For reasons not dissimilar to Guillebaud's ten years before, Morin concludes that 'the Comet of May 68 is nowadays at the opposite pole of our heaven, on the other side of the solar system, in the shadow'.[55] His own fluctuating reactions to it – unique here in being proffered three times at ten-year intervals within one work – can be read together as an important attempt at constructing a refracting telescope with which to observe it, by a paradox of relativity at once bringing it closer and emphasising its distance.

Mai 68; la bréche often adopts what might be rather less loosely than usual described as a deconstructive approach – unpicking the binary anti-theses constitutive of conventional political discourse, or in a different but related manoeuvre voiding them of any referential content and emphasis-ing, as May did, the overdetermined negativity at their heart. Morin in 'Une révolution sans visage/A faceless revolution' undoes the antithesis between *revendication* (the demands on salaries and working conditions beloved of the PCF) and revolution (for those who considered themselves Marxists at any rate a scientifically attainable goal), stating that 'demands [*revendication*] are so broad-based and confused in their origin that they are almost revolu-tionary, while revolution is so far limited to a few groups of youths and intellectuals that it is a virtual Utopia'.[56] Undecidability – 'the *impossibility* of distinguishing',[57] a key deconstructionist theme – is one of the most striking characteristics of May (de Gaulle's '*insaissisable*' suggests this), and it perhaps underlies the paradox articulated by Castoriadis in 'La révolution anticipée':

> The third period of the crisis . . . brought to light the total political emptiness of French society and created an original political phenom-enon: a duality of non-power. On the one hand, the government and the ruling party in final decomposition, hanging without real faith on the breath of a 78-year-old man: on the other, the manoeuvres and wheeler-dealing of the 'Left's' lackeys, incapable even in these circumstances of putting forward anything more than governmental schemes or even of appearing 'united'.[58]

It was, in other words, impossible to decide where 'real' power lay because there were no organisations capable of exercising it – a criticism of the PCF in particular made yet more wounding by Castoriadis's assertion that 'the condition of this void [was] the total political inertia of the workers, who conducted the greatest strike ever recorded in any country's history as a straightforward strike for higher wages'.[59] The PCF's reclaim-ing of the events as a 'strike' is here cruelly turned against it and its supporters, and the workers implicitly held responsible for the Party's shortcomings rather than (as in, say, a Trotskyist analysis) the other way round.

One binary antithesis called massively into question by May was that between word and action. If a hostile critic such as Aron could deliver a tirade against the endless 'talking-shop' of the events, it was legitimate to retort that the freeing of language from the institutional straitjacket of Gaullist France was, precisely, an *act* of emancipation. (The importance assumed in French intellectual life from the early 1970s by the performative linguistics of J.L. Austin, whose *How to Do Things with Words* is translated into French as *Quand dire, c'est faire/When speaking is doing*, seems less arbitrary in this context than it might otherwise.) Thus it is that for Lefort in 'Une révolution sans visage'/'A faceless revolution' 'if there was a vibration leading to a rupture, it was because there was at the same time Action and Word'.[60] Notions of rupture and discontinuity are figured in the work's very title, with its echoes of a 'breach' in the hull of the Gaullist ship of state or the Maginot line of bourgeois society after which nothing could be the same even if most things remained unchanged.

A breach, by definition, challenges and violates the existing ordering of space, and we have seen in work on the 'night of the barricades' in particular how important to May such a challenge was. Henri Lefebvre – a colleague of Touraine's in the sociology department at Nanterre, but unlike him a former member of the PCF – develops this idea in *L'Irruption: de Nanterre au sommet/The Irruption: from Nanterre up to the summit*. The work's very title is a spatial paradox, for we might have expected an eruption, as of a volcano, rather than the more implosive 'irruption'. Nevertheless, French society did in a very real way burst in upon itself in May, as Lefebvre indicates in his gloss of the term 'event(s)' ('The event thwarts predictions, and insofar as it is historic overturns calculations . . . The movement was born where it was least expected').[61] This is seen as at once lesson learnt from structuralism and performative refutation of it ('What did the students learn from the then dominant structuralism? – that only pure violence can shatter those famous structures presented to them as objects of pure science'),[62] so that when 'praxis gives the lie to ideology'[63] Lefebvre is also giving the lie to Althusser. This is not to reduce the events to a symbolic staging of intellectual rivalries, but to stress how they appeared at the time as elusive referential touchstone for this or that conceptual *parti pris* and how their 'irruption' in the student milieu seemed to challenge every Left-wing species of orthodoxy with every other, in a discursive carnival whose plurality was at once stimulus and threat.

Lefebvre mimes this challenge by way of an imaginary dialogue between a *contestataire* for whom the return to work was a betrayal ('the whole of bourgeois society was crumbling')[64] and a voice whose more sceptical stance on *autogestion* would seem to place it with a (comparatively) sympathetic PCF view of events:

B: ... I'd still like you to be clearer [sc. on what you mean by *autogestion*].
A: I can't be.[65]

This seeming emptiness is not, for Lefebvre, matter for condemnation; rather, it corresponds to the vacuum at the heart of French political society, a vacuum whose corollary was the crowds endlessly filling the street ('the street became a political space, thereby indicating the political emptiness of specialised places. . . . Social space changed its sense').[66] The Paris street has a long history of becoming a political space, most famously in 1789, and Baron Haussmann's laying-out of the boulevards in 1860 was largely designed to make expressions of dissent in the street easier to control. What was remarkable about the politicisation of the streets in May was that it did not spring from a lack of representative institutions, but from their suddenly, and it seemed all but unanimously, perceived inadequacy. His subsequent work (notably *La Révolution urbaine/The Urban Revolution*) was to deepen and extend his analysis of urban space, an analysis that has remained Marxist in its problematic but implicitly anti-Leninist in its rejection of centralised apparatuses. In this respect, and bearing in mind his youthful association with the Surrealists, it could well be said that Lefebvre has for over half a century been a profoundly *soixante-huitard* thinker.

SPIRITUALITY AND LANGUAGE IN MAY

The insistently spiritual tone of so many accounts of May is a major potential source of embarrassment in writing about it – not simply because of its apparent incompatibility with orthodox Marxism (the vast majority of the participants, after all, were not Marxists), but because of the difficulty in knowing how to deal with a testimony at once as powerful and as elusive as that of a student on the 'night of the barricades' reported by Andrien Dansette ('I was happy, never in my life had I had such a sense of strength, such a feeling of happiness . . . I was making history, or rather defying it').[67] Watching hours of newsreel and documentary footage of May at the Paris Vidéothèque, I found myself affected by very similar albeit vicarious emotions – a participant, across twenty-one years and the unwitting distanciation device of the black-and-white image, in a phenomenal psychic and spiritual energy I have partially understood but still cannot fully analyse. The Anglo-American 1960s – the decade of LSD mysticism, transcendental meditation, *Sergeant Pepper's Lonely Hearts Club Band* – were spiritual at least as much as they were political, whereas the self-consciously Cartesian tradition in French culture (ably bolstered by the Catholic Church) has always tended to marginalise or exclude alternative forms of spirituality.

The title of the Jesuit philosopher Michel de Certeau's *La Prise de la parole/The capture of the word*, like the Bishop of Arras's observation that the Holy Spirit had visited Earth at Whitsuntide, suggests that the spirituality of May is closely linked with its linguistic polymorphousness. The work of Mikhail Bakhtin, itself of Christian inspiration, is, as already mentioned, an important pre-text here, with its constant stress on the splitting, multiplicity and heterodoxy of language as correlative to spiritual crisis and revelation. Writing of Plato's *Dialogues*, he refers to their:

> tendency to create the *extraordinary* situation, one which would cleanse the word of all of life's automatism and objectness, which would force a person to reveal the deepest layers of his personality and thought.[68]

This sounds a little like May two thousand and more years a*vant la lettre*, the common thread being the key Bakhtinian notion of the *dialogic*, that which 'wants to be heard, understood, and "answered" by other voices from other positions.'[69] The *carnivalistic* is the supreme form of this, taking literary form in the Ancient Greek Menippean satire at a time when 'disputes over "ultimate questions" of worldview had become an everyday mass phenomenon among all strata of the population and took place whenever and wherever people came together.'[70] Furthermore, during carnival 'all *distance* between people is suspended, and a special carnival category goes into effect: *free and familiar contact among people*';[71] and this provisional abolition of social space has its corollary in time too, which flows 'according to its own special carnival laws . . . finding room in itself for an unlimited number of radical shifts and metamorphoses'.[72]

Any of the above quotations could have come straight from an eye-witness account of May, and de Certeau's celebrated statement that 'last May, the word was captured as the Bastille was captured in 1789'[73] constructs May's 'revolution' as symbolic and carnivalistic through its choice of antecedent (the fall of the Bastille was a jubilantly liberating experience; trials and executions came much later). Yet that is not to say that it was not also performative – that the Word(s) did not also in some sense become flesh – in its 'reintroduction . . . of the *event* into a thought that had been too imprisoned by the development of a system'.[74] This seems to oppose the spontaneous speech of the 'event' to the written constriction of the 'system' in what we have already seen[75] to be a simplistic manner; but that very objection is itself too tendentious by half, potentially complicit with attempts to lead *gauchisme* or critical spiritual energies back to Father Party or Mother Church, and disregarding the fact that events are inescapably written against systems rather than as some impossible pure *parole* outside them.

De Certeau makes this plain when he stresses the need to go beyond narrative and description to an understanding of what events become for 'us' – observers or participants – along with the necessary heterogeneity of such an understanding. The event 'takes place within the field of a *common* language, but one endowed with a *particular* sense by those partners who are in a position of strength',[76] which is to say that system and event together constitute a symbolic battleground. 'A language was breaking up just as the essential link between power and representation was snapping',[77] so that the barricades struck directly at the weak point of late Gaullist society. What de Certeau variously describes as 'the irruption of the unthought'[78] and 'the irruption of language'[79] has what it would be irreverent, but nonetheless accurate, to call a polymorphously Messianic quality about it. Few actions, after all, are more insistently linguistic than the announcement of the Good News – especially when that news turns out to be so difficulty to qualify.

The writer Maurice Clavel – up to 1968 a staunch Gaullist – is the most notorious 'spiritualiser' of May, as in his novel *La perte et le fracas/A song and dance* and the glutinous gushings of *Ce que je crois/What I believe*, where he relates saying to his wife when the first riots broke out: 'Here we are in mid-Foucault!'[80] More interesting from an institutional point of view are developments within – which is also to say against – the Catholic Church. Jacques Marny and others in *L'Église contestée/The contested Church* relate the occupation of the Centre Saint-Yves, in the Latin Quarter, as a permanent *contestataire* Christian base from 10 May. Catholics involved with the events faced three specific problems – their attitude towards Marxism, for so long reviled as Antichrist but beginning to have an effect on the Church in Latin America through the theology of liberation; the implied participation in violence, of however symbolic a kind; and the whole question of Catholicism's relationship to the eminently terrestrial world of politics.

Once Christianity was separated from the Church, much as Marxism was from the PCF, these 'problems' suddenly seemed to matter a good deal less. Linguistic plurality became possible, so that on Whit Sunday in the Church of Saint-Séverin a priest (Father Talec) was able to describe that festival to a self-constituted 'revolutionary forum' as 'the day . . . when we are happiest to proclaim that people expressed themselves each in their own language, and that each person had something to say.'[81] The title of one of Marny *et al.*'s chapters – 'Nous étions l'Église, ces jours-là/We were the Church in those days' – foregrounds the diversity and the throwing-off of existing institutional constraints that made the 'days' in question spiritually as well as politically heady ones.

Three theologies – one Protestant, one Orthodox, one Catholic – discuss the implications of the vents in *Évangile et révolution – au coeur de notre crise spirituelle/Gospel and revolution – at the heart of our spiritual crisis*. The Gospel is here seen as revolutionary because it questions all preexistent and fetichised systems, which prompts the thought that the large numbers of Catholic youth who embraced Maoism rather than traditional Communism were, so to speak, writing a 'New Testament' to the PCF's 'Old'. The three authors co-sign an 'ecumenical message' which identifies the spiritual side of May as 'a thirst to be, and to be together', and overtly sacralises the barricades, which 'delimited a kind of sacred space where miracles seemed possible at every moment.'[82] Sanctity is called for because 'only saints know how to . . . stabilise peacefully the *festive state*'[83] – another echo of Bakhtin.

This kind of talk would have enraged – doubtless did enrage – orthodox churchpeople just as much as May's revolutionary euphoria enraged a Raymond Aron, and nowadays may appear just as dated. Yet only three months later *Humanae Vitae* was to plunge the Church into crisis, and it can be argued that 1968 provided a dual shock from which (in France anyhow) it has never recovered. The decline in orthodox vocation and practice needs to be set against the spread of alternative forms of spirituality, from charismatic Christianity to the 'turn' towards psychoanalysis (Julia Kristeva, in *Au commencement était l'amour/In the beginning was love* and *Histoires d'amour/Love stories*, has suggested connections between psychoanalysis and forms of Christian spirituality). The tongues untied in May, for all the nonsense a good many of them spouted, were not easily to be rebound.

THE 'INDIVIDUALIST' READINGS OF MAY

As mentioned at the beginning of Chapter 3, there is one major qualitatively new type of interpretation of May that came to the fore well after the Bénéton and Touchard article – that which sees the events not as socialist revolution adumbrated or betrayed, but as premonitory stirrings of the renewed stress on individualism that was to be characteristic of the 1980s. That May was in some sense an individualistic movement is hardly in dispute; the linguistic profuseness, the violent rejection of modern social anonymity, the 'taking of desires for reality' all bear witness to that. What the texts we are about to consider suggest is that those assertions of individuality were to tend either away from the political (at least in its Left-wing sense) altogether or towards a reformist politics of accommodation very different from anything clamoured on the barricades.

Jean-Marie Benoist, a forerunner of the 'new philosophers', was among the first to proclaim that *Marx est mort/Marx is dead* – a truism for many in 1993, verging on *lèse-majesté* in 1970. May for Benoist actually goes to prove his thesis (which is why it seems appropriate to consider his work here), in that it caused a 'crack in the discourse . . . known as revolutionary'[84] – as much of a 'breach', if true, as that detected by Morin. Benoist's analysis is primarily a linguistic one, seeing in the 'crazed inflation' of May's revolutionary vocabulary its total severence from the politics to which it purported to refer and its implosion as a subjectless system whose discourses were held together only by their 'ineradicable metaphysical complicity'.[85] The vocabularies of the government, the PCF and the *gauchistes*, trading insults in a morphological game of 'pass-the-parcel' (from *gauchiste* to Gaullist to fascist and round again), sustain rather than undermine one another in a linguistic space that Benoist, in the kind of borrowing from Derrida then becoming *de rigueur*, identifies as that of Western metaphysics. The Marxist donkey is clearly not meant to survive for long the pinning on it of the dreaded metaphysical tail – this despite the fact that Derrida in virtually all his utterances on Marxism has emphasised that it is neither more nor less the prisoner of metaphysics than any other Western philosophical discourse, including his own.[86]

Once the 'drift of/from the Marxist to the mythological signifier'[87] has been established, it is easy for Benoist to mock the symbolic dimension of May, the 'folly of those aberrant, absolute, self-referential gestures and the even greater folly of continuing to situate them in the space of an outdated pseudo-reality, Marxism-Leninism'.[88] That such gestures might have had an emancipatory force going well beyond the particular vocabulary and context in which they were made – that, to adopt/adapt Lyotard, they might be effective as figure rather than as discourse, which is in itself something of a challenge to 'Western metaphysics' – is not a possibility entertained by Benoist, whose praise for Althusser ('For the first time, Marx is a *text*')[89] seems rooted in the possibilities his readings open up for widening the 'crack in revolutionary discourse' and allowing metaphysics and metaphoricity to appear as the overdetermining realities they supposedly are.

MAY AND MODERNISATION

Régis Debray, author of *Modeste contribution aux discours et cérémonies officielles du dixième anniversaire/Modest contribution to the speeches/ discourses and official ceremonies of the tenth anniversary* of 1978, had spent May in a Bolivian prison-cell after being arrested while fighting alongside Che Guevara, so that he cannot readily be accused of facile nostalgia. For him, 'May 68 is the cradle of the new bourgeois society',[90] a condensed and accelerated process in which French society and institutions belatedly caught up with the technological, industrial and economic changes that the nation had experienced since the Liberation. The 'thirty glorious years' of material progress fetched up, in May, against hopelessly hierarchical and outdated social structures, so that:

> The France of stone and rye, of aperitifs and village schoolmasters, of yes-daddy yes-boss yes-dear was given its marching orders so that the France of software and supermarkets, of news and planning, of know-how and brainstorming could spread its wings, home at last. This spring-cleaning felt like a liberation, and indeed that is just what it was.[91]

Debray would probably still have described himself as a Marxist at the time of writing this, and his later work – notably *A demain de Gaulle/De Gaulle for tomorrow* of 1990 – is imbued with a high-cultural disdain for the Americanised mass-media France prefigured in the above quotation, so that he cannot be accused of either enthusiastic acceptance of 'the new France' or post-modern capitulation to it. His pronouncements on the tenth-anniversary celebrations are caustic ('Nothing but emotions and prose poetry – no political analysis'),[92] and Morin and Lefebvre, without being named, are taken to task ('France's entry within the walls of the Western fortress was dubbed a "breach", and the black sheep's return to the fold of developed capitalist countries was an "irruption at the summit"').[93] The tenth anniversary had come at a particularly low ebb for the Left, which (largely through its own disunity) had lost the March legislative elections while the Right 'seemed young and lively'.[94] In those immediately pre-Thatcherite days, when monetarism and privatisation were challenging new ideas while in Germany and Italy the aftermath of 1968 had degenerated into violent terrorism, Debray's analysis had a European as well as a national conviction.

The seeds it sowed did not germinate for a further ten years, when the individualistic reading came close to dominating the twentieth-anniversary retrospectives.[95] Gilles Lipovetsky in *L'Ere du vide/The Era of vacuum* of 1983 expressly relocates the idea of revolution from the political to the cultural sphere:

> Our time has managed to evict revolutionary eschatology only through a permanent revolution of everyday life and individuals themselves: widespread privatisation, the erosion of social identity, ideological and poli-

tical disaffection, the rapid destabilisation of personality mean that we are living through a second individualist revolution.[96]

Vaneigem, were he dead, would doubtless be turning in his grave at so brazen a neutering of the subversive force of his 'revolution in everyday life', for Lipovetsky's process of personalisation'[97] amounts to a joyously polyvalent consumerist acceptance of the 'society of the spectacle' rather than in any sense a challenge to it. The 'overinvestment of the existential'[98] he sees as characteristic of May has political impoverishment as its corollary; cultural difference, indeed, might almost be thought to be dependent on political indifference:

A 'revolution without finality', without a programme, with neither victims nor traitors, without political direction, May 68, for all its living Utopia, remains a laid-back latitudinarian movement, the first indifferent revolution, a proof that the desert is no cause for despair.[99]

The blossoming of new and alternative forms of communication is for Lipovetsky the most prophetic aspect of May, but his analysis appears blind to any actual challenge these might have posed to the structures and distribution of power in the France of 1968. The events are described, in what can only be called a negative or contentless historicism, as 'a hot transition between the age of social and political revolutions where the collective interest dominated those of individuals and the narcissistic, apathetic, deideologised age'[100] – the latter, presumably, capable of continuing if not doomed to continue indefinitely under the weightlessness of its own lack of contradictions. May 68 is less (as for Debray) the storm before the calm than the last burst of heat before the interminable reign of the cool. This kind of argument, echoed in another register by Jean Baudrillard (notably in *A l'ombre des majorités silencieuses/In the shadow of the silent majorities*), may appear to have had the dubious Popperian advantage of being for its moment at least unfalsifiable. From a more recent perspective, the unmistakably social nature of the tensions in French urban communities as in much of liberated Eastern Europe, the French Left's increasing awareness of its ideological impoverishment, the concomitant brutish irruption of Le Pen's racist Poujadism all indicate that that moment, with its inanely comforting vision of a world where jogging and the home computer have made social conflict literally meaningless, has been and gone.

Luc Ferry and Alain Renaut, in *La Pensée 68/The thought of 68*, mounted an attack on the anti-humanism of structuralist thought later compounded by what the cover of their *68–86: itinéraires de l'individu/68–86: journeys of the individual* describes as 'a lively upsurge of civic and republican values which makes the intellectual configuration of the 1960s look thoroughly dated.'[101] The earlier work, in its philosophical dimensions, need not concern us here, other than by way of noting that Épistémon and Lefebvre had covered much of the same terrain more vigorously (and more rigorously) twenty years before. It contains a chapter on interpretations of the events which divides them into three categories – those which took the participants' point of view and saw May as a revolt of subjectivity against oppression (Sartre, Morin *et al.*); those for which it was rather the logic of History working itself out (Debray, Lipovetsky); and those which privileged the *eventfulness* of the events, their status as 'a pure uprising breaking any continuity' (Lefort).[102] Ferry and Renaut's plea is for an interpretative plurality, found above all in the work of Aron (!), that would bring together these different types in the 'articulation . . . between the philosophical discourse of the 1960s, the nihilism of 1968 (the refusal of an order with no vision of what was to replace it) and its individualist continuation'.[103] Such a plurality is of a piece with the hegemonic Left politics of the late 1980s in France and elsewhere in Europe – anti-revolutionary, embracing notions such as electoral democracy and human rights that were sneered at in 1968, and stressing 'the right to be different' – *le droit à la différence*, a key political watchword of the time. Morin's assertion that the 'Comet of 68' was 'on the other side of the solar system' is certainly borne out here; alas, Ferry and Renaut write (for all the world like the structuralists they so detest) as though, history and movement seemingly counting for nothing, that was where it would always stay. Their work in that respect pre-echoes the 'end of history' thesis of such as Francis Fukuyama.[104]

The end of 1986 saw massive student demonstrations leading to the withdrawal of the proposed Devaquet reforms of higher education, which would have introduced student fees and given universities the right to select candidates according to whatever criteria they chose. Inevitably, these demonstrations provoked comparison with May, a comparison Ferry and Renaut counter in *68–86* by referring to their pragmatic, reformist stress on one particular measure rather than any grand ideological design ('"May 68 led to ideologies: we want to get rid of a law . . .". So exit ideology, and with it the whole utopian dimension of May').[105] The stress on the civic and the juridical was certainly a long way from May, though Marcellin's gross abuse of his powers as Interior Minister after 1968 probably helped to restore it to a certain prominence; the notion that law and justice are the products of social relationships of power rather than free-standing abstract entities – a notion articulated by one of Ferry and Renaut's *bêtes noires*, Michel Foucault, and (literally) hammered home on May's barricades – is curiously absent from *68–86*'s analysis. The withdrawal of a law passed by a democratically elected government as a result of widespread public protest nonetheless illustrates how important those relationships of power had remained. The Chirac government (Mitterrand, as minority President, remained superbly above it all) 'ring-fenced' discontent in the student milieu by capitulating to it, for reasons clearly connected with memories of eighteen years before. The students wanted to get rid of a law because they knew full well that they could, and that knowledge went straight back to 1968.

WEBER: FROM TROTSKYISM TO THE PS

Henri Weber in *Vingt ans après: que reste-t-il de 68?/Twenty years after: what is left of 68?* does not so much disparage the inheritance of May as attempt to prove that it is alive and well in the France of Mitterrand. His text is at the same time a dialogue with his former political self – a leader of the JCR in May and co-author of the previously discussed *Mai 68: une répétition générale*.

For Weber, history began to prove (his) Trotskyism wrong in about 1975, with 'the collapse of revolutionary culture among workers and young people'.[106] (His analysis here is sufficient similar to that of Guillebaud not to need further elaboration.) What is interesting is that unlike many other disillusioned militants he did not leave politics altogether; he is now a close adviser to the former Socialist Prime Minister (and Mitterrand's supposed choice as dauphin) Laurent Fabius. The Trotskyists, for Weber, were right in predicting the near-collapse of the PCF and the consequent reshaping of the Left, wrong in supposing that they and not the PS would be its benefi-ciaries.

Weber ascribes to May four main characteristics: internationalism, the importance of youth, anti-colonialism, and a long-lasting historical dimen-sion ('we have to insert May 68 into a long ideological and political cycle to see it *in perspective*').[107] To see May as a moment that came and went tends to lead to one of two opposing conclusions: either that it was an aberration of no lasting importance, or – pressing a 'Stalinist' theoretician into the service of a Trotskyist reading – that it was what Georg Lukàcs would have called a 'world-historical moment', a specific revolutionary conjunction of circumstances that once past or betrayed would need to be laboriously recreated. The Weber of before 1975 would assuredly have written the above quotation with the second reading in mind, but in 1988 the 'long ideological and political cycle' of which he speaks is a reformist and electoral rather than a revolutionary one.

His justification for this change of perspective appears less political than cultural, largely because, as we have seen, the PS owed so much of its 1980s success to its articulation of politics and culture. May's impact was the result of its combining three major movements, one libertarian and democratic, one hedonistic and communitarian, and one romantic and messianic. For Weber, the two first are still in some sense at work (the answer-in-a-nutshell to the question of his title), the third 'fell apart, in the second half of the 1970s, under the threefold impact of post-May disappointment, the liberalisation and democratisation of Western societies and the snubs administered by "existing socialism".'[108] The said ' "existing socialism" ', of course, was not to exist for much longer, and it would take a very different *parti pris* from Weber's to see in Thatcher's Britain much evidence of 'liberalisation and democratisation'. His division of the May movement nevertheless does much to illustrate its historically contradictory nature and to clarify the profound ambiguities of its legacies. He criticises Lipovetsky for misreading the individualism of May, which is 'Promethean and communitarian, not apathetic and narcissistic',[109] adducing the work of the women's movement as an example, and describing the democratic individualism of the 'active citizen' as 'the only coherent and consistent kind'.[110] This is a fairly clear example of how much of the discourse of May has been absorbed into that of the Socialist Party. Bolshevism, and its attendant reprobation of individualism, are swept aside, and the absence of May's 'romantic–messianic' side is identified as the major difference between the 1968 events and the 1986 demonstrations, which 'kept [May's] democratic and hedonistic, but not its revolutionary, inspiration'.[111] Weber's autobiographical investment smacks of patronisation when he asks himself 'what might have been going on in [my old comrade] Alain Krivine's greying head'[112] as he watched the 1986 marches – a question answered in Krivine and Bensaïd's already-discussed *Mai si!*, written *inter alia* as a riposte to Weber.

The 1986 demonstrators, for Weber, had abandoned the idea of revolution largely because of the very events that had brought it to the fore ('This generation grew up in 1970s France, a society profoundly democratised and liberalised by the combination of the "thirty glorious years" and the May movement').[113] It is for all the world as if the more grandiose aspirations of May had served only to pave the way for the discovery that 'the democratic ideal is the great revolutionary idea of the West'[114] – a discovery that, in the period of the 1789 bicentennial celebrations, was to be the Socialist Party's major ideological weapon. The 'new mode of economic and social regulation'[115] that Weber calls upon the May generation to devise in response to the economic crisis can be understood, in opposition alike to Leninist centralism and to market anarchy, as a deepening and extension of existing democratic institutions – reviled in May, now shining forth in their true colours – along the lines the libertarian impetus of 1968 suggested. The Socialist Party of the post-Mitterrand era, nowhere overtly mentioned, is clearly figured as the organisation through which this change is likely to be brought about.

HOSTILE CULTURAL VIEWS OF MAY

It would be wrong to suppose that psychoanalytic discourse on, or influenced by, May was necessarily of a radical or *contestataire* kind, despite Lacan's sympathy with the events and his followers' general identification with the Left. André Stéphane in *L'Univers contestationnaire/The 'contestationary' universe*[116] and Gérard Mendel in *La Crise des générations/ The generation crisis* (both of 1969) deploy psychoanalytic concepts to denounce the events, seen as a rejection of any form of order likely if unchecked to lead to Fascism. ('Stéphane' is a pseudonym for two analysts who elected to remain anonymous for the sake of their patients; one of them was widely rumoured to be Mendel.)

Stéphane's approach is a solemnly literal one, not unworthy of the manner in which such conservative publications as the *Sun* or the *Reader's Digest* draft in tame psychoanalysts from time to time to demolish radical positions by illuminating the supposed neuroses and complexes of their proponents. Left-wing intellectuals are here unceremoniously flung on to the couch to have their selective political indignation (over Algeria or Vietnam but not Eastern Europe or the Gulag) imputed to their rejection of the very idea of Oedipus and hence of the parental function. (Had it escaped Stéphane that intellectuals had moved from the PCF to *gauchiste* movements largely because of their disgust at what had been done in the name of socialism?) The events, in terms clearly influenced by Aron, are described as a vast party 'that the whole of France attended when its parents were off in Afghanistan and Roumania',[117] taking place in an 'atmosphere saturated with narcissistic libido'.[118] This mass regression to the world of the pleasure principle is epitomised by Cohn-Bendit's refusal of the Oedipal dimension and laboriously elucidated in terms of the conflict between narcissism and anality, the point at which the child learns to control its bodily functions. The workers' strike escapes censure because it was 'anal-sadistic',[119] controlling its outpourings and directing them towards constructive ends unlike the intemperate 'faecalisation' of the students. Those who thought that it was merely paving-stones and Molotov cocktails being thrown at the CRS are clearly suffering from hopeless literal-mindedness.

The most serious criticism of Stéphane's work is its total ignoring of the historical circumstances of its time. The 'structure of the *contestataire*', as one of his chapters dubs it, is presented as an unchanging procession of symptoms, with no attempt made to explain why it should have been in May 1968 that cosmic narcissism, oral dominance and other such forms of psychopathology came so dramatically to the fore. The rejection of the Oedipal order is rebuked in tones that suggest the classic reactionary's view of modern society's lack of self-discipline and its attendant ills ('I blame the parents'); but the implications of this are nowhere spelt out, and we are left with relatively little idea of where the stiff dose of anal realism the youth of 1968 were deemed to require was to come from.

The Right-wing novelist and literary critic Pierre de Boisdeffre, author of a diatribe against the *nouveau roman* of Robbe-Grillet and others entitled *La Cafetière est sur la table/The coffee-pot is on the table*, puts himself forward as a candidate for the administration of such a dose in *Lettre ouverte aux hommes de gauche/Open letter to men [sic] of the Left*, one of the influential 'Lettre ouverte' series published by Albin Michel. Boisdeffre is dismissive of May's linguistic liberation, which he reduces to 'the illusion of a liberated Word',[120] and censorious of its anti-patriotism, in terms at times reminiscent of Barrès ('the national I is a fact').[121] For the rest his criticisms are routine – the violence was merely destructive and bereft of political sense, the revolutionary discourse a figment of the imagination, the Left impotently divided and infatuated with the imagination, the Right impotently divided and infatuated with the idea of civil war. The reassertion of order at the end of the events is presented, approvingly, as the triumph of 'the France of small towns'[122] – an ironic phenomenon for a Parisian intellectual straight out of the pages of *Homo Academicus* to applaud.

THE WORK OF GUY HOCQUENGHEM

The gay activist Guy Hocquenghem merits a place apart for his two major texts drawing on May – *L'Après-Mai des faunes/The fauns after May*[123] and *Lettre ouverte à ceux qui sont passés du col Mao au Rotary/An open letter to those who have abandoned their Mao jackets for the Rotary Club*. Hocquenghem had been active in the movement, publishing an article in the first issue of the revolutionary journal *Action* on 7 May entitled 'Pourquoi nous nous battons/Why we are fighting', yet in *L'Après-Mai des faunes* six year later he dismisses the nostalgic heritage of May that had by then become canonical. What many had regarded as hedonistic he sees as dreary ('noodles and omelettes dominated the menu'),[124] normalising ('morality went over to *gauchisme* with its procession of inevitable lies and shady deals'),[125] and – crucially – homophobic. His claim that the 'libidinal or erotic relationship between homosexuals and delinquents'[126] constitutes a major source of revolutionary strength bears the mark of its time – three years after the foundation of the Front Homosexuel d'Action Révolutionnaire (in which Hocquenghem was active), two years after the publication of Deleuze and Guattari's *L'Anti-Oedipe/The Anti-Oedipus* with its extolling of the polymorphous fluxes of desire, at a period when the films of Fassbinder and Pasolini constituted a (critical) *mise-en-scène* of the relationship of which Hocquenghem speaks. His protest that 'only bourgeois imagine that true love finds its reality when a prick is rammed into a vagina'[127] would have carried particularly savage force in the aftermath of a movement that lived on in the memory of many of its (male) participants as a doubtless exaggerated litany of heterosexual conquest. Among the very few posters to be torn down in the occupied Sorbonne had been those put up by a gay group.[128]

Hocquenghem's *Lettre ouverte* is a vehemently exhilarating diatribe against 'the reign of Mitterrand Ier',[129] particularly its cultural recuperation of the heritage of May. Those whom he criticises are apostrophised as:

Neither Right nor Left, but the worst of both; faithful to the most dangerous manipulative style of the revolutionary groups despite having abandoned the generous Utopia that was their goal; worse than 'recuperated', wearing your renegades' medal of spit round your neck, you are the Legion of Dishonour, the badge-wearers of the about-face; and, what is more, you claim to give permanent object-lessons in flexibility.[130]

Serge July, Bernard-Henry Lévy, Marguerite Duras, Jack Lang are among Hocquenghem's targets, along with two writers whose work has been discussed here, Régis Debray and André Glucksmann. Debray is criticised for having accepted a post as adviser to Mitterrand and for moving from advocate of Third World guerrilla action to apologist for European rearmament, Glucksmann for an analogous move from strategist of the forthcoming French revolution to ardent proponent of the character-building virtues of nuclear weapons. It is above all their enthusiastic *realism* that Hocquenghem despises, believing as he does like a *gauchiste* Oscar Wilde that '"it is far more beautiful when it is useless"'.[131] This stance derives its polemical force from his conviction that what the 'May generation' now see as the maturity of realpolitik is simply an infatuation with power – the power they sought to overthrow in 1968 and, now that it lies with the 'court' of Mitterrand, brazenly covet at the cost of any ideological or artistic integrity. Thus it is that:

> Between the ages of twenty-five and forty-five, in France now, creation answers: zero. Not one writer, not one film-maker (Godard, who is older, counts only as a hostage carried along for a while by the Maoist tide), no painters (they are younger) and, above all, no novelists with a *gauchiste* past. It is a hole, a vacuum.[132]

This he attributes to the diversion of energies from creation and challenge to administration, intrigue and complicity, illustrated by the number of 'cultural agitators who have become government or counter-government officials'[133] – a phenomenon in turn attributed to he conspiratorial Maoist politics, centering upon the rue d'Ulm, in which so many of his targets (Lévy, July, Glucksmann) were steeped. This 'explanation' is by any objective standards a highly dubious one, constituting as it does a settling of accounts between Hocquenghem's political past and that of the Maoists ('I was . . . a Trotskyist–surrealist when they were Althusserian Stalinists, a spontaneist anarchist when they were Maoists of steel').[134] It does, however, focus upon a question that will preoccupy us in the next chapter – why May yielded so little in the way of major artistic reproductions. That may be regarded as paradoxically endemic in the movement itself: the call for 'power to the imagination', for creativity to be liberated from its institutional confines into and for society as a whole, came close to implying the death of 'art' as a specific human activity altogether. It did not, however (except for the Situationists), actually imply that, for the 'liberation' called for issued instead in the massive interpenetration of culture and politics – for Hocquenghem as we have seen a diluting and corrupting one – so characteristic of the 'Mitterrand/Lang era'. On this reading, those who ought to have been carrying on the challenging work of the 'new novelists' or the *nouvelle vague* cinema cravenly opted for the 'King's shilling' of the governmental commission or the *Maison de la Culture*. The facilitation of creativity became an alibi for the absence of creation – an argument not without its echoes on the Right and its calls for the pruning or abolition of cultural subsidy.

This is not to say, however, that reproductions of May – written, broadcast and filmed – did not, particularly at the time of the twentieth anniversary, abound. Our next chapter will look at the form(s) these took and the image(s) they propagated, to see if such a thing as a taxonomy of genres of May might be possible.

5 Reproductions of the May Events

If May lives on as image rather than narration, that is because its story is such an ambiguous and inconclusive one. The events may have been lived through by many of their participants in the epic–heroic mode resoundingly distilled in the endless singing of the *Internationale*;[1] but that in turn has become part of the image of May, or at least of that image's soundtrack, returning time and again across the footage of march and occupation in such a way as to call the apocalyptic finality of its own words into question. The very plurality of interpretations to which this book bears witness shows how unclosed a narrative that of May was.

This of itself probably accounts for the lack of works recounting or celebrating May as Sartre's novel *La Mort dans l'âme/Iron in the Soul* or Melville's film *L'Armée des ombres/The Army of the shadows* did the – in every sense more decisive – struggle against Nazism. The 'social novel' in France was in any event a genre in eclipse by 1968, certainly in the intellectual milieux from which May sprang. Questioning of the status and even the possibility of narrative, largely though not exclusively in the work of the 'new novelists' (Butor, Robbe-Grillet, Sarraute and so on), had all but made committed literature in the Sartrean sense impossible. This is not to say that their work was bereft of a political dimension (Jean Ricardou and Stephen Heath have powerfully argued the opposite), but rather that that dimension had so insistently located itself in the problematic of writing that the notion of 'writing *about*' (a) historical event(s) would necessarily have seemed a suspect one, implying the kind of textual transparency against which the 'new novelists' and the *Tel Quel* group had long argued.

By the time of the twentieth anniversary, this point of view certainly no longer dominated as it had done; but by that time May was (to quote Morin yet again) 'on the other side of our solar system', and that combined with the popularity of oral history and first-hand testimony to ensure that the dominant style in which May was reproduced was that of ironic/nostalgic recollection. The upsurge of interest in oral history (well documented by Philippe Lejeune in *Je est un autre/I 'is' another*) owed much to the 'freeing of the word' characteristic of May; it is ironic that that freeing should issue, twenty years later, in a mode itself ironic when it was not full-bloodedly elegiac.

FRACTION(S) AND TESTIMONY

The 'faction(s)' referred to are of a twofold kind: on the one hand, the
different parties (or groupings, or absences/refusals of groupings) to which
the leading May activists belonged; on the other, the 'factional' genre of
narrative reconstitution embodied by the most influential twentieth-
anniversary text, Hervé Hamon and Patrick Rotman's *Génération*. This was
published in two volumes, *Les Années de rêve/The years of dream* appearing in March 1987 and *Les Années de poudre/The years of powder* in
January 1988, and formed the basis for a series of fifteen one-hour television programmes later commercially marketed on video. *Génération* was
described as 'the best novel of the summer', recounting as it does the
biography of *gauchisme* in France from Alain Krivine's first voyage to
Czechoslovakia in 1957 through to the late 1980s. The term biography'
(rather than 'history') is intentional; Hamon and Rotman follow a cohort of
individuals committed to various revolutionary groups through an itinerary
– what Bourdieu would call a trajectory – of which May is only a moment,
albeit a crucial one. They offer no definitive interpretation of their own,
leaving it to participants as varied as Krivine (who now sees May as 'an
uneven revolt with no organisation and only a superficial political dimension')[2] and the former Maoist and editor of *La Cause du peuple* Jean-Pierre
le Dantec, for whom with Mitterrand 'the Left had come to power just as its
ideology had become obsolete'.[3]

What makes *Génération* such mesmerising reading is thus precisely what
also makes it analytically dubious. Alain Prost in *Le Mouvement social*
describes it as 'archivists' work',[4] suggesting that the work's literary approach at once lengthens and weakens its analysis, and highlighting in
particular its failure to make clear the criteria by which the group Hamon
and Rotman follow were chosen. 'The definition of the historical object is
inseparable from that of the problematic'[5] – a criticism to which Hamon and
Rotman could perfectly well have responded by reminding Prost that they
were jobbing intellectual journalists, not social scientists or (even) historians. The point is that the 'factional' – biographical genre implied by the
very title *Génération*, whose founding question might be couched as 'What
does it mean for (the) you (of) now to have believed and acted as you did
then?', appealed to a wider audience in the France of 1988 than the type of
social and political analysis on which we have hitherto been concentrating.
Such conclusions as Hamon and Rotman themselves offer are similar to
those we have seen elsewhere: the swansong of revolutionary culture, the
final isolation of the PCF and the PS's inheritance of the movement's
cultural energies, the movement away from the narrowly political to the

social. Where biographical testimony and analytical conclusion most interestingly converge is in their explanation of why French *gauchisme*, unlike its German and Italian counterparts, did not degenerate into bloody violence. The Maoist Gauche prolétarienne engaged in direct action (notably kidnappings of industrialists) in the early 1970s, but the murder of one of its own militants, Pierre Overney, by a security guard (himself murdered some years later) in 1972 brought this to a traumatised halt. Virtually all those Hamon and Rotman interview suggest that the GP acted as a safety-valve for violence rather than a catalyst to it, and that it was some of the elements most derided in and immediately after 1968 (the republican tradition as heir to 1789, the 'humanist mould of the *grandes écoles*')[6], along with the fear of self-appointed revolutionary elitism that had been an important factor in May, that accounted for the lack of violence in France. The Left's return to republican and electoral politics can thus be understood as an accommodation to the aftermath of 1968 in France as well as to the failure of revolutions elsewhere described by Guillebaud.

Génération began as a book and later became a television programme; the reverse is true of Cohn-Bendit's *Nous l'avons tant aimée, la révolution,*[7] (1986) in which the 'generational' mode of reproducing 1968 is in some ways even more marked. The cover of the paperback depicts the Cohn-Bendit of eighteen years on, photographed in colour and with the hint of a proudly wry grin, propping on his knee the famous (black-and-white) photograph of him gripping broadly and insolently at a riot policeman in 1968. This 'then-and-now' approach had already been used by Cohn-Bendit in Philippe Alfonsi and Maurice Dugowson's television programme *Paris – histoire d'un jour/Paris – the story of one day* in 1985, where he 'told' his 1968 filmed image that was advocating a boycott of the elections: '"Dany, you're being a prat."' He declares in his introduction to the 1986 book that he agreed to make the television programmes to get rid of the heritage of 1968, enabling himself to say: '"Don't ask me any more questions. Look at these images, you'll find everything I have to say about the 1960s. From now on, I shall speak only about the present and the future."'[8]

Cohn-Bendit's current political involvement – as Green Party journalist and local councillor in Frankfurt – so obviously continues his involvements of the 1960s that it seems unlikely that he will ever be able to 'speak only about the present and the future'. Those he interviews in *Nous l'avons tant aimée* are on the whole much equivocal about the 'inheritance of 1968' – its validity or quite simply its existence – which often enables Cohn-Bendit as interviewer to cast himself in a kind of 'Jiminy Cricket' role as impudent voice of conscience. Thus, with former gauche proletarienne Ceroni:

D. C-B.:   So, Gaby, now it's yoga, jogging and macrobiotics?
G.C.:   Macrobiotics – not quite.
D.:   The class-struggle is over and done with?
G.C.:   Not quite either. In 1968, for me, the class-struggle also meant rediscovering oneself – changing as we tried to change things around us.[9]

Cohn-Bendit here, interviewing somebody whose current preoccupations might seem to align him with the Lipovetskyan brand of individualism, reinjects a political dimension into Ceroni's neo-personalism, much as he does more overtly with the former American 'yippie' Jerry Rubin, now a staunch advocate of capitalism:

J.   What you don't understand, Dany, is that we won in the 1960s. We won! America has been defused, it's anti-militarist. We can go further now.
D.   You can't say that! Look at what's going on in Nicaragua. Look at how America intervened in Grenada. Look at the spirit of films like *Rambo* . . .[10]

'Dany' thus represents that part of his constructed spectator (constructed by the 'we' of the title) that remains loyal to the attitudes and memories of May – on one kind of Freudian reading one might almost say that he 'is' the pleasure principle as against the reality principle embodied by those he interviews. Their attitudes run from the brazen capitalism of Rubin, through that, outwardly more tempered, of Serge July (who 'invests today in *Libéra-tion* the same energy I used to in other activities'),[11] to the 'new man' epitomised by Ceroni, the imprisoned Red Brigades members who now embrace a gradual process of reform, Cohn-Bendit's former partner Barbara Koster for whom 'women are still in struggle everywhere',[12] and the 22 Mars activist Jean-Pierre Duteuil, now a member of the libertarian autonomist movement in the Basque country. The different itineraries have already begun to take on an exemplary, nearly archetypal value, so that Cohn-Bendit's first question to himself in the 'auto-interview' with which the work almost inevitably concludes appears somewhat disingenuous ('Can you feel sincerely concerned by people as different as a New York careerist, a French metal-worker and an Italian terrorist serving a life sentence in a Rome prison?').[13] His answer underlines the exemplary character of the different mini-narratives at the same time as it constitutes him as a kind of meta-text for them, the ultimate Man (!) of 1968:

Each of those to whom I have spoken chose a journey on which I could have embarked if the chances and the necessities of the time had so constrained me – though to be sure the personality of each individual played a determinant part.[14]

His concluding sentence, with its call to 'abandon the "I know . . . you listen!"' for '"Let us bring our lives, hopes, dreams together and thus find the necessary energy to continue to change the world"',[15] reasserts the 'we' of the title in a modified *soixante-huitard* spirit emblematised in the use of 'continue'; in May the old world had seemed about to be overturned and replaced overnight. The text (which, alas, has never been made commercially available on video, unlike *Génération*) is thus on the whole a more polemical one than Hamon and Rotman's; but the star-system cult of Cohn-Bendit, already criticised by its object in his earlier *Le Grand Bazar/The Great Bazaar*, may be thought to blunt its subversive force. It is an open question how far Cohn-Bendit, like the British figure he in many ways most resembles, Ken Livingstone, is now recuperated by the system against which he continues to fight.

Elisabeth Salvaressi's *Mai en héritage*, with its 'fourteen portraits and 490 itineraries' (to quote the front cover), is the most thorough attempt known to me to chart the different aftermaths of the events. Her introduction stresses the PS's debt to May ('fed by *gauchisme* with ideas and men [sic], the PS did more than recuperate 1968: it swallowed it')[16] and the events' significance as 'the symbol of a change in mores and of an upheaval in political and private morality'.[17] She does not go on to define what this change might have been; the whole, here, is the sum of its parts plus whatever (if anything) the reader chooses to make of them. Her fourteen portraits include 'stars' (Guy Hocquenghem to whom the work is dedicated, Serge July) side by side with comparative unknowns. Christian Valls's commitment to Buddhism and study of Japanese shiatsu massage represent the spiritual aftermath of May as clearly as Jean-Pierre Duteuil's anarchism and Basque nationalism stand for fidelity to 'the movement' or Claire Wolf's Damascene illumination after eating a hashish cake ('I realised that everything that had seemed obscure to me was simply absurd')[18] epitomises the reaction of Lipovetskyan individualism. Many of the 490 itineraries make grimly humorous reading, such as the erstwhile Maoist who after a brush with mysticism now runs a hotel in the USA, or the co-founder of the Renault (Flins) Action Committee last seen stewarding a Le Pen demonstration; many, such as the number of suicides, are simply grim.

The shortcoming of this anecdotal approach is that its criteria for selection and classification are not explicit. Bernard Lacroix's critique of Bénéton and Touchard's approach[19] suggests the possibility of a more systematic method, using Bourdieu's concept of the 'constructed individual' (v. *Homo*

Academicus) along with extensive empirical data to produce a series of typical itineraries; but this remains, for the moment at least, unexplored.

It is Christine Fauré, one of five women in Salvaressi's named 'portraits', who – after a journey through the JCR, the MLF and psychoanalysis – occasions the most poignant and acute comment on the aftermath of May ('She has not changed her opinions, but the places in which they can be lived out have disappeared one by one').[20] The 'deltaisation' of May, the splitting up of what fleetingly appeared a single river into a variety of streams, was a continuation and development of the heterodox logics of the movement; but all too many of those streams have now either silted up or flowed into what increasingly seems the Dead Sea of the PS. Salvaressi concludes the main part of her work with an 'auto-itinerary' (cf. Cohn-Bendit's 'auto-interview') in which she states that 'May 68 really died for me in 1981'[21] because of the break-up of the MLF, which she connects with the Socialists' victory. The conquest of state power, for Salvaressi, had at any rate for the time being stifled or pulverised the search for an alternative politics.

MAOIST ACCOUNTS

Both the tenth and the twentieth anniversaries of May yielded autobio-graphical accounts by *établis* – Maoist militants who had gone to work in factories (the term is also French for a workbench). These are not strictly speaking accounts of the events; Robert Linhart's *L'Établi* of 1978 begins in September 1968, Daniel Rondeau's *L'Enthousiasme/Enthusiasm* of 1988 mentions May briefly but its main action starts in an unspecified July of the early 1970s. They are nevertheless included here because they represent the most directly eloquent testimony to the aftermath of the events, and because they evoke a form of action which can only be understood in the light of the ambiguous relationship – *rapprochement* or not? – between student and working-class movements in May.

L'Établi echoes Simone Weil's *La Condition ouvrière/The working-class condition*, based on the time the author – like Linhart a graduate of the École Normale Supérieure – spent working in factories in 1934–5. Linhart, unlike Weil, wanted less to empathise with exploitation than to organise its overthrow – a concern that had led to his physical and mental collapse in May, when he had refused to participate in the Latin Quarter events because it had been conclusively proven theoretically that revolution could only come from the workers. The book gives an account of his ten months working under an alias in a Citroën car factory until he was unmasked and discreetly dismissed, and in so doing highlights what was doubtless the founding contradiction of the notion of *établissement* – that between the scientificity of Marxism and the necessarily partial lived experience of the individual *établi*. Linhart at Citroën appears less to have organised the working class (though he had some success in that) than to have encountered workers, an experience that leads him to denounce the bourgeois monopoly of speech and to draw an implicit comparison between the exploitation of workers and that of women in an adaptation of Simone de Beauvoir's celebrated line from *Le Deuxième Sexe/The Second Sex:*

> The bourgeois always imagine that they have a monopoly of personal itineraries [a conclusion a reading of Salvaressi might well reinforce]. What a joke! They have a monopoly of public speech, that's all. . . . The others live their history intensely, but in silence. Nobody is born an unskilled worker; they became one.[22]

The militant, on this reading, is less a secular worker–priest than a surrogate psychoanalyst seeking to give the worker 'his' – but whose? – language. The journey from Catholic upbringing to Maoist militancy and thence into psychoanalysis was an extremely common one in the post-1968 period, and Linhart's account helps to suggest why. It is eminently consonant with the logic of the narrative that during a largely sleepless night after the start of a strike Linhart has a dream in which:

> The old society, lockjawed and incredulous, sees the spread of an unprecedented, incomprehensible joy.
> We shall shatter the walls of the factory to let in light and the world.
> We shall organise our own work, we shall produce other objects, we shall all be scholars and welders, writers and ploughmen. We shall invent new languages. We shall put to flight weariness and routine. Sadok and Simon [two co-workers] will no longer be afraid. It will be a dawn like nobody has ever seen.[23]

This visionary discourse – perhaps a return of the repressed, for it is considerably more utopian than any Linhart would have allowed himself in May – is broken by 'the February dawn, pale, and cold – the real one',[24] as though in ironic evocation of the withering of so many of May's hopes. The work ends on an optimistic note, for after his dismissal Linhart meets a worker, Kamel, who has always been hostile to him but tells him that he has refused money offered by management to start a fight with Linhart and give them an excuse to dismiss him. The final line – 'Kamel is the working class too'[25] – suggests the contradictions within that class, but also the hope that they may one day be overcome.

Rondeau's *L'Enthousiasme* takes one of its epigraphs from Paul Nizan's *La Conspiration/The Conspiracy*, about Left-wing plotting among École Normale Supérieure students in the late 1920s who set up a journal called *La Guerre civile/Civil War*. The sense of *déjà vu* is even more marked than with Weil. Rondeau, however, did not come from such a privileged milieu; he participated joyously in May largely because he was on the point of failing his university examinations in Nancy. The bulk of the text is an account of his experiences as *établi* in the steelworks of Eastern France, explicitly compared to the religious life:

> Poverty had been a vocation. We had thrown ourselves as young men into the secular world with principles largely drawn from early Christianity. *Établissement* was our cross, a unique point of view on the world rather than a burden on our shoulders – a short cut.[26]

Rondeau distils the self-immolatory paradox of the intellectual Maoist in explaining that 'there was no room for books among our impedimenta; we were strange shepherds, dreaming of being swallowed by our flock'.[27] Benign mockery seems instead to have been his lot, side-splittingly evoked when he plucks up the courage to tell his workmates who and what he really is ('Him, a student . . . A shithead like you who can't even hammer in a nail . . . . You'd be better off buying us a drink!').[28] Friendship, warmth, even solidarity in struggle – a strike after which he is dismissed – develop much as for Linhart, but even more than in *L'Établi* what dominates is a gallery of (often memorably drawn) individual portraits, so that the book appears as an elegy to *gauchisme*. The last chapter – 'Farewell youth' – makes this explicit, as Rondeau's dismissal coincides with the break-up of the *Gauche Prolétarienne* even as Solzhenitsyn's revelations about the Gulag close down the revolutionary option forever ('*Gauchisme*, they had said, was an infantile disease of communism – infantile perhaps, but deadly. It was our final tribute to politics.')[29]

The work's ultimate trivialisation comes in a concluding conversation between the author and an old friend who suggests that his political commitment was the result of his having been in love ('I was thunderstruck. What if he was right?').[30] Between Cupid and History as embodied by Solzhenitsyn, what chance for the committed individual? Between lyrical evocation of camaraderie and embarrassed explaining away of a now-inconceivable past, how – if at all – can that past's political and social values be understood and (re)asserted? Nobody to the best of my knowledge has written a (post-) 1968 novel (fictional or factional) that, rather like Butor's *L'Emploi du temps*,[31] sets then and now on each other's trail by techniques of chronological interrogation, displacement and juxtaposition. That is a pity, for such a text might have revitalised both the 'new novel' and the 'social novel' by questioning the boundary between them, as well as going some way towards answering the questions posed above.

ON THE OTHER SIDE OF THE BARRICADES

The factional texts by participants in the May movement we have thus far considered are not (so to speak) the whole story; there are two eyewitness accounts from senior police officers, *En mai fais ce qu'il te plaît/In May do just what you like* by the then Prefect of the Paris police, Maurice Grimaud, and *De l'autre côté de barricades/On the other side of the barricades* by André Gaveau, one of the senior commanding officers in the Latin Quarter. Neither of these, despite their titles suggesting respectively a sardonic disdain for disorder and the overlooked voice of a 'silent majority', adopts the condemnatory attitude that might be expected. Grimaud was later to become a close collaborator of the Socialist politician, at the time of writing President of the European Commission, Jacques Delors, and circulated an open letter to all Parisian police on 29 May condemning 'excessive use of force' and pointing out that 'whenever a demonstrator is the victim of unlawful violence, dozens of his comrades will want to avenge him – an escalation without limits'.[32]

Too little, too late, it is tempting to retort – but Grimaud reveals a startling understanding of the symbolic intensity of the violence in saying in his book, 'I genuinely believe that violence was the price we paid for the refusal, on both sides, to kill.'[33] His letter, written at a time when that violence might have seemed to be going on forever, can be seen as an attempt to head off the real bloodshed that still seemed likely to occur. His own conversations with policemen revealed their anxiety for their families, often the victims of insults (this is borne out by Gaveau), and their general condemnation of violent excesses – a variation on the 'rotten apple' theme beloved of police officers through the ages, with its despairing gesture towards the corruptibility of human nature. There are conversations with students too, from which an attempt at generational connivance ('at their age I was on their side against the police')[34] emerges along with severe criticism of any "conspiracy-theory' analysis. For Grimaud, the student movement and the strikes alike were mass expressions of grievance against a régime that left the police to do its dirty work for it ('for six weeks, almost the only visible image of the government was that of its police').[35] His major perceptions of the events – their verbally liberating force, their generational importance, their end as unexpected as their beginning – have nothing remarkable about them other than the place from which they are uttered; and that, at a time when, as Hervé Hamon has said, the dominant question was, 'Where are you speaking from, comrade?',[36] is precisely their importance. Even from within the ranks of violent repression, dissent and critical analysis were not unthinkable.

Gaveau – understandably for one who had been based in the Latin Quarter – sees May primarily in generational terms rather than as a wider social or governmental crisis. This both enables and determines his son's role in the fictionalised retelling, which opens at 7 a.m. on 11 May when policeman father and demonstrator son meet, exhausted, over coffee in their suburban home ('"Were you there tonight?" – "Of course (. . .) Were you there too?" – "Of course"').[37] Gaveau goes on to emphasise that 'the "generation gap" has never separated the two of us',[38] before telling us that his son, following a by-now-familiar itinerary, has given up a promising financial career to 'return to the land of his ancestors in an uncomfortable little farm in the Lot [South-Western France]'.[39] Gaveau describes himself as 'a retired policeman who has had a very busy career, devoted to the public good'.[40] So citizenly a father, so talented yet unmaterialistic a son – the differences of May are here without its contradictions and the violence and destruction to which those elsewhere led.

This is not to denigrate, or in any way to comment on, the real-life Gaveau (father and son). My concern is simply to show how the would-be documentary spontaneity of this opening is actually a highly constructed, 'literary' narrative which begins by suggesting an exemplary microcosmic solution before its main story even starts. (The fact that Gaveau's faithful aide-de-camp is named Mouton – 'sheep' – and 'possesses the memory of an elephant'[40] may strike a less exemplary chord.) Gaveau's analyses for the rest have much in common with Grimaud's, seeing May as an appeal that he hopes will lead to a more understanding society. Of particular interest as one of the few attempts to see the position of the police in class terms is the published communiqué from the Communist sympathisers' organisation within the police force (Bureau de l'Amicale des Communistes de la Police) on 8 May, denouncing the government:

> Just as it sets the police against the working class, it is today opposing them to the students. Yet experience shows that there are no solutions for workers or students that go against policemen's interests. The fact that the police's most pressing demands have been left unsatisfied is a very significant one.[41]

That the PCF leadership (at the time still preoccupied with denouncing the students) should find itself effectively outflanked on its Left by its sympathisers in the police of all places may not be the most significant of the multiple paradoxes of May; but it is certainly among the most bizarre.

The only major Right-wing political figure to produce a 'factional' account of May was Édouard Balladur, whose *L'Arbre de Mai/The Tree of May* (subtitled an 'alternative chronicle') appeared in 1979. Balladur – an adviser to Pompidou at the time of the events as well as a member of the ORTF's governing body – was to become Finance Minister in the Chirac government of 1986–8. It is thus not surprising that he sees 'no cause to feel proud of what happened that month in France',[42] nor that he pre-echoes the title of his later book *Je crois à l'homme plus qu'en l'état/I believe in man more than in the state* by restating the classic Right-wing humanist notion that 'revolutionaries love humankind, not men'.[43] The text sets side-by-side characters from real life and invented ones, such as the student François Ramel who finds refuge from over-tolerant parents (!) in the *gauchisme* of Nanterre or the liberal journalist Calomet (whose name resembles 'calumet', the French for a pipe of peace). The fiction is as cumbersome as might seem from these examples or Balladur's view that 'consumer society was persistently criticised at the same time as a great many demands expressed an appetite for bliss [*jouissance*], and for selfish expansion'.[44] The equation of *jouissance*, whose essence is non-quantifiable, with consumerism – the quantifiable *par excellence* – is an elementary category mistake, the 'appetite for selfish expansion' an odd target for criticism from one later to become France's leading ideologue of privatisation. Of greater interest is the construction of historical characters – de Gaulle of whom the Élysée General Secretary is alleged to have said on 29 May 'It's the flight to Varennes!',[45] evoking Louis XVI in 1791, and Pompidou, clearly for Balladur the hero of the hour. His heroic status is asserted through the time-honoured dramatic device of our being made privy to his innermost thoughts at moments of destiny:

> From time to time, Pompidou emerged from his thoughts, setting aside his reading of dispatches to listen to the speakers. But he very soon returned to his musings: had he been right, the previous evening, to encourage de Gaulle to leave for Romania?[46]

Those who might have expected from the only work of its kind some hint of self-doubt will be disappointed. Balladur proudly avers that he was never plagued by uncertainty, posing the rhetorical question: 'What could a psychiatrist say that one did not already know?',[47] as though in ignorance (and quite conceivably in ignorance) of the fact that 'what one already knows' is by definition all a psychoanalyst at least can say. His conclusion that 'May was more important for what it meant than for what it said'[48] can neatly be applied to *L'Arbre de Mai* itself, appropriately wooden in its writing but significant as a major testimony from one who was seven years later to become the second most influential Right-wing politician in France.

LITERATURE AND THE EVENTS

Patrick Combes observes in *La Littérature et le mouvement de mai 68/ Literature and the May 68 movement*: 'There exists no "(hi)story" of May; by common agreement, that is an impossibility.'[49] Combes is here using the French 'histoire' in its literary sense(s), and his argument is one already suggested here – that May's widespread questioning of the status of writing and of intellectuals subsumed any more specifically literary reflection or interrogation of it. The very term 'literary reflection', indeed, was at the time a doubly suspect one – among Left-wing intellectuals for the reasons mentioned above (p. 117), among participants in the events because of the all-encompassing passion for *la parole* suggested in Jacques Durandeaux's preface to his collection of first-hand accounts, *Les Journées de mai 68/The Days of May 68*:

> We are going to speak a little of what we are living through: that is all. But we should not go so far as to say that some of us necessarily speak poorly about it. They speak about it, and it is this word – *their* word – that counts . . . . They are living words, with all that implies, and we have deliberately refrained from correcting them.[50]

Speech here, even as it is written down, appears to drive out writing, whilst in the work of Barthes, Derrida and the *Tel Quel* group writing was asserting itself over against speech. Literature was the 'excluded middle', too unspontaneously belletrist for the ones and insufficiently scientific (or at any rate specific) for the others, while at the same time the growing importance of the mass media, for Combes as for Debray, was challenging its sway from yet another quarter. Yet it is clear that the 'May-text', made up of all the accounts and readings of May we have considered here along with all the others, is a literary phenomenon, its 'pulverised corpus'[51] constituting the very kind of mythical literary discourse with neither author not metatext that was one of the *Tel Quel* group's Holy Grails.

Discussion of literature in May is inseparable from literature as a social institution, which was violently called into question and often rejected in the discussions and commissions of May. (Combes provides invaluable extended documentation here). The shift, associated above all with Barthes, from author to reader was a critical one. 'Society' – Gaullist, capitalist or just *tout court* – was read and reread in and through all its institutions, and Combes's statement that 'a new type of reader was born in 1968'[52] is true in more than the short term, for there was a major and enduring upsurge of interest in critical theory and the social sciences after May. Literature, henceforward, had to compete on the same terrain as other, less 'aristo-cratic' discourses, and even suffer their critical definitions and redefinitions, rather than having the field to itself as its Deloffrean[53] advocates would have wished.

Constraints of space and disciplinary competence mean that I shall be confining myself almost entirely to narrative fiction about the events, and a small selection at that. About fifty works of fiction had appeared at the time Combes wrote, mostly in 1971, and characterised on the whole by their 'skein of voices'[54] – a term appropriate both to the experience of May as speech and to contemporary work on the plurality of writing. The early and mid-1970s were characterised by more accounts from women and Maoists for whom May was coming to appear as 'an obligatory moment on their itinerary'[55] and thirty texts appeared for the tenth anniversary. Those I discuss here fall into four more or less arbitrary categories: texts by PCF members or sympathisers, for whom the interrogation of May was doubt-less easier in fictional(ised) than in overtly political form; novels set within the world of education; satirical works; and texts from or after the twentieth anniversary. The working-class movement seems largely conspicuous by its absence, because of the bourgeois origins of the writers but also perhaps because of the difficulty of integrating (in however contradictory a manner) its 'story' with that of the students.

One text that makes an attempt to do this is *Mai 68 en France*, by Jean Thibaudeau (like Philippe Sollers at the time it was written a member of the PCF). This was broadcast as a play on German radio before being published in 1970 with a preface (*Printemps rouge/Red Spring*) by Sollers, for whom the text reconstructs the 'impossible *junction* between idealistic verbalisa-tion and the materialist tracing of a language that is not yet widespread, between sublimated immediacy and experienced, lived practice'[56] – be-tween May as clash of languages and May as renewal of revolutionary praxis.

It does this by techniques of juxtaposition similar to those of Eisensteinian montage in the cinema – at once geographical (1968 here is nothing if not worldwide), citational (extracts from newspapers of every stripe), and vocal. The text is to be read by eight female and six male voices (within which are 'set' the other textual voices quoted), divided into three catego-ries according as they 'express subjectivities, provide information or mani-fest a non-individual political choice'.[57] The contrast between the reactionary bourgeois press (*France-Soir*, which 'reduces the reader to the fixed, blinded spectator of a typographical fact'), that of the liberal bourgeoisie (*Le Monde* which 'introduced its reader into a vast conversation where it is up to individuals to interpret facts'), and *L'Humanité* whose 'photographs and headlines are slogans for action'[58] maps *Tel Quel*'s analysis of 'closed' (reactionary) and 'open' (progressive) types of text on to objects, precisely, less literary than those it habitually considered. *Le Monde* breaks the dichotomy only at the cost of making the implied 'political choice' an individual one, unlike the 'non-individual' ones on which the work closes with the assertion that May was:

> not a Revolution – wasted or betrayed – but much more than an image of Revolution – quite different from a collective psychodrama – a genuine attempt at revolution in its successive phases . . . the interplay of class contradictions that might have been able to come together for Revolution.[59]

Neither Trotsky/Barjonet nor Aron, then, but an open enactment of contradictions (themselves enacted by the text of *Mai 68 en France*) cut short only by the ambiguously conditional 'might [could? should? when if not then?] have been able'. . . . A montage of quotations from Lenin follows to conclude and close the text, stressing the importance of revolutionary party discipline and ending: 'the victory of socialism is fully and absolutely guaranteed'.[60] These final two paragraphs – the open text side-by-side with the closed Party – figure the *rapprochement* between French intellectuals and Marxism-Leninism along with the tensions that were to lead to its demise.

Raymond Jean's *Les Deux Printemps/The Two Springs* (1971) sets before us one such tension – that between the May events and the August suppression of the 'Prague Spring'. The fact that both these in different ways incurred the PCF's disapproval was scarcely enough to allay the anxieties of Communist intellectuals such as Jean, whose central character – an academic visiting Prague in 1969 – consoles himself rather unconvincingly with the assertion that 'nobody has called socialism into question'.[61] The novel is a montage of fantasies – tepidly erotic and cinematic as well as political – the decline of whose revolutionary hopes is figured by the departure of the narrator's mistress (Blandine) for California. Archetypally for such a text, *Les Deux Printemps* ends on the narrator's decision to return to the book he has been writing; he looks back on his experiences – political and with Blandine – as 'the memory of a memory. The memory of a period when everything seemed *possible*, in Paris as in Prague.'[62] Nostalgic encapsulation here, with the 'memory of a memory', folds back in/upon itself, so that the narrator's book – on the Paris Commune – represents history as escape from the contradictory present rather than effort to understand and change it.

The logic of Jean's text thus seems ultimately that of solipsistic regression, which has to do with its being written in retrospect but also with its univocal, first-person perspective. Robert Merle (a professor at Nanterre and PCF member at the time of the events) justifies his use of a very different narrative form, 'simultaneism', in the preface to *Derrière la vitre/ Behind the window-pane*:

> Characters are presented with no connections between them, living in parallel isolation, at the same time and in the same place, separate existences. It is because the theme of solitude and incommunicability appeared to me from the start (. . .) as the major theme of student life at Nanterre that I used this type of narration. I did not choose it arbitrarily; it was imposed on me by my project.[63]

The action of the novel takes place on 22 March 1968 (the date on which 'May' may be said to have begun), but its 'project', according to Merle, dated back to November 1967, when he invited his students to speak to him about their lives and preoccupations, in a manner reminiscent of the schoolteachers Pierre Vernier in Michel Butor's novel *Degrés/Degrees* (1960). Merle's narrative form, however, is a long way removed from the *nouveau roman* experimentation of Butor; the classic use of an omniscient narrator is one major reason why *Derrière la vitre* might at the time of its publication (1970) have appeared, as Merle himself says without accepting the term's implied reproach, '"old-fashioned".' It is difficult not to perceive in his otherwise disingenuous comment – 'I am surprised (. . .) that an intellectual can consider fashion a legitimate criterion for evaluating a literary work',[64] in 1970s Paris of all places – a gibe at the *nouveaux romanciers* and their theoretical allies the *Tel Quel* group which, despite Sollers's and Thibaudeau's adherence to the PCF, was identified with a politics of form and theory that many in that party would have considered *gauchiste*.[65] Merle's association of his narrative technique with the 1930s appears as an implicit attempt to reclaim the heritage of socialist realism.

A key character is this regard is the PCF's student *éminence grise* at Nanterre, Jaumet, whose pipe-smoking calmness clearly connotes political maturity, and whose discourse at the very end of the novel – after he has been one of the only two students to vote against the continued occupation of the administrative block – *could* be seen as representing or guaranteeing the 'truth' of the text through its ironic framing of the claims of *gauchisme*:

' . . . if the small groups manage to arouse a substantial number of students through their actions, this mass, infectiously, will arouse the proletariat, and the revolution will come about of its own accord, spontaneously, without central command, with no overall perspective and nobody to guide it.'[66]

The earlier 'could' is italicised because the status of Jaumet's analysis is called into question in (at least) two ways. Firstly, what he says does accurately prefigure what was to happen in May – except, of course, that 'the revolution' did not (quite, actually) 'come about'. Secondly, his adoring ally Denise Fargeot goes on to have significant reservations about that analysis:

'I know what he's going to tell me,' Denise thought, 'I know the record: *"The objective conditions for an insurrection are not present."'* (. . .) But what are these famous *"objective conditions"*? And how do we ever know that they are *"present"*? Were they in France in 89? In Russia in 17? In China in 34, during the Long March? In 57, in the Sierra, with Castro? A question: what if we tried to create these conditions, instead of waiting for them to be miraculously present?' But she said nothing, she felt tired, her neck hurt.[67]

'She said nothing' – the woman's political voice, and its potentially *gauchiste* evolution, remains, for Jaumet at least, silent, as it has been throughout (Denise is characteristically shown as a subservient consumer of political knowledge, asking Jaumet for clarification of this or that point). When she finally speaks, it is to ask, heart a-flutter, whether Jaumet would like to join her and friends on a summer car-holiday in Scotland. Between 22 March and that summer, of course, was to come May, and with it – though not necessarily coincident with it – the growing audibility of the voice that in *Derrière la vitre* speaks only to and for itself.

As the text stands, the all-but-comical ascription of 'the personal' to the woman here is of a piece with the rest of the novel, and closely linked with Jaumet's status as object of sexual desire. Thus, the suicidal Jacqueline Cavaillon seeks consolation and friendship with Ménestrel (= 'minstrel'), whose wanly romantic surname figures the unwilling chastity that obsesses him; but it is to Jaumet that she turns for her own sexual initiation. She is entirely identified with the emotional sphere, but Jaumet (withdrawing a post-coital pipe from his mouth) is there to provide paternal reassurance ('"All day long, I think only of myself" (. . .) "Your attitude will probably change when you've solved your personal problems"')[68] that there is life beyond the personal. There was, indeed, in May and after, but of a kind the Jaumet we encounter here could not possibly have foreseen.

Meanwhile, further to the Left, we encounter David Schultz, of wealthy parents and a sociology student, and his partner Brigitte (not dignified with a surname). Here again, the male is in possession of a political truth with which he deigns to enlighten the woman (David to Brigitte: "'Understand, comrade, that with us there are no leaders, only spokesmen – if that'").[69] It is the male too who possesses the vocabulary to denounce monogamy ("'If you're not entitled to dispose of your body as you choose, you're not a human being, you become a consumer object'"),[70] and who indulges the fantasy of cross-class sexuality ("'Ah!' thought David, gripping the boiling mug hard in his right hand, "to go to bed with a working-class woman!'").[71] Once again, however, the superiority of this male discourse is partially – though only partially – undercut, for it is Brigitte who actually crosses the ethnic as well as the class sexual divide in her relations with the Algerian worker Abdelaziz. The latter is the first character we meet in the novel (after a socio-historical introduction to the town of Nanterre, we read an excerpt from his diary), as though to foreground the importance of the working class. We do not discover what later becomes of the David–Brigitte–Abdelaziz triangle, so that Brigitte's acting-out of David's fantasies, like Denise's questioning of Jaumet's political omniscience, remains of uncertain weight in the text.

Derrière la vitre's 'cast of extras' gives a comprehensive view of the world of Nanterre in 1968 – the junior lecturer frustrated in his hopes of promotion, the Maoist determined to leave and become an *établi*, the real-life characters (Jean-François Duteuil, Cohn-Bendit . . .) there to provide realist credibility. It stands out from other '68 novels' in being set before the events took place; the two other texts with educational settings considered here, Pascal Laîné's *L'Irrévolution/The 'Irrevolution'* (a pun on 'revolution' and 'irresolution'), which won the prestigious Medici Prize in 1971 and François George's *Prof à T. . ./A teacher in T . . .* of 1973, both take place afterwards, dealing with the problems of their central characters in attempting to live out the lessons of May in far-flung outposts of the French secondary educational system. 'May' here is thus generational, to do with existential crisis and personal/professional/political identity, rather than the historical moment at which it was clearly impossible to write it fictionally. For Laîné's teacher, exiled from Paris to a technical high school in Sottenville (an invented hell-hole that owes much to Sartre's Bouville in *La Nausée/Nausea*), May was in the first instance a spiritual rather than a political phenomenon ('I had believed for the first time. I had found something like grace at the corner of the Boulevard Saint-Michel and the Rue Soufflot').[72]

His pupils, predictably, disappoint him through their lack of revolutionary aspiration ('to become "executives" – that sums up in an almost magic word all their dreams'),[73] but more interestingly through their inability to understand, let alone identify themselves in, his condemnation of the place from which he speaks:

> And when I pillory the bourgeoisie in what I say, they give me looks of surprise: am I not one of those bourgeois I so vehemently condemn? I look like one, I talk like one, and above all there is one rôle I assume whether I choose to or not: that of the master.[74]

The Sartrean voice is not far away, never more so than when he asks himself the insoluble question: 'What must I do for them to revolt against me?'[75] The narrative resolves itself through a threefold *mise-en-scène* of writing: first, when he decides (like Antoine Roquentin in *La Nausée*) to write the book we are now reading; then when he encourages the pupils to found a school newspaper in which the headmaster is referred to as a '"pig"' and he himself as a '"third-rate revolutionary"';[76] finally, when he leaves Sottenville in disgust and as the train pulls out throws the pupils' essays from the window. Conventional academic work is scattered in a potlatch more despiring than affirmative, militant polemic falls short of its goal, and literature alone survives.

George's protagonist in *Prof à T*... is a philosophy teacher, dispatched to the unnamed provincial town after failing his *agrégation* at the oral stage. Parisian dismissal of the provinces, as with Laîné, is a given, here in dandyish form ('I loved the provinces . . . only in the provinces can one be truly bored'),[77] and the questioning of the educational institution, of dominant modes of thought ('structuralism is the Gaullism of ideas'),[78] of the gap between his pupils and his expectations of them are again major themes. The confrontation between his views and those of one of his students, a workerist member of the PSU, is that of the classic Marxist analysis with one that, while conceivably prefigured in (a reading of) Bakhtin, was not fully to emerge until after 1968, notably in the work of Hocquenghem. The irony here – history running as so often in and for May back to front – is that it is the younger generation that puts forward the older analysis:

> For him, there are only manual workers. He thinks the revolution can only be brought about by the workers, with the help of small farmers and tradespeople, while I am convinced that if ever it comes to pass it will be through the coming together of all kinds of anti-social elements, drugtakers, madmen, criminals and even, in the last resort, tatty junior teachers such as myself.[79]

'If ever it comes to pass'. . . . Laîné's 'irrevolution', two years after his book and five after the events themselves, reappears more ambiguous than ever. It would have come as no surprise to find George's protagonist, or indeed his predecessor, joining the intellectual exodus from revolution to the Socialist Party in the early 1980s. The self-questioning fictionalisation of May exemplified by these texts was very rapidly, for the reasons we have seen, to become unwriteable.

SATIRE AND ANNIVERSARY

Satires of the events seem to have been few and far between; May's superabundance of irreverence and parody clearly rendered them superfluous. Bertrand Poirot-Delpech's *Les Grands de ce monde/The Great and the Good*, of 1976, is a 'coals-to-Newcastle' picaresque which has de Gaulle on 29 May, not with Massu in Baden-Baden but picnicking incognito and smoking marijuana with a Republican Guard in a Métro station. Of more interest, for its even-handed lampooning of de Gaulle and the students, is *Le Général en Sorboone/The General at the Sorbonne* (published almost immediately after the events), by the veteran Right-wing satirist Alfred Fabre-Luce, who had been imprisoned after the Second World War for collaboration. The events here end with a show-trial (needless to say symbolic) of Malraux and de Gaulle in the occupied Sorbonne, lyrically extolled by Malraux as 'the imaginary museum of which I had so often spoken [. . .] I saw literature start all over again on your walls',[80] Malraux's aesthetic grandiloquence and self-conscious innovativeness (exemplified by his setting up of the Maisons de la Culture) are the twin targets here for an older, more sardonic and conservative Right. The trial's 'psychoanalytic report' on de Gaulle accuses him of 'inflicting a neurosis on France by placing her in the shadow of his abusive "superego" and [. . .] attempting incestuous relations with her by proclaiming himself at once her father and her husband';[81] but the General's final self-assertion – at the very limit, surely, of parody – reads much more 'psychoanalytically', as the signifying absence of his 29 May speech:

'Like France, I was bored. I lacked the enemy that makes it possible for a leader to be a strong ruler. You found it for me. The enemy I was seeking outside our frontiers was within ourselves.'[82]

Such a symbiosis between General and students once established, the text concludes with its prolongation into a festival the rival of Salzburg or Avignon, which ensures its own survival by asserting the principle that 'alienation [. . .] will never come to a stop'.[83] This solves the major problem of how to end a narrativisation of May by the simple expedient of extending it indefinitely, prolonging its distortion of time until time and history (unlike alienation . . .) cease to be.

The other major satirical text to have emerged in 1968 – *Si Mai avait gagné/If May had won* by Frédéric Bon and Michel-Antoine Burnier – tackles the same problem, more acute still from their Left-wing point of view ('if May had won', what new kind of society would/should they be describing?), by stretching chronological distortion to the limits of science fiction. Their narrative is supposed to be discovered in June 2155 during excavations under the ruins of Paris, destroyed in 1984 (!) by the World War of Liberation. Key pages of it are missing, notably those describing the period from 11 to 24 May – a device which enables the authors (formerly active members of the Communist students' 'Italian' wing) to sow some agreeably piquant semantic misunderstandings. Thus, the PCF is deduced to have formed part of the Pompidou government, the label 'false revolutionaries' taken to be the *gauchistes*' self-description (not so far, after all, from the demonstrators' cry: 'We are all *groupuscules*'), and de Gaulle's proposed 'referendum' interpreted as meaning that he was proposing to ask his ministers' advice.

Bon and Burnier really get into their stride, however, with the fictionalised rejection of de Gaulle after his 30 May speech (illustrated by a Wolinski cartoon showing a man urinating into a ballot-box). The movement – whose continuing bases and demands remain necessarily, but tantalisingly, undefined – gathers strength while an increasingly beleaguered Georges Marchais describes participants as '"playing at revolution as Marie-Antoinette played at being a shepherdess"'[84] and the PCF's new anthem sets the words of the *Marseillaise* to the tune of the *Internationale*. Farmers release a lorryload of pigs to disrupt a demonstration of Gaullist housewives; Waldeck Rochet flees to Belgium; after more and more violent demonstrations, the CRS refuse to charge and de Gaulle (on 19 June) steps down. His replacement, the Centre-Left senator Gaston Monnerville, appoints Mitterrand Prime Minister; the movement is no more willing to be instantly mollified than in 1936, and the 'Estates-General of self-management and workers' power' meet at the Sorbonne while in Britain Wilson is forced to resign and the slogan 'Mitterrand, c'est du vent!' ('Mitterrand is a windbag!')[85] gathers force. On 30 June the 'real' dénouement of the events is published as fiction in *Le Nouvel Observateur*; revolutionary forces appear to have taken power in February of 1969, but the record of those years has, alas, been lost.

This is splendidly knockabout invention, but it is not only that. The 'Marie-Antoinette' metaphor is wickedly characteristic of Marchais's own (and continuing) flight to a workerist Varennes; the words of the *Marseillaise* can be sung to the tune of the *Internationale*, and that juxtaposition shrewdly prefigures the PCF's 1970s insistence on 'a socialism in the colours of France'; the growing number of deaths shows a refusal to evade the likely consequence of a continuation of the events; Mitterrand's imaginary utterances are reminiscent of many he has actually made in power, and the dismissive slogan is finding increasing echoes in France at the time of writing. That the revolutionary (as opposed to pre-revolutionary) narrative is missing is scarcely a surprise, nor even a disappointment, so far has May's diagnostic outstripped its prognostic value.

The challenge to the very notion of literature that was to be so important in the cultural development of the '68 generation' is ironically turned back upon itself by Jean-Louis Curtis's *La Chine m'inquiète/China worries me* (1972), which parodies the events by relating them in the imagined words of celebrated writers. The effect is rather like a protracted *New Statesman* competition, though unlike that journal (whose then-editor Paul Johnson, now a pillar of the still-Thatcherite Right, wrote an embarrassingly dithyrambic piece on the events in May) Curtis, an associate of the Right-wing anarchist group of writers known as the *Hussards*, shows little or no sympathy for the movement. His 'Proust's-eye view' of May taxes the *gauchistes* with anti-semitism (they 'had been on the Jews' side for as long as the latter had had the decency to get themselves massacred *en masse* by totalitarian regimes'),[86] though for the Proustian aesthete Charlus, as for Fabre-Luce's Malraux, the walls of the Sorbonne represent 'a sublime blossoming of poetry'.[87] The *nouveau romancier* Nathalie Sarraute is another recipient of irony directed against the salon *gauchisme* of the literary world (her aesthete Louise Derval asks the clearly rhetorical question 'Who will take power tomorrow if not the Parisian intelligentsia?'),[88] while Aragon's appearance on the barricades is derided by way of a celebrated quotation from Flaubert's *L'Éducation sentimentale/Sentimental Education* ('And Frédéric, open-mouthed, recognised Sénécal'[89] – Sénécal being the fanatical republican turned Bonapartist hired gun after the failed revolution of 1848).

Anger (Malraux's supposed 'cry of sedition ordering the sacking of ancient cultures'[90] notwithstanding) is less marked in Curtis's unfavourable parodies than disdain, rooted variously in Giono's eternal Mediterranean verities ('Paris is a long way away. They can kiss their revolution goodbye [. . .] Truth is the sun and the stars, the scents of the mountains, love')[91] or in Céline's Parisian street that is not just a boulevard slumming it ('Your barricade . . . I'll stick it up my arse. The street belongs to everybody').[92] 'Céline's conclusion – 'Revolutions come and go, and in the end everybody gets screwed'[93] – is one reinforced by the work's supposed anthological quality, which by making May merely the pretext for one style of literary creation after another absorbs it into a cyclic process that could quite easily go on for ever.

A genuine anthology, published under the auspices of the LCR for the twentieth anniversary, is *Black Exit to 68*, which brings together short stories by twenty-two writers. The book's 'Anglo-American' title, evocative of Hubert Selby Jr's *Last Exit to Brooklyn*, reflects its authors' involvement with the private-eye genre, though this looms nowhere near so large as might be expected. The texts are grouped thematically and their authors' brief autobiographical itineraries appended, functioning almost as a metatext by which to read and understand the stories themselves. It is significant that the first group is entitled 'Les tendres'/'The sentimental ones', and that its stories all deal with May as setting for loves that end in frustration, romantic fantasy or bitter disillusionment. May, from being the ultimate love affair, becomes successively linked with death ('Les morts de Mai'/ 'The deaths of May'), revenge ('Les implacables'/'The remorseless ones') and enduring generational conflict ('Les papis'/'The old guard'). The latter section all but takes the May-myth outside history and preserves it in aspic, through Eric Kristy's 'In MAI moriam', about a sixtieth-anniversary television retrospective that culminates in a brawl between its aged participants, and Thierry Jonquet's 'Les gars du 16'/'The guys on Block 16', relating the death and burial in an unmarked grave of the last surviving militant of May (aged 112). The story that most suggests any sense of continuing historical struggle, and of the interaction of the personal and the political as opposed to their mere juxtaposition, is Joseph Périgot's 'L'embardée'/'The car that swerved', in which a father still faithful to the 1968 ideals learnt from his son (who has needless to say abandoned them) runs over and kills a Right-wing politician who also bears an uncanny resemblance to his dead wife's lover. The difficulty in narrativising 1968 historically – which a book from a Trotskyist publishing-house might have been expected to try to do – is strikingly figured not only in the individual texts that make up *Black Exit to 68*, but in their arrangement and presentation.

Julia Kristeva's *Les Samouraïs* (1990), like Simone de Beauvoir's *Les Mandarins* of 1954, is a *roman à clef* about the leading Parisian intellectual lights of its time, which begins with Olga Morena/Kristeva's arrival to study in Paris in the early 1960s. May, inevitably, figures primarily as (one) context for a number of interrelated cultural, ideological and emotional crises. Thus, the Maoist Martin and Olga's husband Hervé Sinteuil/Philippe Sollers differ on the correct attitude to adopt towards the PCF before seeming to agree that 'in any case, the spring is red'[94] – in every sense a flourish of local colour. Hervé announces that he will be going to the Renault works at Flins the next day, but we are not told whether or not he does, and by the following chapter the events have resumed their rightful place in the superstructure:

> Since last spring, the country had calmed down, but peoples' minds had not. Discussions and debates were still feverish: philosophers, writers, artists all had a 'destructive ultra-leftist', or at least a 'subversive', streak to them.[95]

In this light the observations of the psychoanalyst Joëlle Cabarus (presumably an additional *alter ego* for Kristeva, herself a psychoanalyst) acquire particular importance:

> (in a diary entry dated 15 May 1968) What effect do revolutions have on the psychoanalyst's couch? First of all a reflux; people who have been lying down get up, go to demonstrations and public meetings, stop coming for their sessions [. . .]. During revolutions, the 'innermost self' goes on strike, to be replaced by talking together, psychodramas, acting-out or quite simply love. Yet, after a few days' absence, Frank and other activists came back. They had to talk about it all in private, to find themselves in a dark room once more, to identify more precisely their enemy (and my supposed complicity with the forces of oppression), to find fresh resources for that imagination which is being called upon to take power.[96]

That Joëlle will later describe feminist groups, in a letter to Olga dated 1 May 1974, as 'the sole survivors of 1968 in Paris'[97] is scarcely surprising, since by then women's movements were the major organisational bearers of the complex, at once powerful and fragile, interaction of public and private suggested in her 1968 diary.[98] That interaction would provide the most effective counter to what would doubtless be the classic Anglo-Saxon dismissal of the work as a piece of narcissistic navel-gazing, since it suggests that what constitutes narcissism at the individual psychic level, no less than what constitutes 'navel-gazing' as a term of reproach, is socially – thus in some sense politically – defined. Yet at the same time, as Diana Holmes points out in her review of the novel, French feminism actually appears 'only in parodied form', with 'no [. . .] representation of collective feminist action, no contextualisation [. . .] within the wider movement'.[99] This ties in with Holmes's contention that 'that world of *Les Samouraïs* remains abstract: the conflicts of May 68; the suspicion that the Maoist regime might be profoundly repressive; these questions are debated but scarcely materialised in the narrative.'[100] For a work dealing with a group so long obsessed by materialism (in its Marxist sense) and materialisation, this might appear a profoundly disabling criticism. If, however, one looks (as I

am doing) as *Les Samouraïs* as one among a number of fictional texts
dealing with May, the work's abstraction becomes symptomatically important, mapping as it does a theoretical impossibility – that of any kind of
exhaustive or omniscient narrative – on to a conjunctural one – that of
writing the narrative of May. It does not seem to me in any sense necessary
to 'choose' between criticising *Les Samouraïs* for being economical with
the concrete (if not the truth) and reading that economy as part of a wider
crisis of representation. Both points seem to me valid; their interplay is
what gives the text (as in varying degrees others discussed here) its major
non-referential interest.

MAY IN THE CINEMA

> The great ferment of the Estates General was all an illusion – wind and
> empty words [. . .] Claude Chabrol, who had endorsed project 4 of the
> Estates General, considered by many as the only revolutionary one [. . .]
> ends the page in his autobiography devoted to May 68 by saying: 'May
> 68 has had absolutely no influence on my film-making, my philosophical
> conceptions or my personal life.'[101]

> You think you're recovering while really you're just getting gently used
> to mediocrity. After a crisis you have to forget everything quickly, wipe
> everything out. Like France after the Occupation, like France after May
> 68. You're recovering like France after 68. My love.[102]

The Estates General[103] would not have been the only reason for believing
that the cinema would have been among the areas of French cultural life
most affected by May. Jean-Pierre Jeancolas, before drawing the negative
conclusion quoted above, describes the importance of (often semi-
professional) film-makers in recording the events. Their role was all the
greater because of the industrial action that restricted television coverage,
but it also derived much of its impetus from the transformative energy that
fuelled the Estates General and the Marxist theoretical work that went on
around *Cahiers du Cinéma.* Thus, to quote Jeancolas again:

> May 68 was one of the first historical events in which the cinema
> intervened, not only with a view to bearing witness – to recording,
> sometimes neutrally, more often from the 'documentary point of view'
> advocated as early as 1930 by Jean Vigo – but also as the agent of a
> militant action that it fully intended to influence.[104]

Much of the footage thus shot was distributed through the parallel and alternative networks set up after May by various *gauchiste* groups. This has inevitably meant that much has been lost, though the Paris Vidéothèque has a fairly substantial holding of documentaries (including the *Cinétracts* series with which Jean-Luc Godard was involved). Given that most of these films had a specific and local utility, their disappearance or marginalisation is not *per se* disturbing. Much more so is the collapse of this militant enthusiasm after 1968 and its relative lack of impact on the work even of those film-makers who had become committed during the Langlois affair (or earlier the Algerian war) and remained so through the events. The survival of capitalism in France meant the survival of the existing networks of cinema production and distribution, on which virtually all film-makers, whatever their political persuasion, were dependent and which proved more than capable of stretching to incorporate 'post-1968' topics such as feminism and *contestation*. Films such as André Cayatte's *Mourir d'aimer* (1970), based on the real-life love-affair in May between a schoolteacher and her 16-year-old pupil which led to her legal hounding to suicide, or Maurice Pialat's *Nous ne vieillirons pas ensemble* (1972), in which a woman abandons her (married) lover because of his galloping male chauvinism, show only too well how the capitalist distribution system, far from repressing and annihilating difference and heterogeneity, was to prove perfectly capable of accommodating them to itself. In this sense, the 'effect of May', as socio-cultural change and political anti-climax, is present in diffused form throughout French cinema after 1968.[105]

The dearth of feature films about May immediately after the events is doubtless to do with the difficulty of narrativising them on the one hand and the abundance of documentary footage on the other. Two feature-length documentaries shown well after the events were *Grands soirs et petits matins* (William Klein, 1978) and *Mourir à trente ans* (Romain Goupil, 1982). Klein's film (whose title ironically combines the *grand soir* of revolution and the exhausted small hours of the morning) is a montage of footage of the events described at the beginning as 'fragments of a film that ought to have existed'. Such a film, presumably, would have been the triumphant narrative of revolutionary social change; what Klein has to give us instead is a tantalising juxtaposition of images whose narrative component remains in the background. Among the film's last shots is one of Alain Geismar (broadcasting on Radio Sorbonne on 4 June) saying: 'The militants no longer understand one another, no longer speak the same language.' This acquires added poignancy if counterposed to the scene – for me perhaps the most moving of all the sounds and images of May – where the occupied Odéon (occupied, we are told, eighty per cent by 'intellectuals') listens to a café waiter, weeping with a frustration that is also an assertion of dignity, saying that he is 'not a dead loss', although socially and culturally he 'has nothing'. For a moment, we are reminded, not speaking the same language was not a barrier to people understanding one another.

The film's title, inevitably, invites us to read it narratively, as the erosion of the *grand soir* by or into a series of *petits matins*. There were, of course, other, more optimistic narratives than this; the successive Trotskyist interpretations are among the most striking examples. These, however, are called into question by Goupil's film, about his friend and JCR/LCR comrade Michel Recanati who committed suicide on 23 May 1978. The film opens with Goupil's recollections of other militant friends who died accidentally or by their own hand, and incorporates extracts from Recanati's diary ('I'm fed up with making love with women') as well as, near the end, a reference to the early death of the woman he loved above all others. Revolutionary romanticism here comes close to Romanticism *tout court*, with its cortège of unhappy loves and premature deaths, but without being entirely subsumed into it. The extensive footage of school students' meetings in May and of Trotskyist demonstrations afterwards details Recanati's rise to 'the top of his profession', but also provides it with a specific political context. Recanati's key strategic role was as organiser and steward of demonstrations (a role the earlier JCR had successfully fulfilled in May itself), culminating in the June 1973 march against a rally held by the neo-Fascist group Ordre Nouveau. Footage of this – line after line of demonstrators wearing crash-helmets and carrying bricks and iron bars – brought back to me the memory of watching from a café the demonstration march past and repeating to myself the Duke of Wellington's 'I don't know what effect these men will have upon the enemy, but by God, they terrify me.' The violence of that night's clashes, in which a hundred people were injured, led to the dissolution of the FCR (as it was then called) and of Ordre Nouveau, marking the end of what Henri Weber in the film terms the Trotskyist movement's *gauchiste* phase and Recanati's leading role with it. Goupil, a film-maker's son, was able to begin filming 'Reca' from an early age; *Mourir à trente ans* is thus all at once a political documentary, a biographical film and a tribute of friendship, that threefold dimension giving it the strength hinted at in Goupil's statement: 'I had to make this film to conquer his death', and suggesting why for all its elegiac plangency the film has about it more of the generous self-assertion of May than almost any other on the events. A film such as *L'An 01* (1972, Jacques Doillon, with sequences directed by Alain Resnais and Jean Rouch) represented a conscious attempt – ironically just as the violence belatedly precipitated by *gauchisme* was bringing about its demise – to capture that generosity in a series of utopian vignettes, reenactments of the mood of the events. Claude Bouniq-Mercier's summary ('What if one day we stopped everything? [. . .] We'd take the time to stroll along, to talk, to sing, to make love, to pick a flower')[106] suggests how dated the film now appears, not to say also racist in its portrayal of black African workers who pause to eat a mango before reading the telegram announcing Utopia. French culture was, after all, far better at producing Maoists than hippies.

The agent, producer and distributor Gérard Lebovici, a close friend of Debord's and founder of the Champ libre publishing-house, encouraged coproductions among the actors he represented and even bought the Cujas cinema (in the heart of the Latin Quarter), solely to screen films made by Debord. His (still unsolved) murder in 1984 brought to a halt this curious neo-Situationist incursion into the world of the spectacle, more accessibly manifested – the film is in the Paris Vidéothèque – by Gérard Cohen's *La Dialectique peut-elle casser des briques*? of 1973. This announces itself as 'the first misappropriated or "hi-jacked" film' (the French 'détourné' has both meanings), and grafts on to the print of a Kung Fu movie (of unacknowledged provenance) a soundtrack identifying the various warrior bands with different leftist groups – all, of course, complicit with the dominant bureaucracy like their gurus Foucault and Lacan, and duly trounced at the end, Godard's roughly contemporary work on the dislocation of image and soundtrack finds a bizarre, and almost certainly unwilling, kind of ally here.

The films mentioned hitherto are all in different ways marginal to an anglophone audience (none has ever had commercial distribution in Britain). The only two available commercial features dealing with the events – both can be bought on video in France – are Diane Kurys's *Cocktail Molotov* (1980) and Louis Malle's *Milou en mai* (1989). This somewhat bathetic conclusion – especially contrasted to the taxonomising fervour I have brought to the rest of this work – speaks through its very lameness of the particular problems the cinema faced in dealing with May. Kurys's feature is a European road movie (a genre very popular at the time), which begins with the theatre scene-painter Fred leaping on stage before a performance and haranguing the audience, in particular Anne whom he loves and her well-heeled mother and stepfather who have forbidden her to see him. Anne, Fred and their friend Bruno leave for an Israeli kibbutz, can get no further than Venice because of the political situation, are robbed of their car and possessions by a militant Left-wing acquaintance (!), and have in any event decided to return to Paris after hearing of the events on the radio (Bruno: 'It's a strike – it's war – I don't know what it is' – revolution, here, clearly the unspoken term). The bulk of the film takes place while they are hitching up to Paris, so that 'May' remains off-screen until the very end, present only in the various discourses on it they encounter on their journey, An older couple say: 'In 1940 they had the Resistance; we had the Algerian war; they have to have their little war too, don't they?' Lorry-drivers disagree over whether what is happening is 'just' a strike or the start of a revolution. A policeman weeps at the violence shown to him and is inclined to blame Gaullist *agents provocateurs* for the ball-bearings that have been thrown. Her father interrupts trying to break a strike at the factory he owns in Lyon to drive the pregnant Anne to Lausanne, reflecting the while that the students are 'in too much of a hurry and don't speak the same language as the workers'. The first on-screen appearance of May is when children are shown playing 'students-versus-CRS', reducing the events to the status of a game that nonetheless has its dangers, as the two males discover when arrested. A happy ending ensues as the three, together once more, drive off in a graffitised car to the strains of Californian music and the reflection that 'petrol was back . . . For us, the journey had just begun.'

The film's positioning within the road-movie genre, in which travel is its own goal, makes it all but senseless to ask what this post-May journey will be. The ending – like the fate of the eponymous cocktail (found in the Venice militants' headquarters and later thrown down an empty embankment), like the characters' belated 'arrival at/in May' and minimal participation (no sooner there than arrested . . .) – seems to suggest that it will be one towards a non-political self-realisation, but even so tentative an extrapolation is made problematic by the patchwork quality of the discourses within the film – views of May as discrete and fragmented as the individual lifts or stops for coffee. It becomes possible at this point to question whether *Cocktail Molotov* (whatever its other qualities) is really a film 'about' the events at all.

Milou en mai goes one better by including no footage representing the events whatever. The action takes place in South-Western France, where the Vieuzac family are gathered for the burial of the octogenarian Madame. She is played by Paulette Dubost, best-known for her portrayal of the maid Lisette in Renoir's scathing social satire *La Règle du jeu* of fifty years before; this piece of casting, and even more so that of Michel Piccoli (known for his consistently Left-wing views) as her son Milou, might suggest a much more subversive film than Malle has actually given us. The film is described by Henri Gueiysse as 'an ever so slightly nostalgic tale of the behaviour of the provincial bourgeoisie in May 68',[107] and that behaviour – squabbling over the inheritance, family tensions rising to the surface over an expansive dinner-table – is not so very different from what it has always traditionally been. The lesbianism of Milou's daughter Claire loses such subversive charge as it may have had through being portrayed in caricaturally sado-masochistic form, much as Camille/Miou-Miou's adulterous roll in the hay with a childhood friend – literally, for it takes place in a loft – does not so much challenge the institution of marriage as hark warmly back to a time of youthful innocence.

The events make their absent presence felt with the arrival of Milou's nephew Pierre-Alain, a student in Paris; he has hitched down with a friendly lorry-driver (Gilbert Grimaldi) who joins the family meal. The worker–student liaison is (predictably?) an abortive one, for Grimaldi shows no sympathy for Pierre-Alain's lyrical enthusiasm (' . . . you simply don't realise what's going on, precisely because it's like nothing else! It's completely new! People are talking! Just like that, without coordination, quite spontaneously!'),[108] regaling the company instead with a macho sexual discourse ('At the Sorbonne, it seems you slip in the spunk')[109] about his life on the road that functions as an inverse stereotype to Claire's lesbianism. Hocquenghem's strictures on the sexism of May are all too sadly confirmed here. Grimaldi reinforces his role as 'French *Sun*-reader' by inveighing against 'Commies' and preferring a Gitane to a joint ('No, thanks, I smoke French').[110] The film is clearly laughing at the working class rather than with them.

Malle evens out the class balance somewhat, however, by turning the full force (such as it is) of his derision against the bourgeoisie in the second half of the film. They are successively scandalised when it proves impossible to hold a proper funeral because the gravediggers are on strike and terrified when the neighours predict Bolshevik atrocities (' . . . the Russan tanks are two days away from Strasbourg!')[111] – the irony here, of course, being that May was anything but murderous or 'Communist'. Their flight to the hills and subsequent sheepish return situate the dénouement in the tradition of social farce far more tellingly represented by *La Règle du jeu* evoked again at the end as Mme Vieuzac/Paulette Dubost 'returns from the dead' in Milou's imagination to share a tender waltz with him. Romantic fantasy, finally, predominates; was this (by implication) all May was really about?

Godard and May

Jean-Pierre Jeancolas, in his negative view of the influence of May on the cinema, makes a major exception for Godard, 'who did not make afterwards the kind of film he had been making before'.[112] There is one sense in which this remark is paradoxically untrue, for it is the two films Godard made immediately before May – *La Chinoise* and *Weekened*, both 1967 –

that most strikingly prefigure the events. Godard himself says: 'I fell in love with a student at Nanterre, so I started going over there myself, and that's how *La Chinoise* came to be.'[113] The student in question was the actress Anne Wiazemsky, granddaugher of François Mauriac and to become (for a while) Godard's wife, who plays one of the film's leading roles. *La Chinoise* tells the story of a group of Maoist militants living in a 'borrowed' Paris flat over the summer, whose lives are devoted to a literal acting-out of Mao's dictum: 'Put politics in command.' The *Internationale* on cassette is their reveille, while their communal gymnastics take place to the chanting of Marxist-Leninist slogans. The group eventually falls apart over the decision to assassinate a visiting Soviet minister; Kirilov ('from' Dostoevsky's *The Possessed*) commits suicide because he is not chosen to carry out the killing, Henri – whose technical training puts him closer to the working . class than almost any of the others – has to leave the group because he disagrees with the plan (and contemplates returning to his native city, Besançon, and joining the PCF), and the wrong man is killed because the number of his hotel room is misread.

The terrorist temptation, that – closely related? – of suicide, the *gauchiste* hatred of the PCF and the workers' ambivalence towards it (Henri says that the communists are 'the only people in France to talk about the price of a television or a fridge'), the fascination with (a certain idea of) Mao's China were all, we have seen, major themes in and after 1968. The backwardness of May's sexual politics is likewise suggested when Juliet Berto/Yvonne mentions that she is a former prostitute and still sells herself from time to time if the group does not make enough from the sale of its newspaper.

The events' disruption of orthodox chronology and synchronicity is nowhere better illustrated than in Godard's prefiguring of these themes here, most of all in the scene where Anne Wiazemsky/Véronique expounds her view in a conversation with the Communist philosopher Francis Jeanson (playing himself) that revolution will start with and from the closing – by violent means if need be – of the universities. This conversation, in which Jeanson puts forward the PCF line that mass working-class support will be required before any major social transformation can occur, takes place on a train (one of the very few at the time) travelling from Paris to Nanterre; the partially-built campus and the station's name La Folie (= madness), so often bandied about in 1968, come into view as the conversation ends. Even a writer so hostile to May as Marc-Édouard Nabe acknowledges Godard's prescience ('Through the poverty of his discourse nobody has shown better – and in pictures too – what a political fraud May 68 was, how deeply tedious and lifeless, how emotionally and intellectually worthless, how ludicrously boy-scoutish in its ideology').[114]

Nabe's bile might have been better saved for the central couple (played by Jean Yanne and Mireille Darc) in *Weekend*, whose avarice disposes them to murder and caricatures the mindless acquisitiveness against which the events reacted. The tracking-shot of an immense traffic-jam on the road from Paris to Normandy is quite literally a sweeping indictment of what May rejected (and, through the absence of petrol, made briefly impossible), while the wife's final devouring of her murdered husband in the company of the 'Seine-et-Oise Liberation Front' hints at the complex interconnections between consumerism and *gauchisme*. The whole of Godard's work from *Alphaville* of 1965 through to *Sauve qui peut (la vie)* of 1980 – which marked his return to the commercial cinema after a number of years working independently, largely in video – can be seen as a sustained (and, inevitably, contradictory) development of the changes in cultural practice figured in May. This has been stimulatingly developed elsewhere at greater length than I can spare here;[115] if it has attracted so much attention, it is perhaps not (just) because Godard had been a renowned director since 1959, but because his films shine out like a good (*pace* Nabe) artistic and political deed in a dark post-1968 cinematic world. Eustache's *La Maman et la putain* – a three-and-a half-hour flow of words that in the end seem to affirm nothing but themselves – is, as the epigraph to this section suggests, the greatest testimony to that darkness. It could hardly have been made at any other time than 1972–3 – the years in which *gauchisme* died.

6 Women and the Events of May 1968

Over the past two-and-a-half decades the May 1968 events in France have continued to provoke commentaries from political observers and actors, historians and scholars of French society and culture. It was not surprising that the events' tenth and twentieth anniversaries were marked by various conferences and debates, TV and radio programmes and publications which reviewed and (re)interpreted what had taken place.

One may choose to believe, like Pierre Viansson-Ponté, that: 'Sur les journées de mai–juin 1968, tout a été dit, raconté, étalé, répété et trituré – et puis le contraire de tout.'[1] But one might add to Viansson-Ponté's remarks that everything or almost everything that has been written and said about May 1968 has been written and said from a masculine point of view. Very little space, if at all, has been given to the words and actions of the women who took part in the events. Marguerite Duras argues that women were not given the chance to write and speak about May 1968:

> One has scarcely the time to experience an event as important as May '68 before men begin to speak out, to formulate theoretical epilogues . . . to speak alone and for everyone else, on behalf of everyone else as they put it. They immediately forced women . . . to keep silent. They activated the old language, enlisted the aid of the old way of theorising in order to relate, to recount, to explain this new situation: May '68.[2]

Duras's sentiments are shared by many if not the majority of women who had participated in and lived through the events.

When I was asked to contribute to this book marking the events' twenty-fifth anniversary, I had already realised that much remained unsaid and ignored as far as women were concerned. What I had not realised, however, was the extent to which women had been excluded from both primary and secondary source commentaries, histories and interpretations. Trying to find out what women had been thinking, saying and doing in May 1968 is not a straightforward exercise and one is forced to rely upon snippets of information and women's words scattered over a variety of sources. Often such information is not contained in the main body of works but lies buried within reference notes or appendices. Furthermore, even when all the fragments of information one can gather are assembled, a complete picture fails to emerge. This may seem paradoxical, given that many of the demands and issues articulated during the events of 1968 concerned sexual revolution, the heterosexual couple, the family, which in turn were directly related to women and their role in society. Similarly, where images are concerned, it would appear that newspaper photographs, television cameras and poster art, through the subtle effects of ideology, focused mainly upon the male form: men at barricades, at meetings, at demonstrations made news, made history. When the female form was present it was, more often than not, unfocused, drowned in a sea of demonstrators[3] or trivialised.[4] The absence of women in images of 1968 is particularly glaring given that more than any other events those of May 1968 were dominated by visuals.

However, one of the paradoxes of the events of 1968 is that despite the fact that women were ignored, feminism was to emerge as the most active and imaginative of radical and subversive ideological forms; one which was to influence if not change the lives of thousands of French women.

The first part of this chapter constitutes a modest attempt to redress the imbalance whereby women have not shared centre-stage along with men in the histories of 1968. Hence it is about what women were doing in 1968 – what they were thinking, how they reacted to the events, to the men involved and towards each other.

The second part of this chapter moves away from the events of 1968 and examines the impact that they have had on women's lives. The following questions are, therefore, addressed: how have feminist ideas been received by women? Have these ideas led to changes in notions of femininity and in representations of women? How have they affected the *rapport des sexes*? Dealing with these questions has been easier as the events themselves acted as a springboard for the desire among women to find out more about themselves and to record their findings. Since 1968, then, a new theme and practice had emerged within the arts, humanities and social sciences where material on women's words and actions has increased and some of which, furthermore, has been taken up and reproduced by the media.

The third part of this chapter asks where women are today: does the 'new woman' (*la femme nouvelle*) exist and if so what is her principal sphere of operation in French society today?

While this chapter does not uncover new views, facts or material, it is hoped that it will provide a clear focus upon women in the context of May 1968 and its impact upon French society.

WOMEN IN MAY 1968

There is a lack of statistical data on women's participation in the events of

May 1968[5] but it would not be an exaggeration to claim that their participation was massive and unprecedented. Female strike and occupation rates were never as high as those among men but this is to be expected. Young women students and *lycéennes* in particular, found it far more difficult than young men did to flout parental authority and stay away from home for long periods of time. Asking her parents' permission to join a demonstration or occupation was often far more traumatic for a young woman than being caught smoking her first cigarette. Parents, for their part, wanted to keep daughters under lock and key, fearing that these young women were learning about politics and promiscuity at a time when they ought to have been revising for important summer examinations.

Where women workers were concerned, the problems of participation were different. In many instances where women were affected by workplace action, they were obliged to stay at home, as schools were closed and children had to be looked after or because without public transport they were less able to rely upon personal means (women car-owners were few while many were reluctant to hitch lifts). Often women hesitated in participating because they were simply not wanted by trade-union officials who viewed them as a hindrance in the thick of action: a young woman chanting slogans at a gathering of 5000 metal workers, outside a Parisian factory, is pulled away from the microphone and severely reprimanded by CGT officials, 'Calme-toi, tu es complètement hystérique'.[6] Trade-union attitudes towards women workers were generally hostile as women were seen to be robbing honest working-men of jobs. In the March 1968 issue of the CGT's women's magazine, *Antoinette*, Benoît Frachon (CGT leader) had declared that an ideal society was one in which the family man earned enough to keep his wife at home.

Nevertheless, in certain industrial sectors, female participation rates exceeded those of their male counterparts: for instance, in both the textiles and manufactured electrical goods industries, 53 per cent of strikers were women while in the food industry, women accounted for 51 per cent of the strikeforce.[7]

However, while women may have participated in great numbers for the first time, their experience of participation was altogether different from that of their male peers. On the whole, women were forced to be content with their role of second-class ground troops who could not expect to gain even the most modest of leadership positions.

In May 1968, women who participated in the events were active within political parties and trade unions; in the various *Comités d'Action* [8] which had sprung up in lycées, universities, factories and neighbourhoods; in street action. Women students and workers were involved in direct confrontations with the security forces: from mounting barricades and hurling paving-stones to launching raids upon the edifices of 'bourgeois power'. Together with the men, women were beaten and arrested – on 6 May *France-Soir* deplored the fact that '[les] jeunes filles soient sauvagement matraquées'. Some were raped in the back of riot police vans and at police stations.[9]

There were cases of women carrying out acts of boldness: for instance the evacuation of children, via the rooftops, from the Sorbonne on 30 May when the CRS (riot police) stormed the occupied university or the evacuation of injured protestors from hospitals in Paris, on 24 May in order to avoid mass arrests.

Women striking and occupying workplaces also made an impact during this period. For example, at the central Paris postal cheques division (CCP) of the Post Office, where 7000 women constituted the majority of the workforce and strikeforce, 1000 women occupied management offices. They made notable gains with bosses agreeing eventually to a reduction of the working week from 41 to 37 hours.[10] Similarly, women at the central Lyon division of the CCP gained one free Saturday per fortnight with further promises from bosses to reconsider working hours, maternity leave and retirement arrangements. These gains were also made following the occupation of work premises.[11]

It would be true to say that women were effective whenever they felt strength in numbers and where they were able to organise and lead action for themselves. Young *lycéennes* from single-sex girls' schools (e.g. the Lycée Racine in Paris) made efficient organisers, setting up *Commissions de Travail* on politics, school rules, reform of the *baccalauréat* and pupil–teacher relations, just as in other lycées. However, at girls' lycées additional commissions were often set up to examine the questions of abortion, contraception and sexuality among others. Unlike their counterparts from mixed schools, *lycéennes* from single-sex schools became confident negotiators and orators in a milieu which was not dominated by young men.[12]

Women workers too, testified to the fact that the organisation of strikes and occupations where they were in the majority and in control was less hierarchical and more democratic. At the central Lyon division of the CCP, where the occupation lasted three weeks, women set up bodies, *intersyndicales*, which were responsible for liaising with the trade unions and for the regular dissemination of information to the workforce so that demands could be formulated collectively. The *intersyndicales* were also responsible for the organisation of meetings where discussion of broader political issues took place. And while women were not organising or attending meetings or carrying out picket duty they found time to read, discuss and sing together in order to keep up morale or overcome fears that many had of violent confrontation with the police.[13] Children who could not be left at home on their own or with fathers were brought along to the occupation and looked after collectively. The women felt comfortable to be themselves and to express their political beliefs in their own way; here, no one could tell them that bringing in their children or knitting or sewing was a diversion from the serious business of industrial action.

Accounts such as these have, for the most part, remained uninvestigated and undocumented, thus denying women the chance to be seen and to speak out and act as subjects in their own right. However, situations where women found themselves in the majority and therefore in control were few and most female participants of the events found that in addition to being considered second-class combatants they were unable to escape from certain traditional feminine roles ascribed to them: that of the mother figure; the secretary; the sex-object.

The Mother Figure

During the events it was women who supplied food to young 'revolutionaries', cleaned occupied premises, nursed those injured in clashes with police and supervised children in improvised crèches.

In lycées all over the country, female pupils organised *services de garderie* which were responsible for the supervision and teaching of younger pupils who were not allowed to join the protest. In universities, too, crèches were set up and run by women – at the Sorbonne, for example, a 24-hour, 60-place crèche was set up on 16 May by a primary school teacher with the help of women medical students and nurses.

Women also found themselves having to look after young men at the barricades. At the height of the disturbances, women residents of the Latin Quarter of Paris provided 'revolutionaries' with coffee and blankets, make-shift masks (dishcloths, towels and even nappies) to counter the effects of tear-gas, and first-aid. In these circumstances women ran great risks of being injured themselves as they dodged paving stones and tear gas canisters and yet 'fragile' young women workers and students were not allowed to join the various *services d'ordre* which were responsible for controlling the excesses of 'revolutionaries', among other things.

The Secretary

In political meetings women held back from speaking, either through fear of being shouted down or because they were aware that their physical appearance would attract greater attention than their words: 'C'était un effort gigantesque d'oser apostropher une salle comble et goguenarde', recalled Evelyne July.[14] Consequently, women appeared to face a choice between making themselves subservient to the men or denying themselves and becoming 'honorary men': 'les femmes doivent jouer les secrétaires ou se viriliser'.[15] Many women, believing they were incapable of leading, found it easier to play the secretary. These 'anges de la polycopieuse' as they were called, typed and copied bulletins and leaflets, prepared coffee, took telephone messages and generally looked after their 'bosses'. This secretarial role is aptly captured in William Klein's film of the events, *Grands soirs, petits matins*.[16] Klein had filmed a meeting of a Comité d'Action Lycéen where strategy and tactics were being discussed. When the telephone rings a young woman who has been taking minutes at the meeting answers:

> Votre fils, madame, il est parti se battre. Avec son manteau, oui. Non il n'est pas malade. S'il lui arrive quelquechose comptez sur moi pour vous prévenir.[17]

It was a role almost impossible to escape from. A few women tried to question their own position within political and other organisations and to raise broader feminist issues but were accused of acting as 'bourgeois degenerates' who were acting against the interests of the oppressed and their struggle. On the other hand, women who tried hard to fit in felt trapped by a language and attitudes alien to them:

> je portais des paroles qui n'étaient pas les miennes . . . J'avais voulu qu'on parle normalement dans les tracts, mais je n'osais plus le réclamer . . . J'avais la trouille, il y avait un côté jeu de mecs . . . je croyais à la révolution, mais les hiérarchies d'organisation c'était grotesque, la guéguerre me révulsait.[18]

Those who escaped from the role of secretary did so by colluding in the hierarchical division between men and women, treating the secretary 'type' with contempt.

The Sex-Object

The assumption that women who became activists did so through romantic or sexual motivation was widely held amongst participants of the events and was exploited by the press in reports on 'orgies' and 'love-ins' which were supposed to have taken place in buildings occupied by students in particular. The national theatre of the Odéon in Paris (occupied mainly by young men) was especially the focus of such attention.[19] The cellar of the theatre had apparently been transformed into a permanent orgy-room in the belief that sexual, political and social revolt were all deeply linked: 'Il faut baiser au moins une fois par nuit pour être un bon révolutionnaire' proclaimed grafitti at the Sorbonne.[20] Hence women came to play an instrumental part in a process whereby young men became more 'revolutionary' and any woman who entered the occupation at the Odéon was, it was rumoured, promptly led down to the cellar.

The 'shock accounts' of events at the Odéon and other occupied buildings meant that women were not seen as serious activists. Women students, especially, bore the brunt of hypocritical male attitudes which disapproved of their seemingly liberated lifestyles and which, at the same time, regarded them as desirable sex-objects.

Relations between middle-class women students and working-class men were particularly tense and many a female activist overcame social barriers and a sense of guilt relating to her privileged background by becoming involved in romantic and sexual relationships.[21] Numbers of women saw this as a problem which required discussion within their political organisations. Their 'leaders', however, refused to acknowledge that a problem existed at all; it was implicit in their attitudes that this was a convenient means of boosting the working-class membership of their organisations. In the meantime women were reminded over and over that only the triumph of the working class over capitalism would bring with it true liberation for them.

However, gradually, as the events progressed some women activists came together, finding the courage to criticise their political organisations and unions for not addressing women's issues. The impact of the actions and writings of American feminists was not lost on them either and the first signs of a fight-back emerged on 21 May 1970 when Anne Zelensky[22] and a small group of women intellectuals organised a meeting at Vincennes. The meeting, which was attended by both women and men, quickly degenerated into chaos as men began to jeer talk of male oppressors. Nevertheless, determination to hold more meetings only hardened and by the autumn of 1970 women's discussion and consciousness groups had multiplied rapidly, especially in student and intellectual circles and as more women joined such groups, the smaller *gauchiste* parties saw their numbers drop until some (for example, the Maoist grouping Vive la Révolution) were forced to dissolve. These women's groups, of differing tendencies but all of whom wished to challenge and change the power relations between the sexes, came to be referred to collectively as the Mouvement de Libération des Femmes (MLF).[23]

THE FEMINIST CHALLENGE OF THE SEVENTIES[24]

Inspired by the spirit of May 1968, which may be summed up as anti-bureaucratic, anti-hierarchic, anti-authoritarian, spontaneous and imaginative and by a belief in the immediacy and indivisibility of individual and collective action, the MLF set out its objectives. Among its general objectives were: the politicisation of the private sphere and particularly of sexual relations, the rejection of hierarchical organisation; separatist action and organisation. Issues over which campaigns would be waged included free abortion and contraception on demand, the removal of sexist images in advertising especially, the recognition of rape as a crime punishable by law and the protection of women from violence inflicted by the state and individual men.

While French women, in great numbers, listened, watched, understood or became involved in MLF activities, the media seized upon the spontaneous and dramatic actions carried out in pursuit of the above-mentioned objectives: for example, the honouring of the 'Unknown Soldier's Wife'; the invasion by feminist activists of the Etats-Généraux de la Femme held by *Elle* magazine at Versailles in November 1970;[25] the publication of the *Manifeste des 343* in April 1971;[26] the procession down the Champs Elysées against Mother's Day in May 1972. Despite media hostility and insults from former male comrades (name-calling ranged from 'malmenées', 'ménopausées', 'névrosées' to the supreme insult 'mal-baisées') and in spite of the dissensions which existed within the movement itself, the MLF's ideas and actions had important cultural and political repercussions.

A feminist-inspired culture was created in various domains of cultural and intellectual life. One of the areas in which the most intense endeavour took place was that of writing and publishing. The 1970s saw the establishment of about a dozen publishing houses for women's writing of which the earliest, Des Femmes, was set up in October 1972. While these publishing houses were not set up to reach the majority of French women, their productions brought a blast of fresh thinking which was taken up by mainstream publishers who began to set up their own 'collections femmes'. It is estimated that between 1975 and 1979 women writers published 150 different works with an average print-run of 5000 per title.[27]

The seventies also marked the emergence (and demise) of several feminist journals and newspapers reflecting the views of the different currents within the MLF. The most well-known included: *Le Quotidien des Femmes* and *Des Femmes en Mouvement*;[28] *Histoire d'Elles, Questions Féministes, Le Temps des Femmes* and *Les Nouvelles Féministes*;[29] *le Torchon Brûle, Les Pétroleuses, La Revue d'en Face* and *Les Cahiers du Féminisme*.[30] This is by no means an exhaustive list and many more could be added to it. Statistical information on the size of the readership of these magazines is unavailable but in their heyday, an estimated 150 000 women are said to have regularly bought at least one of these titles.[31] Again, these magazines did not aim to create a mass readership but the constant focus that they afforded to the issues of sexual liberation, contraception and abortion, homosexuality, rape and prostitution was bound to influence the mainstream women's magazines. For example, *Elle* and *Marie-Claire* attempted to arrange the marriage between feminism and femininity[32] and two new types of women's magazines were launched in the late seventies. The first, *Comment* which called itself the monthly magazine of 'la femme libre qui a évolué au sein de la société actuelle' had a very short life. But *F Magazine*, launched by the group Expansion in January 1978 and put together by Claude Servan-Schreiber and Benoîte Groult, initially enjoyed two very successful years with its campaigning tone and refusal to collude in the objectification of women.

Communication between women, on women, was not limited to books, newspapers and magazines. Other information and message services included: the *Répondeuses* (an answerphone message service); the *Radioteuses* which at the time were illegally operating *radios-libres*; cafés, art galleries, and bookshops also provided space where news and views could be swapped. Furthermore, women were also able to put their creative skills to use within groups such as La Spirale [33] founded by the journalist Catherine Valabregue, Musidora, Vidéa, Femmes-Média and Les Muses s'amusent which brought together women film-makers, actresses and other artistes and which, jointly, organised the first women's film festival in April 1974.

In academic life too, women researchers, teachers and students came together to discuss and create a feminist–feminine culture which would counteract sexism within their institutions of work and challenge masculine approaches to the study of the humanities, social and natural sciences. Thus in 1972 an Etudes Féminines route of study was introduced at the University of Paris VIII to cover the disciplines of history, philosophy and literature while 1975 saw the establishment of the Centre Lyonnais d'Etudes Féministes at Lyon III. In 1976 a Centre d'Etudes Féminines was set up at the University of Provence and in 1978 the University of Toulouse agreed to house the Groupe de Recherche Interdisciplinaire et d'Etude des Femmes.

All of this activity on the part of women academics culminated in a conference held in December 1982, at Toulouse, to assess the state of women's studies in France and to put forward strategies for the further development of research in this field. A four-year programme was to last from 1983 to 1987 to include a total of 68 different research projects.

Although this programme was not renewed after 1987, it brought women's studies into the mainstream of Higher Education teaching and scholarly activity.

It was not only cultural and intellectual life which was marked by feminist action and activities. Women's groups and organisations mush-roomed and battled on the social front too. Campaigning for free abortion and contraception were organisations such as Choisir and Mouvement pour la Libération de l'Avortement et de la Contraception (MLAC)[34] while groups like SOS Femmes-Alternative, SOS Femmes-Violées (operating under the aegis of the Ligue du Droit des Femmes) and later the multi-racial Commission pour l'Abolition des Mutilations Sexuelles (CAMS) organised against violence against women.

In trade unions, women began to gain a growing awareness of the injustices and discrimination that they were subjected to and the seventies bore witness to several conflicts in which women played a leading role: in Thionville in 1972, women workers at Les Nouvelles Galeries went on strike; between July 1975 and December 1978 women employed by the Confection Industrielle du Pas-de-Calais occupied their factory while at Lip, in Besançon, women workers took part in meetings, demonstrations, strikes and occupations. With the increase in numbers of women's groups within trade unions, the latter were forced to consider the question of women's equal rights with those of men via specially set-up *commissions féminines syndicales*.[35]

In the countryside also, women did not remain immune to the influences of feminist ideas and forms of action. In the Larzac, for example, women became involved in the fight against the proposed extension to a military base in their region. Having played the traditional wife/mother role within a largely isolated community, the fight to save the Larzac brought them into contact with women engaged in other battles (with women workers at Lip in Besançon, for example) and led them to organise rallies, speak at meet-ings and carry out the type of direct action (planting trees on the proposed extension site, for example) which had become associated with feminist activism. The formation of networks and exchanges with women outside their community was to bring irreversible change to the lives of Larzac women.[36]

Finally, where the sphere of mainstream politics is concerned, feminism made limited advances in the aftermath of the May 1968 events. This is partly because large numbers of women political activists believed that political parties colluded in women's oppression and that their efforts and interests would be better rewarded by the MLF and other specific women's issue groups and partly because the very structure and organisation of political parties within a highly-centralised political system made it very difficult for women to gain access to decision-making processes. However, it was within the parties of the Left that feminist politics found some space in which to operate. This was particularly so in the run-up to the legislative elections of 1978 when women came to be regarded as an important political constituency by the Left. From 1977 onwards feminist groups emerged within the two main parties of the Left: in the Communist Party (PCF) feminists came together in the Elles voient rouge collective; in the Socialist Party (PS) they grouped around the publication *Mignonnes, allons voir sous la rose*. While these women were held in contempt by many within their respective parties, their presence embarrassed party leaders into breaking their silence over women's issues. Thus in the PCF, leaders began to talk about 'objectifs spécifiques des femmes' and accepted the term 'féminisme', albeit redefined to strip it of its 'bourgeois' content:

> si cela veut dire défendre á fond les droits des femmes, agir pour créer une société d'égalité, de justice, oú encore les hommes et les femmes seront plus libres et heureux.[37]

In the PS, where feminism found a more respectful audience, the Secrétariat à l'Action Féminine, set up to promote women's rights, began to campaign more vigorously through the organisation of meetings, debates and study days. The political activism of these women, within their parties, bore some fruit: for example, in June 1978, a parliamentary bill criminalising rape, put forward by the two main parties of the Left, was enacted after being passed unanimously by the Senate.

While feminist action did not gain women positions of power within political decision-making, there is no doubt that it forced political leaders to consider women's demands for equal rights and in the seventies a number of laws, designed to improve the status of women, appeared on the statute books:

1970   law replacing 'paternal' authority with 'parental' authority within the family
1972   law recognising the principle of equal pay for equal work
1974   introduction of limited *free* contraception[38]
1975, 1979   repeal of previous laws forbidding abortion
1975   law against sex discrimination in recruitment procedures
1979   repeal of previous laws forbidding women in industry (managerial and supervisory posts only) from undertaking night work.

These and other more minor laws were enacted under the guidance of the secrétariat d'état à la Condition féminine set up in July 1974.[39] They were supplemented by further key women's rights legislation with the arrival of the Left in government and the establishment of Yvette Roudy's ministère des Droits de la femme in 1981.[40] The ministry's most notable achievements included free abortion on demand (1982); equal rights and equality of opportunity for women in work (1983);[41] equality between spouses as far as property and children were concerned (1985); extension of the 1972 race discrimination law to include sanctions against incitement to hatred, discrimination and violence on grounds of sex (1985).[42]

The 1970s represented a period when the major part of militant feminist action and the most important pieces of women's rights legislation took place. By the beginning of the eighties, however, French feminism had lost its élan and intense militancy.[43]

The defeat of the Left at the legislative elections of 1978 marked a turning-point at which the ideological crisis within the Left in France and elsewhere, the rise of the New Right and deepening economic problems all combined to make it impossible for a movement as heterogeneous as the MLF to continue effective involvement in pressure politics. The ideological crisis of the Left affected a number of groups within the MLF (particularly those of the *lutte de classes* current) which suffered paralysis of discourse and strategy before finally disappearing, while the rise of the New Right brought with it a wind of anti-feminism. In addition to this, the aggravation of the economic situation meant that women became more concerned to hold on to hard-fought-for gains than to mount new campaigns or publicise new issues. Hence, the feminist activist, it seemed, gave way to the feminist individual who began to believe that the only effective way of serving the collective good was through individual endeavour and success – if the private had once been political then the political could now become private.

The Left's victory in 1981 and the establishment of Roudy's ministère des Droits de la femme drew the final curtain on post-1968 feminist militancy: 'le féminisme militant a cédé la place à un féminisme tranquille'[44] Roudy herself concluded. But if Roudy's ministry had provided concrete support for the projects of numerous feminist groups[45] and had initiated positive women's rights legislation, thus marking the beginning of a phase of 'féminisme tranquille', then for many others such recuperation and institutionalisation of feminist-inspired thinking and action, 'le féminisme d'état', signalled a retrograde step from revolt to reform and the end of something new which had begun in May 1968.[46] However one chooses to view this, what remains incontestable is that the feminist challenge of the seventies contributed in no small way towards fracturing the image that women had of themselves and to changes in the way they were viewed by society.

FEMININITY, FEMINISM AND THE 'NEW WOMAN'

Dominant ideology through mainstream culture has instructed women what to think about themselves and how to conduct relationships with those around them: their parents, their husbands and lovers, their children, their bosses and other women. In other words dominant ideology has instructed women on how to achieve femininity. Moreover, this femininity is defined in terms of a woman's ability and willingness to identify with a man in a way which is conducive to his happiness and well-being and which ensures the survival of his family line through nurture of his children. In this feminine role, then, a woman must place her own desires and needs last, while often renouncing their specificity and individuality. Thus, marriage, motherhood and home have come to represent the main accomplishments of femininity, on the one hand, while a childlike virginal beauty is essential if a woman is to capture her man in the first place.

In May 1968, the ideology of femininity was confronted by feminist ideology which searched for a feminine identity which did not define itself in relation to masculine criteria. For feminists, motherhood became the main stumbling-block of true liberation for women because it represented a permanent reason for inequality between the sexes.[47] Consequently contraception and abortion as a means to voluntary and autonomous motherhood constituted key issues over which feminists campaigned in the seventies. Control over motherhood, feminists argued, represented the most fundamental of liberties from which all others followed. If motherhood was controllable rather than 'natural', if it became a matter for discussion and deliberation, then nothing really distinguished women from men.

Feminist questioning of motherhood therefore provided the basis of the demand for a complete and radical change in the relations between women and men whereby women as subjects of their own motherhood and sexuality could choose whether or not to live in marriage, to have children, to serve the family or to work outside the home and whether or not to conform to definitions of beauty and sexual behaviour as set out by the ideology of femininity.

May 1968 proved to be a turning-point as far as the reception of feminist ideas by French women was concerned. The ground upon which the ideology of feminism had sprung up had been prepared prior to the events. The expansion of the French economy in the fifties and sixties had led to changes in the world of work so that although the proportion of women in the working population had remained constant between 1954 (34.83 per cent) and 1968 (34.93 per cent),[48] the pattern of women' recruitment had altered. Greater numbers of middle-class women were entering the liberal professions, managerial and supervisory functions and office administration.[49] Consequently women's objective relations with home and family were also beginning to change. This had, to some extent, been recognised, first, by the law of July 1965 which gave a married woman the right to administer family property in the absence of her husband and to seek work without her husband's permission; second, and more importantly by the Neuwirth law of 1967 which legalised the sale of contraception. Women were gradually beginning to speak as subjects and the events of May and the feminist challenge emerging from them were to greatly accelerate this process. On the one hand, women, in vast numbers, wanted to be active outside the home[50] and this had led them to support feminist demands linked to conditions of work, salaries, child-care, and so on. On the other hand, women wanted to express themselves sexually and this had led them to question marriage, the family[51] and the sexual identity imposed upon them. While it was not always easy to dismiss the resignation implicit in the idea that women had been subjugated for centuries and that this could not change, thousands of French women, nevertheless, claimed to be feminist (in spirit at least if not in the way that they were able to live their lives). The success of the MLF was that many women found it quite difficult not to want to be even 'a little bit' feminist because to be feminist meant being forward-looking and progressive, meant being independent and not being 'owned', it meant being in control, it meant a new, different way of experiencing real life:

> Ce qui est fantastique au M.L.F., précisément, c'est que les filles avec qui l'on est, c'est des copines, c'est-à-dire des filles avec qui on va s'acheter des fringues: c'est très sympa de s'acheter des fringues avec des nanas, ou bien avec qui l'on se raconte des histoires. On ne se sent pas du tout culpabilisées de ne pas faire de la 'politique', tu vois ce que je veux dire, de vivre, un point c'est tout.[52]

LA FEMME NOUVELLE

The fact that feminism appeared to offer women a different way of living was not lost upon the purveyors of mainstream feminine culture. In an economy suffering from the effects of the oil crisis of the early seventies, the media and advertisers were desperate for new ideas in order to gain new audiences and pull themselves out of the rut of stagnating profits. These new ideas, to the dismay of many feminists, were appropriated from the MLF.

Throughout the seventies a number of women's magazines whose explicit role it is to perpetuate and confirm accepted images of femininity, had been reacting to feminist ideas in an attempt to keep up with the changing attitudes and behaviour of their public. This was particularly true of a magazine such as *Elle* which saw itself as progressive and innovative. The magazine had, since 1968, taken up the issues of contraception and abortion and women's equal rights in general. However, this liberal approach continued to coexist with traditional themes of femininity which in particular were presented through the fashion pages and advertisements. The seemingly easy marriage of feminism and femininity produced the message 'liberated but feminine': thus alongside serious articles such as 'Que savez-vous du président' by Maurice Duverger or 'Les femmes comment votent-elles' by Monica Charlot one could, quite easily, have also come across Triumph bras representing 'une nouvelle manière de vivre, une nouvelle découverte de la liberté . . .' for the 'femme nouvelle . . . femme féminine'.[53] This 'femme nouvelle' became the media's mascot.

She appeared everywhere – on posters, in the press, on small screens, on large screens . . . young, beautiful, sporty, sexy, intelligent, mother, wife, lover, professional woman.

. In January 1978 an entirely new magazine was launched in her honour – *F Magazine* was billed as 'féminin mais non bétifiant, féministe mais non militant'[54] – while in January 1979, Bernard Pivot's famous *Apostrophes* programme devoted an hour-long prime-time slot to 'Les nouvelles femmes'. But who exactly typified this 'new woman' and what did she believe in?

Contrary to the impression, given by the media, that she was everywoman, everywhere, the 'new woman' was in fact most typically middle-class, aged between 25 and 45, married with one or more children, well-educated, in work (or looking for work) and more often than not lived in the Paris region.[55]

While the majority of 'new women' placed themselves on the Left of the political spectrum[56] they were particularly concerned about women's issues and the position of women in society. Hence most were sympathetic towards the aims, if not always the practice, of the MLF and a large proportion believed that change in favour of women could only occur as a result of the MLF's demands and actions.[57] It is not surprising then that 'new women' rejected certain traditional notions of femininity. They were among those who had called for the right to enjoy control over motherhood. The overwhelming majority, over 80 per cent, considered the legalisation of contraception and abortion to be a major progress as far as women's liberation was concerned and 75 per cent believed that having children was not a necessary condition for a successful life.[58] Furthermore, the freedom to express themselves sexually also represented an important and hard-fought-for right and 'new women' rejected images, put forward by the media and mainstream culture, of women being subjected to a man's desires, women carrying out housework, women being fulfilled by the tasks of motherhood, women as empty-headed sex-objects.

Finally, gaining control over motherhood meant that the focus of the 'new woman's' life no longer lay in the home but in work outside the home. For most 'new women', 79 per cent, the satisfaction gained from work came from the knowledge that they were financially independent, in control of their own lives and that their qualities and skills were recognised by society.[59] However, while 'new women' had claimed the right to control motherhood and their own sexuality and to work outside the home, it would seem that the majority preferred to enjoy these rights within a marriage of equality between spouses.[60]

Generally, then, 'new women' were more opposed to authority in all spheres of their lives, felt less bound by social norms, conventions and morals, they were more open to pleasure and saw themselves as multifaceted individuals. While these changes were not accurately reflected by real life, what was certain was that women's perception of themselves had changed and that on the eve of the 1980s society seemed to have accepted a diversification of feminine models.

STATE FEMINISM AND THE RETURN TO FEMININITY

The victory of the Socialists in 1981 and the creation of the Ministry for Women's Rights marked the beginning of what many feminists saw as the recuperation and normalisation of feminism by the state. The emergence of state feminism was to hasten the fragmentation of the MLF as differences between groups became increasingly irreconcilable and considerable numbers of activists, who had hitherto provided the focus of the movement, decided to work in an individual capacity with the new ministry and related institutions. Two important reactions seemed to flow from this change.

Firstly, while more women than ever before were calling themselves feminist, there was nevertheless an assumption among many that this was sufficient and did not need to be followed up by militant action. After all, some of the most important of women's demands had been met and there were laws to prove this. Furthermore, many women felt that having fought collectively for over ten years it was time to consolidate and conserve the gains made – the Ministry for Women's Rights could take up the fight where they had left it.

Secondly, in the austere eighties, the setting up of a ministry devoted solely to the furtherance of women's rights sent alarm bells ringing in the male-dominated establishment – among government bureaucrats, political parties, employers, the judiciary and the media to name but a few institutions. State feminism appeared to represent a far greater threat than the militant MLF of the seventies ever had. Yvette Roudy's anti-sexist bill, for example, challenging the right to portray women in degrading ways was particularly badly received. Roudy and the 'emasculatory' bill became targets of vituperative attacks: 'Quelle différence entre Roudy et un ayatollah?' asked the head of one advertising agency[61] while Alain Decrucq, head of the Conseil National de la Publicité affirmed:

> Je suis certain que les femmes sont d'accord avec les images que l'on donne d'elles . . . Elles préfèrent être perçues comme jeunes, jolies, aguichantes plutôt que comme des repoussoirs.[62]

The war against feminism had begun.

Mainstream culture, through the media, announced the end of feminism and the return of femininity. Women, it was claimed, had become weary of the tensions, the austereness and the excesses of feminism; they wanted a return to secure, traditional values. Women's magazines which had embraced feminist themes in the seventies now seemed relieved to be able to return to their original vocation of promoting the virtues of femininity. Several magazines changed direction. While *Elle* replaced pages on news and current affairs with 'show-biz' type articles and casual, comfortable fashion with lace, silk and satin, *F Magazine* underwent a change of names from its original title to *Le Nouveau F* in 1980, to simply *F* in 1983, to *Femme* in 1984. Under the editorship of Annick Geille, recruited from *Playboy*, *Femme*'s main concerns were to do with the new-found relationship between women and men, based upon trust, confidence and fun! Furthermore, 1984 also saw the launch of the weekly *Madame Figaro* – 'le magazine des valeurs sûres'.

Advertisers who had successfully seen off Roudy's anti-sexist bill also got down to the work of promoting the 'new feminine woman' who had come to terms with herself and consumer society.

The 'new feminine woman' represents the return of the 'good girl'. In the era of AIDS there has been a constant reminder to women to re-embrace traditional sex roles or suffer the consequences. The 'new feminine woman' has, therefore, integrated the main gains of feminism into her life but refuses to be marginalised by its more 'vulgar' or 'excessive' aspects. She no longer calls herself feminist. But she has successfully married her career with a stable, monogamous relationship and her confidence with her femininity and moreover, her efficacy in doing this is recognised and appreciated by her husband/partner, her boss, by society.

Today we are told 'La révolution est accomplie', 'les femmes sont heureuses'.[63] The overwhelming majority (91 per cent) of French women are happy.[64] Like the media's 'new feminine woman' they have, it would appear, perfected the art of compromise so that while 60 per cent are happy in their relationships with men, 82 per cent believe they could live without them;[65] while 76 per cent feel that motherhood represents one of the most important aspects of a woman's life, 53 per cent could happily live without children;[66] and while French women have ceased the battle against pornography, 'affaire de puritain', and sexist advertising, 65 per cent would be prepared to act collectively against violence directed at women.[67] The conclusion reached? French women are today, above all, 'indépendantes', 'travailleuses', 'aventurières', 'capricieuses', they are not 'inquiètes', 'révoltées', 'égoistes', and most importantly 'soumises'.

The reduction of the situation of French women to half a dozen or so epithets obscures the reality. French society has been feminised, it is claimed. But 25 years after the May 1968 events and the birth of new feminist protests, what does feminisation really mean? For the most part feminisation has taken place at the lower levels of various hierarchies. For example, women may make up nearly half the workforce (44.5 per cent)[68] but they are still, for the most part, concentrated in those sectors of the economy and in those low-paid professions which have traditionally been dominated by them. Furthermore, they constitute the majority of the part-time workforce and are twice as likely to find themselves unemployed as men are.

Today, as has always been the case, women assume the major part of work in the home and are responsible for childcare. French women (in comparison with their European sisters) enjoy the least leisure time (28 hours per week as opposed to 35–50 hours in other countries).[69]

In the political arena too, a certain amount of feminisation may have taken place at the bottom of the pyramid of power but the proportion of women MPs in the Assemblée Nationale only reached 5.7 per cent in 1988.[70]

Finally, women are still the most likely targets of crime, including crimes of sexual violence. Whereas the general crime rate in France dropped by 3.68 per cent between 1986 and 1987, the number of rape cases increased by 8.82 per cent.[71]

There is little doubt that important gains have been made by French women over the last 25 years, but it is also true that those gains are currently under threat and that women continue to bear the burden of inequality. However, while the movement of May 1968 may have ended in reform, more than one feminist has insisted:

Ce mouvement a permis d'imaginer qu'il est possible de bricoler quelquechose, d'expérimenter, de faire autrement.[72]

Epilogue

I returned from a week in Paris, with a sense of timing that has not deserted me since, in April 1968. In January 1970, I went to France for six months (in Caen, provincial beacon of the events) that turned into three-and-a-half years first in Caen, then at the École Normale Supérieure (Parisian beacon of the events) – the intelligence of chance indeed. I am at the time of writing almost exactly twice as old as May. If I drew the diagram of my life it would look like this: ∝. This book has been an attempt to close, in an open way, that diagram.

Which is to say that it has also been a closet, veiled, disingenuous form of autobiography, wherein the belatedness of my May-experience, like its relaying through a cacophony of texts, stands in for as it stands guarantee for its authenticity. 'My generation' – Hamon and Rotman's, but also, since I happen to be English, Pete Townshend's – discovered difference in a flash of lighting. The multifarious subsequent attempts to write that difference are already suggested in Willener's splendid *L'Image-Action de la société ou la politisation culturelle/Society's action-picture: about cultural politicisation* of 1970, which conjugates dada, surrealism, free jazz, the work of Godard or the Living Theatre not simply as reflective examples of an undefinable *Zeitgeist* but as attempts to live and write time differently. In this perspective, the wish of the participants in May to 'affirm themselves as the creators of their own universe'[1] is not merely an attempt to kill God along with the Father – cod-Nietzsche to accompany their cod-Freud, as a more ironic Stéphane might have put it; it powerfully suggests the problematising of existing relationships to time as well as to place that may well be May's most abiding legacy. R. Linbaum, in Willener's chapter 'Entracte ou préfiguration?: un entretien de groupe'/'A pause between acts or a prefiguring?: a group discussion', says that 'the first thing to see about May is that it was a surprise . . . and a surprise doesn't happen twice'.[2] A surprise rewritten, that is to say, is not a surprise any more – or rather it is the same surprise, the same difference, and thus not an *event* any more.

This brings us back full circle (to 'the same surprise, the same difference' . . .) to the quotation from Barthes with which this work began.[3] The problem of writing (the) event(s) has been a major one in contemporary French thought; Geoffrey Bennington's book on Jean-François Lyotard is entitled *Lyotard: writing the event*, and it cannot be innocent that one of Lyotard's major instances of an 'event' (in *Des dispositifs pulsionnels*) is the murder of Pierre Overney at Renault – the end, Hamon and Rotman

167

have suggested, of *gauchisme* and hence perhaps the end of the ('May')
events. For Lyotard and Bennington, 'Overney's death is an "event" not
because of its causes or effects, but because of its senselessness or *inanity*:
despite the efforts of the Renault company's narrative, and even of the
demonstration's organisers, Overney's death is an event in so far as it
refuses to be absorbed into the *order* of a classic narrative, brought to book
in a narrative *account*, its tension exchanged for other tensions.'[4] This
'inanity' has nothing to do with the moralising strictures of an Aron, for it
stems as much from an excess of senses as from a shortage of sense, and
that excess in its turn stems from what Bennington describes as 'the disruption (. . .) in terms of tension and energy, of a restrictive narrative tempo-
rality.'[5]

The story of such a disruption – of probably its major paradigmatic
instance in most living Western memories – is what, self-defeatingly, I have
been trying to tell, in Chapter 1 at any rate. Thereafter, that narrative
complete in its manifest inadequacy, I have been writing the writing of the
events (or even, via the spiral of translation in Chapter 2, rewriting the
writing of the writing of them). The excess of signification that all these
writings have necessarily implied would not, I think, have been possible –
writeable – unless haunted by its Other in the shape of some ultimate
meaninglessness or unsayability. In moments more flush with literariness,
this might sound to me like lines from T. S. Eliot's *The Love Song of J.
Alfred Prufrock*:

> Would it have been worth while
> If one, settling a pillow or throwing off a shawl,
> And turning toward the window, should say:
> 'That is not it at all,
> That is not what I meant at all.'[6]

In others, moving between classes and meetings in an overcrowded
tower-block that might be reminiscent of 1968 Nanterre except that that is
not what it is ('the same surprise, the same difference, and thus not an *event*
any more'), that Other is the rictus of vocationalism and Common Sense,
endlessly snarling: 'Why should I – why should anybody? – want to know
about a collective frenzy that might as well have taken place two thousand
years ago for all the difference it now makes? Why fell trees and bore
students with the "history" of an autobiography of failure?' Because, obviously, I want it to happen again although – because – it cannot; because
also, beyond that, what May was about is also what pedagogy, what history,
autobiography, even failure, especially politics should be about: the renego-
tiation of time and place, not once for all, not here and now, but incessantly

and (dis)continuously. That, along with and underpinning the diversity of analyses and reproductions, is what May 1968, perhaps the contemporary world's most striking moment of asynchrony, so vividly encapsulates.

Notes

1 What Happened in May 1968?

1. R. Barthes, 'L'écriture de l'événement', in special number of *Communications*, 'Mai 68: la prise de la parole' (Paris: Seuil, 1968), p. 108.
2. These all figure at least once – generally, of course, in French – in the titles of books cited in Laurent Joffrin's bibliography in *Mai 68: Histoire des Événements* (Paris: Seuil/Points, 1988), pp. 344–59, apart from 'crisis', significant as the expression chosen by Bénéton and Touchard as the title of their key article (translated here as Chapter 2). There are additional 'one-off sightings' in the bibliography for 'days', 'storms' and the metonymic 'barricades'.
3. See D. Caute, *'68: The Year of the Barricades* (London: Paladin, 1968), for a lively and well-documented survey of these. (The only country where in 1968 the whole structure of society was called into question more than in France was Czechoslovakia, with the 'Prague Spring' and the Russian invasion in August).
4. Quoted in Joffrin, op. cit., p. 9.
5. E. Morin/C. Lefort/C. Castoriadis, *Mai 68: la brèche suivi de Vingt ans après* (Paris: Editions Complexe, 1988), p. 148.
6. Sigmund Freud, 'New Introductory Lectures on Psychoanalysis', *Standard Edition*, Hogarth/Institute of Psychoanalysis, London, 1964, Vol. XXII, p. 113.
7. Morin, op. cit., p. 181.
8. Ibid., p. 33.
9. J. Fourastié, *Les trente glorieuses ou la révolution invisible de 1947*, (Paris: Fayard, 1979).
10. M. Winock, *Chronique des années soixante* (Paris: Seuil, 1987), p. 112.
11. See J. Capdevielle and R. Mouriaux, *Mai 68: l'entre-deux de la modernité* (Paris: Presses de la Fondation Nationale des Sciences Politiques, 1988), p. 25.
12. A. Delale and G. Ragache, *La France de 68* (Paris: Seuil, 1978), p. 11. Capdevielle/Mouriaux and Delale/Ragache both give admirably well-documented accounts of social movements and tendencies at which I have only the space to hint here.
13. For a full account of these developments see H. Hamon and P. Rotman, *Génération I: Les années de rêve* (Paris: Seuil, 1987). For the significance of Mao in France, see K. A. Reader, *Intellectuals and the Left in France since 1968* (London: Macmillan, 1987), pp. 9–10.
14. The situationists' activities up to and in 1968 are more fully documented in R. Viénet, *Enragés et situationnistes dans le mouvement des occupations* (Paris: Gallimard, 1968) (the Strasbourg pamphlet is reproduced on pp. 219–43), and P. Dumontier, *Les Situationnistes et mai 68* (Paris: Gérard Lebovici, 1990).
15. Capdevielle and Mouriaux, op. cit., p. 24. (The original French uses the term

'*insaisissables*', here rendered by 'hard(er) to grasp', which was used by de Gaulle himself while the events were at their height).

16. R. Merle's *Derrière la vitre* (Paris: Gallimard, 1970), to be considered more fully in Chapter 5, gives a vivid fictionalised account of this.
17. According to Joffrin, op. cit., p. 49.
18. Ibid., p. 64.
19. A. Schnapp and P. Vidal-Naquet's fundamental *Journal de la commune étudiante* (Paris: Seuil, 1969; second edition 1988), brings together 362 texts and documents produced between November 1967 and June 1968, representing all shades of opinion and social groupings, including fascist students, Parisian priests and doctors.
20. Joffrin, op. cit., pp. 113–14. (The *Versaillais* were the soldiers who bloodily suppressed the Paris Commune of 1871.)
21. This term, drawn from M. Bakhtin's *Problems of Dostoevsky's Poetics*, trans. Emerson (Manchester: Manchester University Press, 1984), pertains to what Bakhtin calls the 'serio-comical' – an appropriate epithet for May.
22. Delale and Ragache, op. cit., p. 79.
23. A Dansette, *Mai 68* (Paris: Plon, 1971), p. 248.
24. The full text of the agreement is to be found in Capdevielle and Mouriaux, op. cit., pp. 147–52.
25. Delalae and Ragache, op. cit., p. 113.
26. Hamon and Rotman, *Génération I*, p. 666.
27. Quoted in Joffrin, op. cit., p. 254, and Hamon and Rotman, *Génération I*, p. 555.
28. For a discussion of the complex, but by no means irrelevant, constitutional issues Mitterrand's declaration raised, see Joffrin, op. cit., pp. 156–9.
29. J. Thibaudeau, *Mai 68 en France* (Paris: Seuil, 1970), p. 107.
30. J. Massu, *Baden 68* (Paris: Plon, 1983).
31. G. Pompidou, *Pour rétablir une vérité* (Paris: Flammarion, 1982), p. 192.
32. Lacouture, *De Gaulle III: Le Souverain* (Paris: Seuil, 1986), p. 690.
33. Lacouture, op. cit., p. 697.
34. Lacouture, op. cit., p. 713.
35. Joffrin, op. cit., p. 296. De Gaulle's speech is reproduced in its entirety on pp. 295–6.
36. Delale and Ragache (op. cit., p. 230) list nineteen deaths attributable to the events (including a 67-year-old who threw a bottle of sulphuric acid at his son during a political argument and himself died from the fumes!); it is significant that only six of these took place in the month of May.
37. Hamon and Rotman, op. cit., p. 487.
38. E. Pisier, 'Paradoxes du gauchisme', *Pouvoirs*, no 39, 1986, p. 23.

2 The Interpretations of the Crisis of May/June 1968

These notes are all translated from the original French; I have given the French title alone where either the sense is self-evident or the work is referred to, and an English translation provided, in the body of my own text. K.A.R.

1. Individual authors sometimes proffer multiple lines of explanation, so that

we undoubtedly risk simplifying their ideas. It still seemed more useful to bring together the main interpretations, despite the inevitable degree of arbitrariness, than to analyse this or that author's thought in detail.

2. More than 120 books on May were published in France, and this number does not include special numbers and journal articles.

3. In his speech of 10 April 1969, quoted in *Le Monde*, 12 April.

4. Quoted in *Le Monde*, 1 June 1968.

5. Quoted in *Le Monde*, 11 March 1969.

6. Cf. *Le Monde*, 1–2 March 1970.

7. In a broadcast speech of 12 June, *Le Monde*, 14 June 1969.

8. Raymond Marcellin, *L'ordre public et les groupes révolutionnaires* (Paris: Plon, 1969), p. 14.

9. Ibid., pp. 12–13.

10. Ibid., pp. 72–3.

11. *L'éducation nationale et la participation* (Paris: Plon [Tribune Libre], 1968), p. 15.

12. The PCF's position is expounded by Waldeck Rochet, *Les enseignements de mai–juin* (Paris: Éditions Sociales, 1968). This can be contrasted with the conclusion of Annie Kriegel, *Les communistes français* (Paris: Seuil, 1969), which discusses the party's attitude during May, and with Georges Lavau's remarks on the Party's 'tribune function' in the collective work *Le communisme français* (Paris: Armand Colin, 1969). See also the article – far from indulgent toward the PCF – by Marc Goldstein, 'Le PCF du 3 mai au 16 juin 1968', *Les Temps modernes*, November 1968, pp. 827–94.

13. François Duprat, *Les journées de mai 1968, les dessous d'une révolution*, (Paris: Nouvelles Éditions Latines, 1968).

14. On the origin of the *groupuscules*, see Jean Bertolino's lively account, *Les trublions/The troublemakers*, (Paris: Stock, 1969); the different movements' ideologies are analysed by Richard Gombin, *Le projet révolutionnaire*, (Paris: Mouton, 1969).

15. The 'minority' tendency was, in fact, the Left fraction of the UNEF which, despite its name, had been in a majority since 1956.

16. The title of an anonymous document distributed in May 1968 by Jesuits of the Action Populaire group, reproduced in Jean-Raymond Tournoux's *Le mois du mai du Général* (Paris: Plon, 1969), pp. 163–80.

17. Broadcast speech of 24 May 1968, reproduced in *Le Monde* of 26 May 1968.

18. The most precise study of the origins of the university crisis is Raymond Boudon's 'La crise universitaire française: Essai de diagnostique sociologique', *Les Annales*, May–June 1969. See also the same author's shorter 'Quelques causes de la révolte estudiantine', *La Table Ronde*, no. 251–2, December 1968–January 1969.

19. Épistémon, *Ces idées qui ont ébranlé la France* (Paris: Fayard, 1968). The author teaches social psychology at Nanterre. While his work is always interesting, his description of the atmosphere at Nanterre should be contrasted with that of Grappin who, in resigning as Dean, denounced a situation that had become 'intolerable for the very reasons that once led me to fight Nazism' (contempt for culture, intolerance, etc.) (*Le Monde*, 20 September 1968).

20. To counter a common misconception, the organisation of the university dates back not to Napoleon, but to the beginnings of the Third Republic.
21. Jean-Denis Bredin, 'L'application de la loi d'orientation à l'enseignement supérieur', *Le Monde*, 7–8 September 1969. The author, a law professor, was among the main architects of the law in question.
22. This conference occurred in November 1966. Excerpts from it were published in *La Revue de l'enseignement supérieur*, no. 4, 1966.
23. Michel Crozier, 'Révolution libérale ou révolte petite-bourgeoise', *Communications*, no. 12, 1968, pp. 39–40.
24. The conflict between senior and junior lecturing staff was certainly connected with the great rise in the number of the latter over the previous decade (see Boudon, in his *Les Annales* article, p. 741).
25. The figures from 1900 to 1966 are borrowed from Boudon in *La Table Ronde*. The subsequent figures (which do not include students at the Grandes Écoles) come from the Education Ministry.
26. See the sharp rise in failures in the CAPES competitive secondary-school teaching examination, easy to pass only a few years earlier.
27. Boudon, *La Table Ronde*, pp. 172–3.
28. Ibid., pp. 174–5.
29. Ibid., pp. 176–7.
30. Boudon, *Les Annales*, p. 755.
31. Surveys very clearly confirm how deeply worried students are about their professional future – see the IFOP survey in *Réalités*, November 1968.
32. Bourdieu and Passeron's *Les héritiers* (Paris: Minuit, 1964) showed at length that young people from well-off backgrounds had far more chance than those from disadvantaged social groups of entering higher education.
33. Another expression of Paul Nizan's was widely used in May, this time from *Aden-Arabie*: 'I was twenty years old. I will let nobody say that those are the best years of your life.'
34. From the Strasbourg situationist brochure reproduced in R. Viénet, *Enragés et situationnistes dans le mouvement des occupations* (Paris: Gallimard, 1968), pp. 219–43.
35. A speech of 24 July 1968 reproduced in E. Faure, *L'Éducation nationale et la participation* (Paris: Plon 1968), p. 21.
36. In a speech of Lons-le-Saunier, 15 February 1969, reproduced in *Le Figaro*, 17 February 1969.
37. N. Bisseret, '"La naissance" et le diplôme – les processus de sélection au début des études universitaires', *Revue française de sociologie*, Vol. II, special number, 1968, p. 197.
38. B. Kayser and P. de Gaudemar, *Dix années d'une génération d'étudiants de la Faculté des lettres et sciences humaines de Toulouse*, Association des publications de la Faculté des lettres et sciences humaines de Toulouse, 1967: reviewed in *Le Monde*, 27 June 1967.
39. C. Delage, *La naissance d'une université*, thesis at Orléans University alluded to in Boudon (*Les Annales*), p. 754.
40. Cf. Boudon, op. cit., pp. 753–4.
41. J.-C. Passeron, 'La relation pédagogique et le système d'enseignement', *Prospective*, no. 14, 1967, p. 152.

42. These manifestos – like their counterparts on the ministerial side – scarcely clarify the fundamental ambiguities that plague this type of accusation: how precisely should we understand expressions such as 'bourgeois culture', 'class culture', 'the culture of the cultured class'? Is culture spread by elementary-school education also 'bourgeois culture'?

43. Numerous tracts dealing with this problem are produced in A. Schnapp and P. Vidal-Nacquet, *Journal de la commune étudiante* (Paris: Seuil, 1969), pp. 163–73.

44. J. Monnerot, 'De la révolte étudiante à la grève générale', *Le Monde*, 8 June 1968.

45. V. J. Mossuz, 'Le mouvement étudiant dans le monde', pp. 167–204 of J. Meyriat (ed.), *L'Univers politique. Relations internationales* (Paris: Richelieu, 1969).

46. From the title to the first chapter of A. Fontaine's *La guerre civile froide*, (Paris: Fayard, 1968).

47. Cf. Viansson-Ponté's notorious 'La France s'ennuie', in *Le Monde* of 15 March 1968.

48. Certain texts about May are reminiscent of Simone Weil's celebrated writings on the festival of June 1936 and the discovery of joy, though the context of that time was an altogether different one.

49. R. Aron, *La révolution introuvable*, (Paris: Fayard, 1968), pp. 33, 38, 51.

50. Ibid., p. 32.

51. Ibid., p. 47.

52. Ibid., pp. 31–2.

53. Ibid., p. 31. (The authors believe the almost total lack of horizontal structures in the student movement – the result of its major crisis since the Algerian war – to be much more significant than problems of vertical communication between students and lecturers. It is not paradoxical to argue that such communication was much easier in the overcrowded faculties of 1968 than in the Sorbonne of the 1930s.)

54. Tocqueville's *Souvenirs* are abundantly cited in one of Aron's *Figaro* articles of 28 May 1968.

55. The title of an article in *Preuves*, February–March 1969, pp. 74–81.

56. *France-Forum*, October–November 1968, p. 4. This article includes an excerpt from Roger Caillois's *L'Homme et le sacré* that is strikingly relevant to May.

57. Épistémon,.op. cit., p. 129.

58. *Études*, June–July 1968, p. 29 (and also in the same author's *La prise de parole* (Paris: Desclée de Brouwer, 1968).

59. See J. Besançon, *Les murs ont la parole*, (Paris: Plon, 1968).

60. Pascal, op. cit., p. 7.

61. J.-M. Domenach, 'L'idéologie du mouvement', *Esprit*, no. 8–9, August–September 1968.

62. B. Cardonneau, 'L'émeute et le plan', *La Table Ronde*, no. 251-2, December 1968–January 1969, p. 30.

63. E. Morin/C. Lefort/J.-M. Coudray (an alias for C. Castoriadis – *translator's note*), *La brèche* (Paris: Fayard, 1968), pp. 26–7.

64. Cf. M. Faure, 'Le monde rural et la crise de mai', *Paysans*, May 1968.

65. *L'Express*, 17–23 February and 24 February–2 March 1969.

66. Thus, in answer to the question 'Is the May–June crisis a reason for hope or one for anxiety?', 41 per cent said 'hope', 47 per cent 'anxiety' and 12 per cent did not know.
67. A. Stéphane, *L'univers contestationnaire*, (Paris: Payot, 1969).
68. Op. cit., p. 34.
69. Ibid., p. 293.
70. Ibid., pp. 294–5.
71. 'Les retombées', *Le Monde*, 20 December 1968.
72. *Esprit*, no. 6–7, June–July 1968, pp. 965–9.
73. J. Maritain, *Pour une philosophie de l'éducation* (Paris: Fayard, 1969), pp. 118–19.
74. Quoted in Tournoux, op. cit., p. 121.
75. Perhaps surprisingly, the quantity of manifestos and tracts that speak of the 'consumer society' is comparatively small (see Schnapp and Vidal-Nacquet, op. cit., pp. 356, 566–9, 595–8). Nor was the 'consumer society' invented in May (see the work of H. Lefebvre, P. Trotignon's description of the 'great whore of the consumer society' in the special number of *L'Arc* devoted to Sartre in 1966).
76. V. A. Coutrot, 'Des catholiques s'expriment', in *Recherches et débats*, (Paris: Desclée de Brouwer, 1966). Jean Guitton says of Cohn-Bendit: 'I feel very close to him through an aspiration towards infinity', *Que faisaient-ils en avril?* (Paris: Desclée de Brouwer, 1969), p. 168.
77. See the articles of C. Roy, 'La question du bonheur', and J. Le Veugle, 'Une révolution culturelle, oui mais laquelle?', *La Monde*, 23 May 1968.
78. Published in *Réalités*, November 1968.
79. *Esprit*, no. 6–7, June–July 1968, p. 969.
80. Ibid., p. 1030.
81. Speech at the Paris Parc des Expositions, 20 June 1968.
82. Speech in Strasbourg, reprinted in *Le Monde*, 15 May 1969.
83. The title of a book by the anarcho-syndicalist thinker Georges Sorel.
84. A. Touraine, *La mouvement de mai ou le communisme utopique*, (Paris: Seuil, 1968), pp. 14–15.
85. Ibid., p. 20.
86. Loc. cit.
87. Ibid., p. 22.
88. Loc. cit.
89. Ibid., p. 26.
90. Ibid., p. 20.
91. Ibid., p. 16.
92. Loc. cit.
93. Ibid., p. 280.
94. Ibid., p. 193.
95. Ibid., p. 17.
96. See François Bourricaud's critique 'Alain Touraine à la recherche du sujet historique', *Preuves*, July–September 1969.
97. The following paragraphs closely follow a paper given by Jean-Claude Casanova on 30 November 1968 to a day conference organised by the Fondation nationale des sciences politiques.
98. In 1966 and 1967, and even through into 1968, three tendencies combined to

slow consumption: a short-term policy of expansion via exports rather than individual consumption, mid-term planning that favoured State rather then private consumption, and social policies (including the restructuring of social security and the reform of the public sector). The 'consumer society' was thus indicted during a period of reduced consumption.

99. R. Aron concludes a short analysis of the economic situation just before May by saying: 'There would have been less dissatisfaction had the government taken the risk of a temporary shortfall in the balance of payments' (op. cit., p. 95).

100. Waldeck Rochet, *L'avenir du PCF*, (Paris: Grasset, 1969), pp. 9–11 and 12.

101. V. F. Bon's analysis 'Structure de l'idéologie communiste', in the collective work *Le communisme en France*, (Paris: Armand Colin, 1969).

102. Cf. *Sondages*, no. 2, 1968, p. 9.

103. Ibid., p. 16.

104. Reprinted in Aron, op. cit., pp. 167–8.

105. Ibid., p. 97.

106. P. Avril, 'L' amplificateur de crise', *France-Forum*, October–November 1968, pp. 21–4.

107. In a speech given to the Club Nouvelle Frontière at Gif-sur-Yvette in November 1968.

108. *Le bipartisme, est-il possible en France?*, Association française de science politique, February 1965, p. 6.

109. *France-Forum*, no. 65–70, January–February 1966, p. 18.

110. See, for instance, J.-L. Chardin, *Revue française de science politique*, February 1966.

111. To quote Witold Gombrowicz in *Le Monde* of 2 November 1968: 'They say that behind Stokely Carmichael at the start there were 500 Blacks and 5000 journalists, and for Cohn-Bendit it is exactly the same. At that age it is hard not to take oneself for an instrument of History when one sees oneself on the front page of every single magazine. Young people believed this, they became too self-important; and adults took fright and backed down. The monster of youth as we see it now is our own creation as adults.'

112. To cite the title of P. Combs's *La crise mondiale de l'éducation*, (Paris: Preses Universitaires de France, 1968).

113. A few eye-witness accounts (A. Rouède's 'La révolte des lycéens' in *Esprit*, June–July 1968), partial reports (Ch. IX of S. Zegel's *Les idées de mai* [Paris: Gallimard, 1968] and such texts as *Les lycéens ont la parole*, [Paris: Seuil 1968], and *Partisans*, no. 49, September–October 1969). There are scarcely any overall analyses, and the most interesting study – G. Vincent's 'Essai sur la perception de la politisation des lycéens', *Revue française de pédagogie*, April–June 1969) – does not, on its own author's admission, close the debate.

114. Tournoux, op. cit.; P. Alexandre, *L'Élysée en péril* (Paris: Fayard, 1969); C. Paillat, *Archives secrètes 1968–1969* (Paris: Denoël, 1969).

115. Such as A. Barjonet, *La Révolution trahie* (Paris: Didier, 1968).

116. Paillat, op. cit., is an example.

117. See Y. Guin's (ideologically biased) *La commune de Nantes* (Paris: Maspéro, 1969).

118. M.-F. and R. Mouriaux, 'La mai des prolétaires à Usinor-Dunkerque', *Politique aujourd'hui*, February 1970; J. Blancherie *et al.*, *Les évènements de mai–*

juin 1968 à travers cent entreprises, Centre national d'information pour la productivité des entreprises, 1968; P. Bacot, *La CFDT et les grèves de mai–juin 1968 dans le région lyonnaise* (Lyon: Agel, 1969). See also the titles listed by D. Woronof, 'Pour une historire de mai', *Politique aujourd'hui*, August–September 1969.

119. Cf. J.-M. Leuwers, *Un peuple se dresse, Luttes ouvrières mai 1968*, (Paris: Éditions ouvrières, 1969).

120. 'Étude statistique des grèves de mai–juin 1968', *Revue française de science politique*, February 1970. This analysis does not corroborate (to put it mildly) theories about the determining role of the 'new working class'.

121. Opinion polls carried out in May highlight two facts: that the population of Paris, by and large favourable to the student demonstrations in the first half of May, had become hostile to them after the 24 May demonstration – well before de Gaulle's 30 May speech; and that there was a striking gap between feeling in Paris and in the provinces, where people had many more reservations about the student movement from the beginning (*Sondages*, 1968, no. 2).

122. J. Gretton's *Students and Workers* (London: MacDonald, 1968), has short appendices dealing with Dijon, Grenoble and Avranches (in Burgundy, the French Alps and Normandy respectively – *translator's note*).

123. G. Chaffard, *Les orages de mai*, Calmann-Lévy, Paris, 1968.

124. Works written before – sometimes well before – May can be thought-provoking: Georges Sorel's work on myth and violence, Tarde's on imitation, Riesman's on the lonely crowd, Sartre's (*Critique de la raison dialectique*) on existential revolt against the world of the 'practico-inert', Michael Crozier's on the 'French model of authority', Marcuse's *Eros and Civilisation*, and so forth.

125. No separate bibliography was provided for this article, whose extensive footnotes made that unnecessary – *translator's note*.

3 Other Interpretations of the Events

1. Capdevielle and Mouriaux, op. cit., p. 168, footnote 1, speak of it as 'an indispensable tool', while drawing attention to some of its lacunae (failure to deal with Sartre or Lefebvre, ignoring the – in my view relative – silence of Althusser and Bourdieu).

2. B. LaCroix, 'A contre-courant: le parti-pris du réalisme'/'Against the current: the *parti-pris* of realism', in *Pouvoirs*, no. 9, 1986, p. 119.

3. See below, pp. 89–90.

4. Lavoix, op. cit., p. 124. (For discussion of Salvaressi see below, pp. 121–2; Vincennes was the experimental university set up after 1968 as part of the government's response to the upheaval in the universities.)

5. P. Ory, *L'Aventure culturelle française, 1945–1989* (Paris: Flammarion, 1989), p. 61.

6. I use the term 'Socialists' here rather than PS since the latter did not come into existence until 1971.

7. Ory, *L'entre-deux-mai* (Paris: Seuil, 1983), p. 67.

8. Ory, *L'aventure culturelle française, 1945–1989*, p. 181.

9. The role of Jack Lang, the Socialist Minister of Culture, in propagating this ethos is an important one, for which, see D. Looseley, 'Jack Lang and the politics of festival', *French Cultural Studies*, Vol. 1, no. 1, pp. 4–19.
10. G. Debord, *La Société du spectacle* (Paris: Gérard Lebovici, 1987), p. 10.
11. Ibid., p. 11.
12. Ibid., p. 94.
13. Guy Debord, *Commentaires sur la société du spectacle* (Paris: Éditions Gérard Lebovici, 1988), p. 18.
14. Ibid., p. 23.
15. R. Vaneigem, *The Revolution of Everyday Life*, trans. Nicholson-Smith, (London: Left Bank Books/Rebel Press, 1983), p. 192.
16. Ibid., p. 8.
17. Ibid., p. 114.
18. Ibid., p. 209.
19. Ibid., p. 118.
20. In Viénet, op. cit., p. 220.
21. Merle, op. cit., p. 242.
22. Viénet, op. cit., p. 232.
23. Ibid., p. 234.
24. For a much more thorough analysis of the stances taken by the numerous left-wing groups in May than I have space for here, see R. Gombin, *Le Projet révolutionnaire* (Paris/The Hague: Mouton, 1969) and *Les Origines du gauchisme* (Paris: Seuil, 1971).
25. Dumontier, op. cit., pp. 222–3. ('Play' translates the French *jeu*, which understood as both the autonomous 'play' of parts of a machine and 'play' in its ludic sense is an important concept in the work of Barthes and other modern French thinkers.)
26. D. Cohn-Bendit (trans. Pomerans), *Obsolete Communism – the left-wing alternative* (Harmondsworth: Penguin, 1969).
27. I shall use the singular despite the book's joint authorship, both because much of it is written in the first person singular and because 'the Cohn-Bendits' has overtones of the dinner-party couple or (less inappositely) the vaudeville stage.
28. Ibid., p. 16.
29. Ibid., p. 179.
30. Ibid., p. 208.
31. Ibid., p. 12.
32. Ibid., p. 12.
33. Ibid., p. 253.
34. Ibid., p. 11.
35. Loc. cit.
36. E. Pisier, 'Paradoxes du gauchisme', *Pouvoirs*, no. 39, 1986, p. 23.
37. D. Bensaïd/A. Krivine/H. Weber, *Mai 68 – une répétition générale* (Paris: Maspéro, 1968), p. 17.
38. Ibid., p. 179.
39. Ibid., p. 143.
40. Ibid., p. 121.
41. Ibid., p. 177.
42. J. Delperrie de Bayac, *Histoire du Front Populaire*, (Paris: Marabout, 1972), p. 233.

43. Bensaïd *et al.*, op. cit., p. 192.
44. D. Bensaïd/A. Krivine, *Mai si! – 1968–1988: rebelles et repentis* (Montreuil: La Brèche, 1988), p. 46.
45. Ibid., p. 48.
46. A term used, with varying degrees of irony, to describe those active in or influenced by the movement and ideas of May.
47. Bensaïd/Krivine, op. cit., p. 163.
48. A. Barjonet, *La Révolution trahie de 1968* (Paris: John Didier, 1968), p. 22.
49. Ibid., p. 27.
50. J. Jurquet, *Le printemps révolutionnaire de 1968* (Paris: Gît-le-Coeur, 1968), p. 63.
51. Ibid., p. 10.
52. Ibid., p. 49.
53. Ibid., p. 55.
54. S. July, A. Geismar, E. Morane, *Vers la guerre civile* (Paris: Éditions Premières, 1969), p. 16.
55. Ibid., p. 381.
56. Ibid., p. 179.
57. Ibid., p. 158.
58. Ibid., p. 154.
59. Ibid., p. 179.
60. July *et al.*, op. cit., p. 180.
61. Ibid., p. 58.
62. Ibid., p. 204.
63. Ibid., p. 401.
64. Ibid., p. 185.
65. A. Glucksmann, *Stratégie et Révolution en France*, (Paris: Bourgois, 1968), p. 121.
66. Ibid., p. 37.
67. Ibid., p. 27.
68. Ibid., p. 9.
69. Ibid., p. 19.
70. Ibid., p. 22.
71. This will be discussed in more detail in Chapter 4 *à propos* Hamon and Rotman's *Génération*.
72. This term refers to a group of (mostly) quondam Maoists who were led by their reading of Solzhenitsyn in the mid-1970s to reject Marxism as necessarily a philosophy of domination, and moved towards a diffuse spirituality reflected in their numerous books, notably for the publishing-house Grasset.
73. See V. P. Chilton, 'Glucksmannstalk: Packaging the Force', *Modern and Contemporary France*, no. 20 (December 1984), pp. 32–6.
74. July *et. al.*, op. cit., p. 308.
75. Ibid., p. 38.
76. G. Delannoi, *Les Années utopiques 1968–1978/The utopian years: 1968–1978*, (Paris: La Découverte, 1990), p. 90.
77. Ibid., p. 96.
78. Though not an institutional one, for he had been educated at the far more privileged École Normale Supérieure; see J.-P. Sartre, *Situations VIII*, (Paris: Gallimard, 1972), p. 185.
79. Ibid., p. 222.

80. Ibid., p. 184.
81. See ibid., p. 194.
82. Ibid., p. 199.
83. J.-P. Sartre, *Situations X* (Paris: Gallimard, 1976), p. 45.
84. C. Jouriès, 'Les interprétations communistes de mai 68', in *Pouvoirs*, no. 39, 1986, p. 29.
85. Sartre, op. cit., p. 27.
86. Ibid., p. 35.
87. Waldeck Rochet, *Les Enseignements de mai–juin 1968* (Paris: Éditions Sociales, 1968), p. 16.
88. Ibid., p. 32.
89. Ibid., p. 63.
90. Ibid., p. 80.
91. L. Althusser, in M.-A. Macciochi, *Letters from inside the Italian Communist party to Louis Althusser*, trans. Hellmann (London: New Left Books, 1973), p. 301.
92. Ibid., p. 302.
93. Ibid., pp. 302–3.
94. Ibid., p. 303.
95. See Hamon and Rotman, *Génération I*, pp. 480–1.
96. Althusser, op. cit., p. 309.
97. Ibid., p. 314.
98. Ibid., p. 318.
99. L. Althusser, trans. Brewster, 'Ideology and Ideological State Apparatuses', in *Lenin and Philosophy and other essays* (London: New Left Books, 1971), p. 160.
100. R. Martelli, *Mai 68* (Paris: Messidor/Éditions Sociales, 1988), p. 6.
101. Ibid., p. 7.
102. Ibid., p. 228.
103. Ibid., p. 238.
104. *New Left Review*, no. 115, London, 1979.
105. (Ed. A Clark), *Anthologie Mitterrand* (London: Methuen, 1986), p. 99.
106. Ibid., p. 100.
107. Ibid., p. 98.
108. Ibid., p. 99.
109. Ibid., p. 101.
110. Quoted in ibid., p. 22.
111. *Situations VIII*, p. 223.
112. M. Gallo, *Gauchisme, réforme et révolution* (Paris: Robert Laffont, 1968), p. 179.
113. Ibid., pp. 148–9.
114. Ibid., p. 115.
115. Ibid., p. 73.
116. G. Martinet, *La Conquête des pouvoirs* (Paris: Seuil, 1968), p. 8.
117. Ibid., p. 11.
118. Ibid., p. 161.
119. Ibid., p. 104.
120. Ibid., p. 112.
121. Ibid., p. 38.

122. Ibid., p. 59.
123. J.-J. Servan-Schreiber, *Le Réveil de la France* (Paris: Denoël, 1968), p. 23.
124. Club Jean Moulin, *Que faire de la révolution de mai?: six priorités* (Paris: Seuil, 1968), p. 11.
125. Ibid., p. 82.
126. D. Barbet, 'Interprétations syndicales/Trade-union interpretations', in *Pouvoirs*, no. 39, 1986, p. 51.
127. P. Dubois, R. Dulong, C. Durand, S. Erbès-Seguin, D. Vidal, *Grèves revendicatives ou grèves politiques?* (Paris: Anthropos, 1971), p. 472.
128. Ibid., p. 542.
129. Ibid., p. 71.
130. Ibid., p. 150.
131. P. Gavi, *Les Ouvriers: du tiercé à la révolution* (Paris: Mercure de France, 1970), p. 31.
132. P. Bauchard and M. Bruzek, *Le Syndicalisme à l'épreuve* (Paris: Robert Laffont, 1968), p. 91.
133. Gavi, op. cit., p. 15.
134. J. Frémontier, *La Forteresse ouvrière – Renault* (Paris: Fayard, 1971), p. 11.
135. Ibid., p. 155.
136. A. Renaut, 'La Révolution introuvable', in *Pouvoirs*, no. 39, Paris, 1986, p. 82.
137. R. Aron, *La Révolution introuvable* (Paris: Fayard, 1968), p. 26.
138. Ibid., p. 14.
139. Ibid., p. 32.
140. Ibid., p. 43.
141. Ibid., p. 100.
142. Ibid., p. 68.
143. Ibid., p. 122.
144. Ibid., pp. 89–90.
145. Ibid., p. 133.
146. Ibid., p. 110.
147. Ibid., p. 145.
148. Ibid., p. 37.
149. J. Laurent, *Lettre ouverte aux étudiants* (Paris: Albin Michel, 1969), p. 10.
150. Ibid., p. 33.
151. Ibid., p. 120.
152. Ibid., p. 100.
153. A. Griotteray, *Des barricades ou des réformes?* (Paris: Fayard, 1968), p. 24.
154. Ibid., p. 36.
155. Ibid., p. 48.
156. The youngest, Georges Bidault, held power for only five months during the post-Second World War interim.
157. Griotteray, op. cit., p. 68. (The 'red/black' reference can be read as a laboured pun on the two flags omnipresent in May and the title of Stendhal's novel *Le Rouge et le noir/Scarlet and Black*, the tale of an ambitious young man's attempts to rise to power in the ossified France of 1827.)
158. Quoted in Schnapp and Vidal-Nacquet, op. cit., pp. 375–6.
159. F. Duprat, *Les Journées de mai 68 – les dessous d'une révolution* (Paris: Nouvelles Éditions Latines, 1968), p. 98.

160. Though it is confined neither to France nor to conservatives, as the Wodgate scenes in Disraeli's *Sybil* and the 'Cour des Miracles' in Victor Hugo's *Notre-Dame de Paris* respectively demonstrate.
161. Duprat, op. cit., p. 175.
162. Ibid., p. 192.
163. Ibid., p. 202.
164. R. Marcellin, *L'Ordre public et les groupes révolutionnaires* (Paris: Plon, 1969), p. 73.
165. Ibid., p. 12.
166. Ibid., p. 34.
167. Ibid., p. 70.
168. Ibid., p. 37.
169. G. Lange, 'L'exemple caennais/The example of Caen', in G. Dreyfus-Armand and L Gervereau (eds), *Mai 68: les mouvements étudiants en France et dans le monde* (Nanterre: 1988), Bibliothèque de Documentation Internationale Contemporaine, p. 208.
170. Ibid., p. 209. (The 'years of powder' is a reference to the title of the second volume of Hamon and Rotman's *Génération*).
171. Dansette, op. cit., p. 293.
172. Y. Guin, *La Commune de Nantes* (Paris: Maspéro, 1969), p. 93.
173. Ibid., p. 140.
174. Ibid., p. 143.
175. G. Chaffard, *Les Orages de Mai* (Paris: Calmann-Lévy, 1968), p. 101.
176. Ibid., p. 94.
177. Ibid., p. 151.

4 Cultural Interpretations of the Events

1. M. Blanchot, quoted in J. Baynac, *Mai retrouvé* (Paris: Laffont, 1978), p. 218.
2. See above, p. 3.
3. J.-C. Guillebaud, *Les Années orphelines* (Paris: Seuil, 1978), p. 7.
4. Ibid., p. 54.
5. Ibid., p. 77.
6. Ibid., p. 107.
7. P. Bourdieu and J-C Passeron, *Les Héritiers* (Paris: Minuit, 1964), p. 53.
8. Ibid., p. 72. (The 'intellectual consensus' referred to had been a left-wing one in Paris at least since the end of the Second World War).
9. Ibid., p. 75.
10. For which latter see below, p. 104.
11. For more detailed exposition of this see Reader, op. cit., pp. 120–31.
12. See R. Williams, *Marxism and Literature* (Oxford: Oxford University Press, 1977), pp. 121–7.
13. See Régis Debray's *Le Pouvoir intellectuel en France/Intellectual Power in France* (Paris: Ramsay, 1979) for an extended consideration for this phenomenon.
14. Épistémon, *Ces idées qui ont ébranlé la France*, (Paris: Fayard, 1968), p. 47.
15. Ibid., p. 29.
16. Loc. cit.

17. T. Judt, *Marxism and the French Left* (Oxford: Clarendon Press, 1986), p. 194.
18. Ibid., p. 225.
19. Reproduced in Schnapp and Vidal-Nacquet, op. cit., pp. 626–37.
20. Ibid., p. 627.
21. Ibid., p. 632.
22. Baynac, op. cit., p. 82. ('Great moment' renders the French *grand soir* – the 'great evening' on which in anarchist and communist discourse the revolutionary transformation of society would occur.)
23. See R. Barthes, 'Poujade et les intellectuels', in *Mythologies* (Paris: Seuil, 1957), pp. 182–90.
24. Baynac, op. cit., p. 164.
25. A. Dansette, *Mai 68* (Paris: Plon, 1971), p. 167.
26. Épistémon, op. cit., p. 108.
27. 'L'atelier populaire de l'ex-École des Beaux-Arts: entretien avec Gérard Fromanger', in Dreyfus-Armand and Gervereau, op. cit., p. 185.
28. Ibid., p. 186.
29. 'L'atelier des Arts-décoratifs: entretien avec François Miehe et Gérard Paris-Clavel', in Dreyfus-Armand and Gervereau, op. cit., p. 195.
30. Ibid., p. 190.
31. Ibid., p. 197.
32. C. Frédéric, *Libérer l'ORTF* (Paris: Seuil, 1968), p. 144.
33. P. Langlois and G. Myrent, *Henri Langlois* (Paris: Denoël, 1986), pp. 349–50.
34. Ibid., p. 347.
35. See S. Harvey's invaluable *May '68 and Film Culture* (London: British Film Institute, 1978), for fuller information of these proposals and other aspects of the subject.
36. R. Lourau, *L'Analyse institutionnelle* (Paris: Minuit, 1970), p. 73.
37. Ibid., p. 19.
38. A. Touraine, *Le Mouvement de mai ou le communisme utopique* (Paris: Seuil, 1968), pp. 43–4.
39. Ibid., p. 45.
40. All in quotation marks loc. cit.; the descriptions are my own.
41. Touraine, op. cit., p. 9.
42. Ibid., p. 12.
43. Ibid., p. 25.
44. Ibid., p. 22.
45. Ibid., p. 123.
46. Ibid., p. 189.
47. Ibid., p. 285.
48. I use the term here as an (inadequate) rendition of the French *jouir* with its orgasmic connotations, used by Roland Barthes in particular to suggest a kind of bliss more threatening to the secure haven of subjectivity than pleasure (*plaisir*).
49. The quotations from Morin and Castoriadis are taken from sections of E. Morin, C. Lefort and C. Castoriadis, *Mai 68: la brèche suivi de vingt ans après*, (Paris: Éditions Complexe, 1988).
50. Ibid., p. 31.
51. Ibid., p. 32.

52. Ibid., p. 27.
53. Ibid., p. 148.
54. Ibid., p. 152.
55. Ibid., p. 178.
56. Ibid., p. 75.
57. J. Culler, *On Deconstruction* (London/Melbourne/Henley: Routledge & Kegan Paul, 1983), p. 247.
58. Castoriadis, op. cit., p. 124.
59. Loc. cit.
60. Lefort, op. cit., p. 71.
61. H. Lefebvre, *L'Irruption: de Nanterre au sommet* (Paris: Anthropos, 1968), p. 7.
62. Ibid., p. 27.
63. Ibid., p. 169.
64. Ibid., p. 67.
65. Loc. cit.
66. Ibid., p. 87.
67. Dansette, op. cit., p. 128.
68. M. Bakhtin, *Problems of Dostoevsky's Poetics* (ed./trans. Emerson), (Manchester: Manchester University Press, 1984), p. 111.
69. Ibid., p. 88.
70. Ibid., p. 119.
71. Ibid., p. 123.
72. Ibid., p. 176.
73. M. de Certeau, *La Prise de la parole: pour une nouvelle culture* (Paris: Desclée de Brouwer, 1968), p. 27.
74. Ibid., p. 40.
75. V. supra.
76. De Certeau, op. cit., p. 48.
77. Ibid., p. 71.
78. Ibid., p. 12.
79. Ibid., p. 122.
80. M. Clavel, *Ce que je crois* (Paris: Grasset, 1975), p. 140.
81. J. Marny (ed.), *L'Église contestée* (Paris: Le Centurion, 1968), p. 132.
82. M.-J. Le Guillou, O. Clément and J. Bosc, *Évangile et Révolution: au coeur de notre crise spirituelle* (Paris: Centurion, 1968), p. 28.
83. Ibid., pp. 32–3.
84. J.-M. Benoist, *Marx est mort*, (Paris: Gallimard (Idées), 1970), p. 9.
85. Ibid., p. 47.
86. See, in particular, J. Derrida, *Positions* (Paris: Minuit, 1972).
87. Benoist, op. cit., p. 74.
88. Ibid., p. 82.
89. Ibid., p. 194.
90. R. Debray, *Modeste contribution aux discours et cérémonies officielles du dixième anniversaire* (Paris: François Maspéro, 1978), p. 10. (Much of this appeared in an English translation in *New Left Review*, no. 115, London, 1979).
91. Ibid., p. 13. (The French gains much force from the use of *franglais* terms such as *news* and *brainstorming*).

92. Ibid., p. 32.
93. Ibid., p. 48.
94. Ibid., p. 10.
95. For a more detailed overview of these, see K. Reader, 'The Anniversary Industry', in *Screen*, Vol. 29 no. 3, summer 1988, pp. 122–6.
96. G. Lipovetsky, *L'Ere du vide* (Paris: Gallimard, 1983), p. 7.
97. Ibid., p. 8.
98. Ibid., p. 50.
99. Ibid., p. 51.
100. Ibid., p. 245.
101. L. Ferry and A. Renaut, *68–86: itinéraires de l'individu* (Paris: Gallimard, 1987).
102. Ibid., p. 69.
103. Ibid., p. 97.
104. See F. Fukuyama's article 'The End of History' in *The National Interest*, 1989, and his book *The End of History and the Last Man* (London: Hamilton, 1992).
105. L. Ferry and A. Renaut, *68–86: itinéraires de l'individu* (Paris: Gallimard, 1987).
106. H. Weber, *Vingt ans après: que reste-t-il de 68?* (Paris: Seuil, 1988), p. 49.
107. Ibid., p. 71.
108. Ibid., p. 124.
109. Ibid., p. 166.
110. Ibid., p. 175.
111. Ibid., p. 198.
112. Ibid., p. 197.
113. Ibid., p. 208.
114. Ibid., p. 216.
115. Ibid., p. 221.
116. The title is a pun on David Rousset's anti-totalitarian *L'Univers concentrationnaire*.
117. A. Stéphane, *L'Univers contestationnaire: étude psychanalytique* (Paris: Payot, 1969), p. 70.
118. Ibid., p. 73.
119. Ibid., p. 262.
120. P. de Boisdeffre, *Lettre ouverte aux hommes de gauche* (Paris: Albin Michel, 1969), p. 89.
121. Ibid., p. 28.
122. Ibid., p. 111.
123. This title is a pun on Mallarmé's poem (which inspired the Debussy music of the same title) *L'Après-midi d'un faune.*
124. G. Hocquenghem, *L'Après-mai des faunes* (Paris: Grasset, 1974), p. 105.
125. Ibid., p. 109.
126. Ibid., p. 172.
127. Ibid., p. 165.
128. See G. Hocquenghem, 'Subversion et décadence du mâle d'après-Mai', *Autrement*, no. 12, 1978, p. 39.
129. G. Hocquenghem, *Lettre ouverte à ceux qui sont passés du col Mao au Rotary* (Paris: Albin Michel, 1986), p. 14.

130. Ibid., p. 16.
131. Ibid., p. 197.
132. Ibid., p. 48.
133. Ibid., p. 49.
134. Ibid., p. 47.

5 Reproductions of the May Events

1. French words with English translation: 'C'est la lutte finale/Groupons-nous et demain/*L'Internationale*/Sera le genre humain'/'So comrades come rally/ And the last fight let us face/*The Internationale*/Unites the human race'.
2. H. Hamon and P. Rotman, *Génération II* (Paris: Seuil, 1988), p. 627.
3. Ibid., p. 625.
4. A. Prost, in *Le Mouvement social*, no. 143 (April–June 1988), p. 95.
5. Ibid., p. 97.
6. The ex-GP leader (now a novelist) Olivier Rollin, quoted in Hamon and Rotman, op. cit., p. 648.
7. For adequate English translations see above.
8. D. Cohn-Bendit, *Nous l'avons tant aimée, la révolution* (Paris: Bernard Barrault/Points, 1986), p. 8.
9. Ibid., p. 97.
10. Ibid., p. 37.
11. Ibid., p. 88.
12. Ibid., p. 196.
13. Ibid., p. 251.
14. Loc. cit.
15. Cohn-Bendit, ibid., p. 254.
16. E. Salvaressi, *Mai en héritage* (Paris: Syros/Alternatives, 1988), p. 15.
17. Ibid., p. 16.
18. Ibid., p. 112.
19. V. supra, pp. 48–9.
20. E. Salvaressi, *Mai en héritage*, p. 108.
21. Ibid., p. 141.
22. R. Linhart, *L'Établi* (Paris: Minuit, 1978), p. 81.
23. Ibid., pp. 94–5.
24. Ibid., p. 95.
25. Ibid., p. 179.
26. D. Rondeau, *L'Enthousiasme* (Paris: Quai Voltaire, 1988), pp. 128–9.
27. Ibid., p. 49.
28. Ibid., p. 76.
29. Ibid., p. 129.
30. Ibid., p. 150.
31. Literally, an individual's 'timetable', though the English translation is the more passive *Passing Time*.
32. This letter is reproduced in its entirety in A. Gaveau, *De l'autre côté des barricades* (Paris: Jean-Claude Simoën, 1978), pp. 211–12.
33. M. Grimaud, *En mai fais ce qu'il te plaît* (Paris: Stock, 1977), p. 169.
34. Ibid., p. 101.

35. Ibid., pp. 20–1.
36. 'D'où parles-tu, camarade?' – translated as 'What's your angle, comrade?' in D. L. Hanley and R. P. Kerr (eds), *May '68: Coming of Age* (London: Macmillan, 1989), p. 10.
37. Gaveau, op. cit., p. 14.
38. Loc. cit.
39. Op. cit., p. 15.
40. Loc. cit., p. 29.
41. Op. cit., p. 210.
42. E. Balladur, *L'Arbre de Mai* (Paris: Atelier Marcel Julian, 1979), p. 8.
43. Ibid., p. 25.
44. Ibid., p. 178.
45. Ibid., p. 332.
46. Ibid., p. 124.
47. Ibid., p. 144.
48. Ibid., p. 352.
49. P. Combes, *La Littérature et le mouvement de mai 68*, doctoral thesis, pp. 6–7. (This work was published by Seghers in Paris, 1984, but the only form in which I was able to consult it was the original thesis, from which page references are consequently taken.)
50. J. Durandeaux, *Les Journées de mai 68* (Paris: Desclée de Brouwer, 1968), p. 5.
51. Combes, op. cit., p. 59.
52. Ibid., p. 119.
53. V. supra.
54. Combes, op. cit., p. 210.
55. Ibid., p. 214.
56. P. Sollers, *Printemps rouge*, in J. Thibaudeau, *Mai 68 en France* (Paris: Seuil, 1970), p. 19.
57. Ibid., p. 24.
58. Ibid., p. 67.
59. Ibid., p. 116.
60. Ibid., p. 117.
61. R. Jean, *Les Deux Printemps* (Paris: Seuil, 1971), p. 240.
62. Ibid., p. 248.
63. R. Merle, *Derrière la vitre* (Paris: Gallimard/Folio, 1970), pp. 11–12.
64. Loc. cit.
65. See the quotation from the summer 1968 issue of *Tel Quel* in Reader, op. cit., pp. 10–11, and also C. Britton, 'The Nouveau Roman and *Tel Quel* Marxism', *Paragraph*, Vol. 12, no. 1, March 1989, pp. 65–97.
66. Merle, op. cit., p. 539.
67. Loc. cit.
68. Merle, op. cit., p. 297.
69. Ibid., p. 57.
70. Ibid., p. 48.
71. Ibid., p. 54.
72. P. Laîné, *L'Irrévolution* (Paris: Gallimard, 1971), p. 35.
73. Ibid., p. 63.
74. Ibid., p. 66.

75. Ibid., p. 79.
76. Ibid., p. 174.
77. F. George, *Prof à T* . . . (Paris: Galilée/10–18, 1973), p. 40.
78. Ibid., p. 116.
79. Ibid., p. 141.
80. A. Fabre-Luce, *Le Général en Sorbonne* (Paris: Table Ronde de Combat ('Les Brûlots'), 1968), p. 61.
81. Ibid., p. 83.
82. Ibid., p. 110.
83. Ibid., p. 132.
84. F. Bon/M.-A. Burnier, *Si mai avait gagné* (Paris: Pauvert (Collection Enragé), 1968), p. 46.
85. Ibid., p. 112.
86. J.-L. Curtis, *La Chine m'inquiète*, (Paris: Grasset (J'ai lu), 1972), p. 20.
87. Ibid., p. 31.
88. Ibid., p. 153.
89. Ibid., p. 132.
90. Ibid., p. 106.
91. Ibid., p. 85.
92. Ibid., p. 34.
93. Ibid., p. 40.
94. J. Kristeva, *Les Samouraïs* (Paris: Fayard, 1990), p. 119.
95. Ibid., p. 142. ('Destructive ultra-leftists' here translates the French *casseurs* – the term used by the Right, and in particular Marcellin, in preference to the more benign *gauchistes* to stress the destructiveness of their opponents).
96. Ibid., p. 174.
97. Ibid., pp. 267–8.
98. For a good survey of developments in women's movements in France after 1968, see C. Duchen, *Feminism in France: from May '68 to Mitterrand*, (London: Routledge, 1986).
99. D. Holmes, in *Modern and Contemporary France*, no. 44, January 1991, p. 96.
100. Ibid.
101. J.-P. Jeancolas, *Le Cinéma des Français* (Paris: Stock/Cinéma, 1979), p. 172.
102. J. Eustache, *La Maman et la putain* (Paris: Cahiers du Cinéma, 1986), p. 27.
103. V. supra, p. 90.
104. Jeancolas, op. cit., p. 170.
105. Jeancolas, op. cit.; R. Prédal, *Le Cinéma français contemporain* (Paris: Cerf, 1984; and J. Forbes, *The Cinema in France: After the New Wave*, (London: Macmillan, 1992), provide the most comprehensive surveys of French cinema in this period. More specific coverage – of women film-makers since 1968 and of the treatment of the Vietnam war in French cinema – is provided by G. Vincendeau and C. Britton respectively in Hanley and Kerr, op. cit. (The fact that the twentieth-anniversary conference from which these papers are taken did not actually include a contribution on 'The events in/through the cinema' is surely of symptomatic significance.)
106. In J. Tulard (ed.), *Guide des films* (Paris: Robert Laffont (Bouquins), 1990), Vol. I, p. 83.
107. Ibid., Vol. II, p. 191.

108. L. Malle, *Milou en mai* (Paris: Gallimard, 1990), pp. 80–1.
109. Ibid., p. 83.
110. Ibid., p. 109.
111. Ibid., p. 124.
112. Jeancolas, op. cit., p. 172.
113. J.-L. Douin, *Godard*, (Paris/Marseille: Rivages (Cinema), 1989), p. 27.
114. 'Le Cinéma selon Godard', special issue of *CinemAction*, no. 52, 1989.
115. See, in particular, Colin MacCabe, *Godard: Images, Sounds, Politics* (London: British Film Institute/Macmillan, 1980).

6 Women and the Events of May 1968

1. Pierre Viansson-Ponté, *L'histoire de la République Gaullienne: le temps des orphelins*. Tome II (Paris: Fayard, 1972), p. 392.
2. Cited by Elaine Marks and Isabelle de Courtivron, *New French Feminisms* (Brighton: Harvester Press, 1981), p. 111.
3. There are exceptions and one of the most enduring images of 68 must be that of a young woman protester carried shoulder-high, brandishing a banner at the mass demonstration of 13 May in Paris. This image has been used in several documentaries. See, for example, Hervé Hamon and Patrick Rotman, 'Paroles de mai', *Génération* (série télévisée) (Paris: Vision Seuil, 1988).
4. See poster (one of the rare ones to depict the female form) entitled 'La beauté est dans la rue' in Marc Rohan, *Paris 68. Graffiti, Posters, Newspapers and Poems of the Events of May 1968* (London: Impact, 1988), p. 125.
5. The whole question of the statistical analysis of strikes and occupations in May–June 1968 is controversial given that it is difficult to distinguish between those who participated willingly and those who were unable to work due to their workplaces being occupied, or because they were prevented by pickets or because stoppages in other sectors affected activity in their own.
6. While this unreal scene lampoons trade union officials, for many women it illustrated some very real experiences. See Dominique Meunier and Nancy Huston, 'Le mai des saints malgré lui (scenario-agenda)', *Histoires d'Elles*, avril/mai 1978, p. 11.
7. See Gisèle Charzat, *Les françaises sont-elles des citoyennes?* Paris: Denoël, 1972, p. 175.
8. The *Comité d'Action*, following in the tradition of the Paris Commune of 1871, was the basic unit responsible for organising revolution.
9. See Paula Jacques, 'Que sont devenues les filles de mai 68?' *F. Magazine*, mai 1978, p. 46.
10. Ibid., p. 50.
11. See Maria-Antonietta Macciochi, *De la France* (Paris: Seuil, 1977), p. 421.
12. See *Elle* (special issue), no. 1171/2/3, juin 1968, p. 18.
13. See *De la France*, op. cit., pp. 421–2.
14. Evelyne July, activist and in charge of the Centre Culturel de Nanterre at the time, cited in 'Que sont devenues les filles . . .', *F. Magazine*, op. cit., p. 46.
15. Ibid.
16. Klein, an American, Paris-based film-maker shot his film in 1968. It made a great impact when released in 1978 as it contained much original footage which had not been seen until then.

17. 'Que sont devenues les filles . . .', *F. Magazine*, op. cit., p. 46.
18. Nadja Ringart cited by Hervé Hamon and Patrick Rotman, 'Des femmes enfin' *Génération*, tome 2 (Paris: Seuil, 1988), p. 198.
19. See Patrick Ravignant, *L'Odéon est ouverte* (Paris: Stock, 1968), pp. 198–202.
20. Alain Ayache, *Les citations de la révolution de mai* (Paris: Pauvert, 1968), p. 106.
21. See *Génération*, Tome 2, op. cit., pp. 218–19.
22. Anne Zelensky, a 'fellow-traveller' of the Socialist party had, prior to the events, founded the group *Feminin-Masculin-Avenir* (FMA) which constituted a forum for debate and discussion of male–female relations. She was also among the group of women who demonstrated at the Arc de Triomphe in Paris, on 26 August 1970. See note 23.
23. The MLF was thus baptised, by the press, following a demonstration by about 15 women at the Arc de Triomphe on 26 August 1970, when wreaths were laid in memory of 'The unknown soldier's wife'. This was a solidarity demonstration to mark the 50th anniversary of American women winning the vote.
24. This section contains only a very brief summary of the challenge posed by feminists in the seventies as several works devote considerable space to this subject. The following are particularly recommended: Claire Duchen, *Feminism in France: from May 68 to Mitterrand* (London: Routledge and Kegan Paul, 1986); Anne de Pisan et Anne Tristan, *Histoires du MLF* (Paris: Calmann-Levy, 1977); Monique Rémy, *Histoire des mouvements de femmes: de l'utopie à l'intégration* (Paris: Editions Harmattan, 1990).
25. A conference organised by *Elle* magazine on 'La Femme' ('Ce que veulent les femmes de 1970, ce qu'elles refusent') was disrupted in spectacular fashion by feminists whose aim was to demonstrate the falsity of claims solemnly made by the participants on behalf of French women. See *Elle*, nos 1301, 23 novembre 1970 and 1303, 7 décembre 1970. See also Charzat, *Les françaises sont-elles des citoyennes?*, op. cit., pp. 182–90.
26. In April 1971, *Le Nouvel Observateur* published a manifesto signed by 343 women, among them Simone de Beauvoir, Jeanne Moreau and other well-known names, who stated that they had undergone illegal abortions.
27. Monique Rémy, *Histoire des mouvements de Femmes* (Paris: Editions Harmattan, 1990), p. 148.
28. *Le Quotidien des Femmes* (November 1974 to June 1976) and *Des Femmes en Mouvement* (December 1977 to July 1982) were both published by the group Psychanalyse et Politique.
29. *Histoires d'Elles* (March 1977 to April 1980), *Questions Féministes* (November 1977 to May 1980), *Le Temps des Femmes* (March 1978 to 1982) and *Les Nouvelles Féministes* (December 1974 to May 1977), among others, were all set up by small groups within the current Féministes Révolutionnaires.
30. *Le Torchon Brûle* (December 1970 to 1974), *Les Pétroleuses* (January 1974 to December 1976) and *Les Cahiers du Féminisme* (1977 onwards) were published by groups within the current *lutte de classes*.
31. Samra-Martine Bonvoisin and Michèle Maignien, *La presse féminine* (Paris: PUF, 1986), p. 36.
32. See Khursheed Wadia, 'Women's Magazines: Coming to Terms with Fem-

inism post May 68', *French Cultural Studies*, no. 6, October 1991, pp. 261–74.

33. *La Spirale* was set up in 1972 to study women's culture and to encourage women to express themselves through writing and painting.

34. Choisir, founded in April 1971 by Gisèle Halimi, a feminist lawyer, had as its initial aim to help and protect the women who had signed the *manifeste des 343*. The Mouvement de la Libération de l'Avortement (MLA) had been founded in January 1971 and was later, in April 1979, to become the Mouvement pour la Libération de l'Avortement et de la Contraception (MLAC). While both groups campaigned together, divisions were apparent, and Choisir was often accused of having a reformist approach while the MLA/MLAC was criticised for being no more than a 'specialiste de la manif'.

35. See Margaret Maruani, *Les syndicats à l'épreuve du féminisme* (Paris: Syros, 1979) and Jeannette Laot, *Stratégie pour les femmes* (Paris: Stock, 1977).

36. See *De la France*, op. cit., 'Le Larzac et les paysannes', pp. 409–20.

37. Georges Marchais speaking at the Palais des Congrès in Paris, on 4 December 1977. Cited in Gisèle Halimi, *Le Programme Commun des femmes* (Paris: Grasset et Fasquelle, 1978), p. 40.

38. This law modified the Neuwirth law of 1967, which authorised the sale of contraceptives.

39. The secrétariat d'état à la Condition féminine gave way to the délégation nationale à la Condition féminine in August 1976 which became the ministère délégué à la Condition féminine in September 1978.

40. For a detailed account of women's rights legislation in France see: Dorothy MacBride-Stetson, *Women's Rights in France* (Connecticut: Greenwood Press, 1987).

41. This law strengthened the previous laws of 1972 and 1975 and introduced the principle of equality of opportunity which, in turn, embraced the idea of positive discrimination: 'il n'est pas possible d'appliquer des mesures identiques à des personnes placées dans des situations inégales, faute de quoi, il en résulterait une permanence des inégalités.'

42. This law was a weak version of Roudy's failed anti-sexist bill of March 1983 which left out that part designed to impose sanctions against any manifestation of sexism liable to offend individuals or groups of individuals.

43. An official split within the movement had occurred in November 1979 when the current Psychanalyse et Politique, having decided to call itself Mouvement de Libération des Femmes – Politique et Psychanalyse, decided to register 'MLF' as a commercial trademark with the Institut National de la Propriété Industrielle.

44. Yvette Roudy, 'Un ministère pas comme les autres. Un projet, une stratégie pour les femmes', *Le féminisme et ses enjeux. Vingt-sept femmes parlent* (collective authorship) (Paris: Centre Fédera FEN-Edilig, 1988), p. 467.

45. In addition to the 100 or so smaller centres of information which were set up with grants from the ministry, money was provided for the establishment of the Centre de Recherches et d'Information Féministes (CRIF) (a coordinating body for feminist studies), the Centre audio-visuel Simone de Beauvoir (an audio-visual documentation service and film workshop) and the Commission sur la féminisation des titres et des fonctions, among others.

46. For an account of the relationship between feminists and the Ministry for Women's Rights, see Claire Duchen, op. cit., pp. 125–49.

47. For an account of the controversy and debate among feminists, surrounding motherhood, see Claire Duchen, ibid., pp. 49–66. Also Monique Rémy, op. cit., pp. 61–72.

48. INSEE, *Données Sociales*, no. 101, 1973, p. 17.

49. Between 1962 and 1968, the increase in the number of women entering the following aggregate occupational groups was professions libérales et cadres supérieurs – 53 per cent; cadres moyens – 37.5 per cent; employés – 30.6 per cent. Données Sociales, ibid., p. 19.

50. In 1968, 44.6 per cent of women aged 25–54 worked. By 1975 this figure had increased to 53.1 per cent. INSEE, *Economie et Statistique*, no. 171–2, 1984, p. 14.

51. During the period 1964–75 the birthrate had dropped by a third. *Economie et Statistique*, ibid., p. 25.

52. Cited in Pascal Lainé, *La femme et ses images* (Paris: Editions Stock, 1974), p. 184.

53. *Elle*, no. 1485, 3 juin 1974 and no. 1486, 10 juin 1974.

54. Véronique Soulé, 'F. Magazine, une percée réussie dans la presse féminine française'. *Presse-Actualité*, no. 131, novembre 1978, p. 16.

55. This profile of the 'new woman' is taken from Benoîte Groult, *Les nouvelles femmes* (Paris: Editions Magazine, 1979), pp. 187–241. This profile is based upon a survey carried out by *F Mazarine* in April 1978 of the responses of 2060 women. According to the survey, 93 per cent of the women questioned belonged to occupational categories which may be covered by the term middle-class (employées – 26 per cent, cadres moyens – 24 per cent, cadres supérieurs – 5 per cent, professions libérales – 4 per cent, enseignantes – 22 per cent, services médicaux et sociaux – 10 per cent, commerçantes/artisanes – 2 per cent). Only 5 per cent of 'new women' were working-class (ouvrières spécialisées, personnel de service, manoeuvres) – 2 per cent, ouvrières qualifiées, contremaîtres, agents de maîtrise – 3 per cent); 69 per cent were married; 30 per cent had passed the *baccalauréat* while 43 per cent had completed some form of Higher Education; 57 per cent worked full-time while 8 per cent worked part-time; 35 per cent lived in the Paris region and another 24 per cent lived in large towns and cities.

56. In the 1978 legislative elections 23 per cent voted for the Right, 40 per cent voted for the Left (PCF and PS), 13 per cent voted for the Ecologists and 7 per cent for Gisèle Halimi's Choisir movement. Ibid., p. 239.

57. 93 per cent were in favour of the MLF while only 7 per cent were against or indifferent. Moreover 39 per cent of the women believed that the MLF was the main vehicle of change in women's lives as opposed to 3 per cent who believed in the action of political parties. Ibid., p. 220.

58. Ibid., pp. 223–30.

59. Ibid., p. 209.

60. 50 per cent of 'new women' preferred a life sharing equal responsibilities with a married partner, 24 per cent opted for traditional marriage arrangements while 20 per cent preferred just to live with a partner. Ibid., p. 188.

61. Philippe Michel quoted in *Le Matin*, 18 mars 1983.

62. Ibid.

63. Françoise Giroud, 'La révolution est accomplie'. *Le Nouvel Observateur*, no. 1361, 6–12 décembre 1990, pp. 6–13.
64. Ibid., p. 12.
65. Ibid., p. 8 and p. 11.
66. Ibid., p. 9.
67. Ibid., p. 13.
68. Martine Lévy, 'France: vers un équilibre dynamique avec les hommes'. *Femmes d'Europe*, no. 70, 1992, p. 34.
69. Ibid., p. 36.
70. Ibid., p. 33.
71. Marie-Claude Nectoux, 'Femmes violentes, femmes violentées . . .' *Après-Demain*, no. 316–17, juillet–septembre 1989, p. 16.
72. Liane Mozère, 'Le torchon brûle', *Génération* (série télévisé), op. cit.

Epilogue

1. Willener, op. cit., p. 87.
2. Op. cit., p. 98.
3. See note 1 to Chapter 1.
4. G. Bennington, *Lyotard: writing the event* (Manchester: Manchester University Press, 1988), p. 109.
5. Ibid., p. 108.
6. T. S. Eliot, *Collected Poems 1909–1962* (London/Boston: Faber and Faber, 1963). p. 17.

Bibliography

This is not a comprehensive bibliography. It lists all books and the vast majority of articles referred to in the text or footnotes that are 'relevant to May' in the widest sense of the word or to the methodologies I have adopted to write about it (but not e.g. T. S. Eliot's *The Love Song of J. Alfred Prufrock*), plus a few additional ones that may be found useful. I have not attempted a division by scope, genre or approach, since that is implicit in my own text.

More comprehensive bibliographies on May are to be found in Capdevielle and Mouriaux, Joffrin, Schnapp and Vidal-Nacquet, and Wylie *et al.* listed below.

Philippe Alexandre and Raoul Tubiana, *L'Élysée en péril* (Paris: Fayard, 1969).

Louis Althusser (trans. Brewster), *Lenin and Philosophy and other essays*, (London: New Left Books, 1971). See also reference to Macciocchi.

Raymond Aron, *La révolution introuvable* (Paris: Fayard, 1968).

Paul Bacot, *La CFDT et les grèves de mai–juin 1968 dans la région Lyonnaise* (Lyon: Agel, 1969).

Mikhail Bakhtin (trans. Emerson), *Problems of Dostoevsky's Poetics* (Manchester: Manchester University Press, 1984).

Édouard Balladur, *L'arbre de mai: chronique alternée* (Paris: Atelier M. Julian, 1979).

Denis Barbet, 'Interprétations syndicales', in *Pouvoirs*, no. 39, 1986.

André Barjonet, *La Révolution trahie de 1968* (Paris: John Didier, 1968).

Roland Barthes, 'L'écriture de l'événement', in *Communications*, 'Mai 68: la prise de la parole' (Paris: Seuil, 1968).

——, *Mythologies* (Paris: Seuil, 1957).

Philippe Bauchard and Maurice Bruzek, *La syndicalisme à l'épreuve* (Paris: Robert Laffont, 1968).

Jean Baudrillard (trans. Foss/Patterson/Johnson), *In the Shadow of the Silent Majorities* (New York: Semiotext(e), 1983).

Jacques Baynac, *Mai retrouvé* (Paris: Laffont, 1978).

Geoffrey Bennington, *Lyotard: Writing the Event* (Manchester: Manchester University Press, 1988).

Jean-Marie Benoist, *Marx est mort* (Paris: Gallimard (Idées), 1970).

Daniel Bensaïd, Alain Krivine and Henri Weber, *Mai 68 – une répétition générale* (Paris: Maspero, 1968).

Daniel Bensaïd and Alain Krivine, *Mai si! – rebelles et repentis* (Montreuil: La Brèche, 1988).

Julien Besançon, *Les murs ont la parole* (Paris: Plon, 1968).

Josette Blancherie *et al.*, *Les événements de mai–juin 1968 à travers cent entreprises* (Paris: Centre national d'information pour la productivité des entreprises, 1968).

Frédéric Bon and Michel-Antoine Burnier, *Si mai avait gagné* (Paris: Pauvert (Collection Enragé), 1968).

Raymond Boudon, 'Quelques causes de la révolte estudiantine', in *La Table Ronde*, December 1968–January 1969.

Pierre Bourdieu and Jean-Claude Passeron, *Les Héritiers* (Paris: Minuit, 1964).

Pierre Bourdieu, *Homo Academicus* (Paris: Minuit, 1984).

François Bourricaud, 'Alain Touraine à la recherche du sujet historique', in *Preuves*, July–September 1969.

Celia Britton, 'The Nouveau Roman and Tel Quel Marxism', *Paragraph*, Vol. 12, no. 1, March 1989, pp. 65–97.

Jean Capdevielle and René Mouriaux, *Mai 68: l'entre-deux de la modernité* (Paris: Presses de la Fondation Nationale des Sciences Politiques, 1988).

David Caute, *68: The Year of the Barricades* (London: Paladin, 1968).

Centre de regroupement des informations universitaires: *Quelle université? Quelle société?* (Paris: Seuil (Combats), 1968).

V. P. Chilton, 'Glucksmanntalk: Packaging the Force', in *Modern and Contemporary France*, no. 20 (December 1984).

Maurice Clavel, *Ce que je crois* (Paris: Grasset, 1975).

——, *La perte et le fracas ou les murailles du monde* (Paris: Flammarion, 1971).

Club Jean Moulin, *Que faire de la révolution de mai: six priorités* (Paris: Seuil, 1968).

Daniel and Gabriel Cohn-Bendit: *Le gauchisme, remède à la maladie sénile du communisme* (Paris: Seuil, 1968). English trans. by Pomerans, *Obsolete Communism – the Left-wing alternative*, (Harmondsworth: Penguin, 1969).

Daniel Cohn-Bendit, *Le grand bazar* (Paris: Belfond, 1975).

——, *Nous l'avons tant aimée, la révolution* (Paris: Bernard Barrault/Points, 1988).

Michel Crozier, 'Révolution libérale ou révolte petite-bourgeoise', in *Communications*, no. 12, 1968.

Jonathan Culler, *On Deconstruction* (London/Melbourne/Henley: Routledge, 1983).

Jean-Louis Curtis, *La Chine m'inquiète* (Paris: Grasset (J'ai lu), 1972)

Adrien Dansette, *Mai 68* (Paris: Plon, 1971).

Pierre de Boisdeffre, *Lettre ouverte aux hommes de gauche* (Paris: Albin Michel, 1969).

Guy Debord, *La Société du spectacle* (Paris: Éditions Gérard Lebovici, 1987).

——, *Commentaires sur la société du spectacle* (Paris: Éditions Gérard Lebovici, 1988).

Régis Debray, *Modeste contribution aux discours et cérémonies officielles du dixième anniversaire* (Paris: Maspero, 1978; translated into English in *New Left Review*, no. 115, 1979).

——, *Le pouvoir intellectuel en France* (Paris: Ramsay, 1979).

Michel de Certeau, *La prise de la parole: pour une nouvelle culture* (Paris: Desclée de Brouwer, 1968).

Christian Delage, *La naissance d'une université*, Orléans doctoral thesis.

Alain Delale and Gilles Ragache, *La France de 68* (Paris: Seuil, 1978).

Gil Delannoi, *68–78: les années utopiques* (Paris: La Découverte, 1990).

Jacques Delperrie de Bayac, *Histoire du front populaire* (Paris: Marabout, 1972).

Paul de Man, *Allegories of Reading* (London: Methuen, 1983).

Jacques Derrida, *Positions* (Paris: Minuit, 1972).

Jean-Marie Domenach, 'L'idéologie du mouvement', in *Esprit*, no. 8–9, August–September 1968.

Jean-Luc Douin, *Godard* (Paris/Marseille: Rivages (Cinéma), 1989).

Geneviève Dreyfus-Armand and Laurent Gervereau (eds), *Mai 68: les mouvements étudiants en France et dans le monde* (Nanterre: Bibliothèque Internationale de Documentation Contemporaine, 1988).

Pierre Dubois/Renaud Delong and others, *Grèves revendicatives ou grèves politiques?* (Paris: Anthropos, 1971).

Claire Duchen, *Feminism in France: from May '68 to Mitterrand* (London: Routledge, 1986).

Jacques Duclos, *Anarchistes d'hier et d'aujord'hui* (Paris: Editions Sociales, 1968).

Pascal Dumontier, *Les situationnistes et mai 68*, (Paris: Gérard Lebovici, 1990).

François Duprat, *Les journées de mai 68 – les dessous d'une révolution* (Paris: Nouvelles Éditions Latines, 1968).

Jacques Durandeaux, *Les journées de mai 68* (Paris: Desclée de Brouwer, 1968).

Épistémon (Didier Anzieu), *Ces idées qui ont ébranlé la France* (Paris: Fayard, 1968).

Jean Eustache, *La maman et la putain* (Paris: Cahiers du Cinéma, 1986).

Alfred Fabre-Luce, *Le Général en Sorbonne* (Paris: Table Ronde de Combat ('Les Brûlots'), 1968).

François Fajardie *et al.*, *Black Exit to 68* (Montreuil: La Brèche, 1988).

Edgar Faure, *L'Éducation nationale et la participation* (Paris: Plon, 1968).

Luc Ferry and Alain Renaut, *La pensée 68. Essai sur l'antihumanisme contemporain* (Paris: Gallimard, 1985).

Luc Ferry and Alain Renaut, *68–86: itinéraires de l'individu* (Paris: Gallimard, 1987).

Jill Forbes, *The Cinema in France: After the New Wave* (London: Macmillan, 1992).

Jean Fourastié, *Les trente glorieuses ou la révolution invisible de 1947* (Paris: Fayard, 1979).

Claude Frédéric, *Libérer l'ORTF* (Paris: Seuil, 1968).

Jacques Frémontier, *La forteresse ouvrière – Renault* (Paris: Fayard, 1971).

Sigmund Freud, *New Introductory Lectures on Psychoanalysis*, Collected Works, Vol. XXII (London: Hogarth/Institute of Psychoanalysis, 1964).

Francis Fukuyama, *The End of History or the Last Man* (London: Hamilton, 1992).

Max Gallo, *Gauchisme, réforme et révolution* (Paris: Robert Laffont, 1968).

André Gaveau, *De l'autre côté des barricades* (Paris: Jean-Claude Simoën, 1978).

Philippe Gavi, *Les ouvriers: du tiercé à révolution* (Paris; Mercure de France, 1970).

François George, *Prof à T . . .* (Paris: Galilée/10–18, 1973).

André Glucksmann, *Stratégie et révolution en France* (Paris: Bourgois, 1968).

Richard Gombin, *Le projet révolutionnaire* (Paris: Mouton, 1969).

——, *Les origines du gauchisme* (Paris: Seuil, 1971).

Maurice Grimaud, *En mai fais ce qu'il te plaît* (Paris: Stock, 1977).

Alain Griotteray, *Des barricades ou des réformes?* (Paris: Fayard, 1968).

Jean-Claude Guillebaud, *Les années orphelines* (Paris: Seuil, 1978).

Yannick Guin, *La commune de Nantes* (Paris: Maspero, 1969).

Hervé Hamon and Patrick Rotman, *Génération I: les années de rêve* (Paris: Seuil, 1987), *Génération II: les années de poudre* (Paris: Seuil, 1988).

David L. Hanley and A. P. Kerr (eds), *May 68 – Coming of Age* (London: Macmillan, 1988).

Sylvia Harvey, *May 68 and Film Culture* (London: British Film Institute, 1978).

Guy Hocquenghem, *L'après-mai des faunes* (Paris: Grasset, 1974).

——, 'Subversion et décadence du mâle d'après-Mai', in *Autrement*, no. 12, 1978.

——, *Lettre ouverte à ceux qui sont passés du col Mao au Rotary* (Paris: Albin Michel, 1986).

Diana Holmes, review of Kristeva's *Les samouraïs*, in *Modern and Contemporary France*, no. 44, January 1991.

Raymond Jean, *Les deux printemps* (Paris: Seuil, 1971).

Laurent Joffrin, *Mai 68: histoire des événements* (Paris: Seuil/Points, 1988).

Jean Jousselin, *Les révoltes des jeunes* (Paris: Editions Ouvrières, 1968).

Jean-Pierre Jeancolas, *Le cinéma des Français* (Paris: Stock-Cinéma, 1979).

Claude Jouriès, 'Les interprétations communistes de mai 68', in *Pouvoirs*, no. 39, 1986.

Tony Judt, *Marxism and the French Left* (Oxford: Clarendon Press, 1986).

Serge July, Alain Geismar and Erlyne Morane, *Vers la guerre civile* (Paris: Éditions Premières, 1969).

Jacques Jurquet, *Le printemps révolutionnaire de 1968* (Paris: Gît-le-Coeur, 1968).

Bernard Kayser and Paul de Gaudemar, *Dix ans d'une génération d'étudiants de la Faculté des lettres et sciences humaines de Toulouse*, Association des publications de la Faculté des lettres et sciences humaines de Toulouse, 1967.

Julia Kristeva, *Au commencement était l'amour* (Paris: Hachette, 1985).

——, *Histoires d'amour* (Paris: Denoël, 1983).

——, *Les Samouraïs* (Paris: Fayard, 1990).

Jean Lacouture, *De Gaulle III: le souverain* (Paris: Seuil, 1986).

Pascal Laîné, *L'Irrévolution* (Paris: Gallimard, 1971).

Georges Patrick Langlois and Glenn Myrent, *Henri Langlois* (Paris: Denoël, 1986).

Jacques Laurent, *Lettre ouverte aux étudiants* (Paris: Albin Michel, 1969).

Bernard LaCroix, 'A contre-courant: le parti pris du réalisme', in *Pouvoirs*, no. 39, 1986.

Henri Lefebvre, *L'irruption: de Nanterre au sommet* (Paris: Anthropos, 1968).

Marie-Jeanne Le Guillou, Olivier Clément and Jean Bosc, *Évangile et révolution: au coeur de notre crise spirituelle* (Paris: Centurion, 1968).

Jean-Marie Leuwers, *Un peuple se dresse: luttes ouvrières, mai 1968* (Paris: Éditions ouvrières, 1969).

W. Lewino (photographs by Jo Schnapp), *L'imagination au pouvoir* (Paris: Losfeld, 1968).

Robert Linhart, *L'Établi* (Paris: Minuit, 1978).

Gilles Lipovetsky, *L'ère du vide* (Paris: Gallimard, 1983).

René Loureau, *L'analyse institutionnelle* (Paris: Minuit, 1970).

Maria-Antonietta Macciocchi, *Letters from Inside the Italian Communist Party to Louis Althusser*, trans. Hellman (London: New Left Books, 1973).

Louis Malle, *Milou en mai* (Paris: Gallimard, 1990).

Raymond Marcellin, *L'ordre public et les groupes révolutionnaires* (Paris: Plon, 1969).

Jacques Maritain, *Pour une philosophie de l'éducation* (Paris: Fayard, 1979).

Jacques Marny (ed.) *L'Église contestée* (Paris: Centurion, 1968).

Roger Martelli, *Mai 68* (Paris: Messidor/Éditions Sociales, 1988).

Gilles Martinet, *La conquête des pouvoirs* (Paris: Seuil, 1968).

Jacques Massu, *Baden 68* (Paris: Plon, 1983).

Matériaux pour l'histoire de notre temps, special issue, 'Occupations/négociations: les syndicats en mai 68', Bibliothèque de Documentation Internationale Contemporaine, Nanterre, July–September 1990.

Gérard Mendel, *La crise des générations* (Paris: Payot, 1969).

Robert Merle, *Derrière la vitre* (Paris: Seuil, 1970).

Jean Meyriat (ed.), *L'Univers politique. Relations internationales* (Paris: Richelieu, 1969).

François Mitterrand (ed. Alan Clark): *Anthologie Mitterrand* (London: Methuen, 1986).

Edgar Morin, Claude Lefort and Cornelius Castoriadis, *Mai 68: la brèche suivi de Vingt ans après* (Paris: Éditions Complexe, 1988).

R. Mouriaux, M. Rebérioux *et al.*, *1968: Exploration du Mai Français*, 2 vols (Paris: Harmattan, 1992).

Jean-Claude Passeron, 'La relation pédagogique et le systéme d'enseignement', *Prospective*, no. 14, 1967.

Michelle Perrot, Jean-Claude Perrot, Madeleine Rebérioux and Jean Maître, *Mai–juin 1968. La Sorbonne par elle-même* (Paris: Seuil (Combats), 1968).

Évelyne Pisier, 'Paradoxes du gauchisme', in *Pouvoirs*, no. 39, 1986.

Poèmes de la révolution mai 1968 (Paris: Caractères, 1968).

Georges Pompidou, *Pour rétablir une vérité* (Paris: Flammarion, 1982).

René Prédal, *Le cinéma français contemporain* (Paris: Cerf, 1984).

Antoine Prost, article in *Le mouvement social*, no. 143, April–June 1988.

Alexander Quatrocchi and Tom Nairn, *The Beginning of the End – France, May 1968* (London: Panther, 1968).

Keith A. Reader, *Intellectuals and the Left in France since 1968* (London: Macmillan, 1987).

——, 'The anniversary industry', in *Screen*, Vol. 29, no. 3, summer 1988, pp. 122–6.

Alain Renaut, 'La révolution introuvable', in *Pouvoirs*, no. 39, 1986.

Waldeck Rochet, *Les enseignements de mai–juin 1968* (Paris: Éditions Sociales, 1968).

——, *L'avenir du PCF* (Paris: Grasset, 1969).

Élisabeth Salvaressi, *Mai en héritage* (Paris: Syros/Alternatives, 1988).

Jean-Paul Sartre, *Situations X* (Paris: Gallimard, 1976).

Alain Schnapp and Pierre Vidal-Nacquet, *Journal de la commune étudiante* (Paris: Seuil, 1969; second edition 1988).

Patrick Seale and Maureen MacConville, *French Revolution 1968* (Harmondsworth: Penguin, 1968).

Jean-Jacques Servan-Schreiber, *Le réveil de la France* (Paris: Denoël, 1968).

André Stéphane, *L'univers contestationnaire* (Paris: Payot, 1969).

Jean Thibaudeau, *Mai 68 en France* (Paris: Seuil, 1970).

Alain Touraine, *Le mouvement de mai ou le communisme utopique* (Paris: Seuil, 1968).

Jean-Raymond Tournoux, *Le mois de mai du Général* (Paris: Plon, 1969).

Jean Tulard, *Guide des films* (Paris: Robert Laffont (Bouquins), 1990).

Raoul Vaneigem (trans. Nicholson-Smith), *The Revolution of Everyday Life* (London: Left Bank Books/Rebel Press, 1983).

Pierre Viansson-Ponté, *Histoire de la république gaullienne II: Le temps des orphelins* (Paris: Fayard, 1971).

René Viénet, *Enragés et situationnistes dans le mouvement des occupations* (Paris: Gallimard, 1968).

Henri Weber, *Vingt ans après: que reste-t-il de 68?* (Paris: Seuil, 1988).

Simone Weil, *La condition ouvrière* (Paris: Gallimard, 1951).

Alfred Willener, *L'Image-action de la sociéte: de la politisation culturelle* (Paris: Seuil, 1970).

Raymond Williams, *Marxism and Literature* (Oxford: Oxford University Press, 1977).

Michel Winock, *Chronique des années soixante* (Paris: Seuil, 1987).

Denis Woronof, 'Pour une histoire de mai', in *Politique aujourd'hui*, August– September 1969.

Laurence Wylie, Franklin D. Chu and Mary Terrall, *France, the Events of 1968* (Pittsburgh: Council for European Studies, 1973).

Sylvain Zegel, *Les idées de mai* (Paris: Gallimard, 1968).

Index

Ideologies, their founders and their adherents are conflated into a single entry; thus, 'Mao' covers also 'Maoism' and 'Maoists'. Where the terms 'Communist' and 'Socialist' are used in a context that clearly denotes the PCF or the PS, they are indexed under those headings. Endnotes, but not bibliography, are indexed.

Printed in the United Kingdom by
Lightning Source UK Ltd., Milton Keynes
140676UK00001B/34/A